JUNIOR CERTIFI

LESS STRESS
MORE
SUCCESS

History Revision

Dermot Lucey

g GILL EDUCATION

Gill Education

Hume Avenue

Park West

Dublin 12

www.gilleducation.ie

Gill Education is an imprint of M.H. Gill & Co.

978 07171 47137

Design by Liz White Designs

Artwork by Oxford Designers & Illustrators

Print origination in Ireland by Carole Lynch

The paper used in this book is made from the wood pulp of managed forests.
For every tree felled, at least one tree is planted, thereby renewing natural resources.

For permission to reproduce photographs, the author and publisher gratefully acknowledge the following:

© Alamy: 24T, 24B, 25TL, 25BL, 25BR, 31, 36, 38, 39, 49, 54L, 76, 156L, 156C, 156R, 157TL, 157TC, 157TR, 157BL, 157BC, 166TL, 166TC, 166TR, 166BL, 166BR; © The Bridgeman Art Library: 25TR, 54R, 56, 62; © Corbis: 170; © Getty Images: 41, 133TL, 133TC, 133TR, 133BL, 133BCL, 133BCR, 166BC; © Imagefile: 171; © Mary Evans Picture Library: 84; © Rex Features: 133BR.

The authors and publisher have made every effort to trace all copyright holders, but if any has been inadvertently overlooked we would be pleased to make the necessary arrangement at the first opportunity.

CONTENTS

Year Three – Understanding the Modern World

Introduction

Organise for less exam stress – Revising for the Junior Cert exam

Junior Cert students should take plenty of time to revise for their exams. The key to good revision is good organisation. Good organisation helps to relieve the stress of exams. It puts you in control.

What is good organisation?

1. You must work to a **revision plan**, and that plan must be written out. It will take you a short time to lay out the plan.
2. You will begin with an **overall study plan for history**. In this, you break down the subject into separate topics to be studied. (Maybe your teacher has done this for you already.) You will break down the overall plan into a number of topics for each week. (For example, if there are 8 weeks left to the Junior Cert, you should use 7 for the plan and 1 week for overall revision.)
3. After this, you will work on a **daily timetable for studying all your subjects**. Your revision plan for History gives you the topics you want to cover that week. The daily timetable breaks down your study time for each topic.
4. Your daily timetable will differ depending on whether it is a school day or a weekend.

What do you do when you are studying history?

1. Keep your study as active as possible – you don't want to fall asleep.
2. You should vary your study between topics where you have 'learning' to do and those where there is written work.
3. Give a focus to your study. Begin with 'What am I learning for this study period?'
4. Use your notes or your textbook – follow your *Less Stress More Success* revision book.
5. Underline or highlight key information.
6. The *Less Stress* revision notes are divided into **sub-headings** and **points** so that you can study them in short sections.
7. Tick off each topic in your Study Plan after you have studied it.
8. After studying each short section, you should **test yourself** to ensure that you have learnt the information. (Using www.etest.ie can help you here.)
9. Test yourself as you go along by covering what you have learnt and put it into your own words.

10. **Each topic** in *Less Stress More Success: History Revision for Junior Cert* should be **revised** at **regular intervals**.

11. Repeated revision is important in the weeks and months before the Junior Cert.

12. After studying a **chapter or a few chapters**, use the Ordinary level questions and the Higher level questions from your textbooks or from the State Examinations Commission papers (available online at www.examinations.ie) to **understand** how the exam paper is laid out and to **plan** answers. Think about how you will answer questions on the topic you are studying.

- Revise regularly
- Examine for content/information the eTests for *The Past Today* (2nd edition) online at www.etest.ie/subjects/jc-history/the-past-today-2nd-edition
- Test with past exam questions

13. Spend no more than 30 to 40 minutes on any one history topic at a time.

Your notes

The closer you get to the exam, the more you have to depend on notes, rather than the full textbook. Revision notes, such as the *Less Stress More Success* series, summarise the key information. They concentrate on content which is the basis for many of the marks in the Junior Cert exams. You will be able to revise large sections of your courses quite quickly.

Your friends

Your friends are a great support. They can help you with difficult parts of the courses. They will support you when everything is not going well.

Past exam papers

Past exam papers show you the type of questions which are asked in the exams. You may know a great deal of information, but if you cannot apply it to the questions asked in the exams, then that information is of no use. You can use past exam questions to test your information on parts of the course, plan paragraph answers or do a time test by answering a full question in the allotted time.

Higher and Ordinary level

The main differences between Higher level and Ordinary level are the extra topics to be learnt and the amount of information to be learnt in each topic. Ordinary level students should find out the most important parts of the history course from their teachers. They should concentrate on those parts through their revision notes.

 Note: Material that is to be studied only by those taking Higher level is indicated in the text.

Stay in school

Junior Cert students should stay in school until the exams and not take time off to study at home. It is better to use the class structure in school to help with your revision. This is especially true of Ordinary level students, who will benefit from the guidance of their teachers right to the end.

Relieve stress

You will need to feel some pressure because this will spur you to work and to give your best. But you must not let that pressure take over. When you are following your plan, you will feel more confident about your work. As you get to know more about your course, this will encourage you to work more.

Best of luck with the studying, and with the exams!

Revision plan for Higher level History

First Year History	
Week 1: Monday to Sunday	
The Job of the Historian	Use of sources, evidence
	The work of the archaeologist
Our Roots in Ancient Civilisation	Stone Age (Mesolithic, Neolithic) and Bronze Age Ireland
	The Iron Age and the Celts
	Early Christian Ireland
	The Roman Empire
	(Know 'houses, food and family life, work, art, crafts, tools, burial customs' for each of the above.)
Week 2: Monday to Sunday	
The Middle Ages	Medieval society (feudalism and knighthood)
	Town and city life
	The manor (three-field system)
	The castle (lord and lady)
	Monastery and parish
The Renaissance	Causes of the Renaissance
	General information on the Renaissance
	Art and architecture
	Painting and learning (improvements and changes)
	Six main biographies (Gutenberg, Michelangelo, da Vinci, Dürer, Shakespeare, Galileo)
	Results of the Renaissance

HL

Second Year History	
Explorations	Causes of the explorations
	Ships and instruments
	General account of voyages
	Effects/results of the explorations
	Special Study: One exploration (Columbus)
Week 3: Monday to Sunday	
The Reformation	Causes of the Reformation
	Special Study: One reformer (Luther)
	Other reformers (Luther/Calvin, England, Ireland)
	Counter-Reformation (Council of Trent, Jesuits, Inquisition)
	Results of the Reformation
The Plantations	Reasons for Plantation policy
	First Plantations (Laois-Offaly, Munster)
	Special Study: One Plantation (Ulster Plantation)
	Cromwellian Plantation in general
	Results/consequences of the Plantations
Political Revolutions	Causes of Discontent in America, France, Ireland
	Special Study: One revolutionary (Washington and the American Revolution OR Tone and the United Irishmen)
	General account of revolutions in France, Ireland and America
	Results/effects of revolutions
Week 4: Monday to Sunday	
Social Change: From Farm to Factory	Causes of social change
	The Agricultural Revolution (general changes, enclosure)
	The Industrial Revolution (causes, inventions)
	Special Study: Contrast industrial England and rural Ireland in the 1840s (different events, classes and groups: factory and mine owners, workers, landlords, tenant farmers and cottiers)
	The effects of changes in agriculture and industry on people's lives (living and working conditions, factory and mine owners, workers, growth of cities, migration, emigration)
	The Great Famine (general account, causes, government schemes, soup kitchens)
	Results of the Agricultural and Industrial Revolutions

Third Year History	
International Relations	(The Paris Peace Conference and the Treaty of Versailles)
	Mussolini and Fascist Italy
	Hitler and Nazi Germany
	Causes of World War II (especially Hitler's foreign policy and the policy of appeasement)
Week 5: Monday to Sunday	
International Relations (cont.)	The progress of World War II in Europe (German victories, 1939–42 in Poland, Norway, France (Battle of Britain), Operation Barbarossa)
	Allied victories, 1942–45 (Stalingrad and Russia, D-Day)
	Reasons for German defeat
	Results of the war
The Rise of the Superpowers and the Cold War	Causes
	The Berlin Blockade
	The Korean War
	The Cuban Missile Crisis
	(Détente and the End of the Cold War (brief))
Ireland – Social History	Urban and rural life and work
	The role of women
	Leisure and entertainment
	Transport and communications
Week 6: Monday to Sunday	
Ireland – History, 1900 to 1980	Ireland around 1900 (Home Rule, unionism, cultural nationalism (GAA, Gaelic League, Anglo-Irish Literary Revival))
	The Home Rule Crisis, 1912–14
	The 1916 Rising and Republicanism
	The Rise of Sinn Féin
	The War of Independence (political and military)
	Treaty negotiations and debates
	The Civil War
	The Irish Free State (Cumann na nGaedheal in the 1920s, de Valera and Fianna Fáil in 1930s)
	Ireland during World War II (The Emergency)
	Post-war Ireland and the Lemass years
	Modern Ireland, 1966–80 (politics, foreign policy)
	Northern Ireland, 1922 to the present time

HL

Revision plan for Ordinary level History

First Year History	
Week 1: Monday to Sunday	
The Job of the Historian	Use of sources, evidence
	The work of the archaeologist
Our Roots in Ancient Civilisation	Stone Age (Mesolithic, Neolithic) and Bronze Age Ireland
	The Iron Age and the Celts
	Early Christian Ireland
	Ancient Rome/the Roman Empire
	(Know 'houses, food and family life, work, art, crafts, tools, burial customs' for each of the above.)
Week 2: Monday to Sunday	
The Middle Ages	Medieval society (feudalism and knighthood)
	Town and city life
	The manor (three-field system)
	The castle (lord and lady)
	Monastery and parish
The Renaissance	Causes of the Renaissance
	General information on the Renaissance
	Art and architecture
	Painting and learning (improvements and changes)
	Six main biographies (Gutenberg, Michelangelo, da Vinci, Dürer, Shakespeare, Galileo)
	Results of the Renaissance
Second Year History	
Week 3: Monday to Sunday	
Explorations	Causes of the explorations
	Ships and instruments
	Effects/results of the explorations
	Special Study: One exploration (Columbus)
The Reformation	Causes of the Reformation
	Special Study: One reformer (Luther)
	Results of the Reformation
The Plantations	Reasons for Plantation policy
	Special Study: One Plantation (Ulster Plantation)
	Results/consequences of the Plantations

Week 4: Monday to Sunday	
Political Revolutions	Causes of Discontent in America, France, Ireland
	Special Study: One revolutionary (Washington and the American Revolution)
	Results/effects of revolutions
Social Change: From Farm to Factory	Causes of social change
	The Agricultural Revolution (general changes, enclosure)
	The Industrial Revolution (causes, inventions)
	Special Study: Contrast industrial England and rural Ireland in the 1840s (different events, classes and groups: factory and mine owners, workers, landlords, tenant farmers and cottiers)
	The effects of changes in agriculture and industry on people's lives (living and working conditions, factory and mine owners, workers, growth of cities, migration, emigration)
	The Great Famine (general account, causes, government schemes, soup kitchens)
	Results of the Agricultural and Industrial Revolutions

Week 5: Monday to Sunday	
Third Year History	
International Relations	(The Paris Peace Conference and the Treaty of Versailles)
	Mussolini and Fascist Italy
	Hitler and Nazi Germany
	Causes of World War II (especially Hitler's foreign policy and the policy of appeasement)
	The progress of World War II in Europe (German victories, 1939–42 in Poland, Norway, France, (Battle of Britain), Operation Barbarossa)
	Allied victories, 1942–45 (Stalingrad and Russia, D-Day)
	Reasons for German defeat
	Results of the war

Week 6: Monday to Sunday	
The Rise of the Superpowers and the Cold War	Causes
	The Berlin Blockade
	The Korean War
	The Cuban Missile Crisis
	The End of the Cold War
Ireland – Social History	Urban and rural life and work
	The role of women
	Leisure and entertainment
	Transport and communications

Answering exam questions for Higher level

There are **6 questions** in the Higher level history paper. They must be answered in **2½ hours**.

The structure of the Higher level paper is shown in this table:

Structure of the Higher level paper				
Question	Type	Marks	Time	Cumulative time
1	Pictures	15	15 minutes	1 hour and 15 minutes
2	Documents	15	15 minutes	
3	Short answers	20	20 minutes	
4	People in History	40	25 minutes	
5	Sources	30	25 minutes	1 hour and 15 minutes
6	Short answers and essay	50	50 minutes	

Question 1 – Pictures

1. The pictures in this question come from any part of the course.
2. Make sure you answer all parts of the question.
3. Keep your answers short – usually one sentence will do.
4. But **refer to evidence in the picture** when you can.

Question 2 – Documents

1. You will get two documents in this question, again from any part of the course.
2. Read the questions for the first document, then read the document.
3. Read the questions again **one by one** for the first document, then find the answer in the document.
4. **Underline** where you think you have found the answer.
5. Use your own words, but also make sure you **copy parts of the document** into your answer.
6. Now do the same for the second document.

Question 3 – Short answers

1. You must answer **10** out of **20** questions.
2. If you can answer one or two more, do so. But no more than that.
3. There are **20 marks** going for this question, so each question is only worth 2 marks. Do not spend too much time thinking about the answer to each question.

exam focus

One way of preparing for the short-answer questions is to write answers on all the past examination questions. Then learn your answers. Also use the Glossary at the end of your textbook.

4. If you are asked for **one piece of information**, only give that.
   - *Example*: Explain **one** way the . . . .
5. Usually Higher level students are asked for **two pieces of information**, so you must give two pieces of information.
   - *Example*: Mention **two** ways in which . . . .
6. Usually **one sentence** will be enough to answer the question.

Question 4 – People in History

1. You are asked to write about a person in history.
2. You select **one person** from Section **A** and **one person** from Section **B**.
3. You should write **historical information** about that person.
4. Each answer is worth **20 marks**, so it is important to give a full answer to these questions.
5. You should write about **one to one and a half A4 pages** for your answer.
6. **Be careful not to go over time in this question!**

One way of preparing for the *People in History* questions is to write out answers for *People in History* questions from past examination papers. Then learn your answers.

Question 5 – Sources

1. This is a **compulsory question** taken from **Second Year History**.
2. It is based on sources such as maps, documents or pictures.
3. The first parts of the question are usually based on the documents. But how well you answer the last part – 5C – could decide how high a grade you will get in the exam.
4. Write **full paragraphs** in answering 5C to make sure you get all the marks.

One way of preparing for 5C is to revise well the **causes** and **results** (consequences) of the five sections in Second Year History – Explorations, Reformation, Plantations, Political Revolutions and From Farm to Factory.

Question 6 – Short answers and essays

1. You must answer **2** questions out of **4** here.
2. This is the **usual order** of the questions (but it can change):
   - **6A** – A question from First Year or Second Year History
   - **6B** – Social Change in 20th-century Ireland
   - **6C** – Political Developments in 20th-century Ireland
   - **6D** – International Relations in the 20th century

Questions 5 and 6 provide **half the marks for Higher level,** so they must be answered well if you want to get a high grade.

3. In the long-answer questions (essay questions), you should write **five to seven/eight points of historical information**, depending on whether the question is marked out of 10, 12 or 14 marks.

Answering exam questions for Ordinary level

The Ordinary level History paper has **4 questions** which must be answered in **1½ hours**. The structure of the Ordinary level paper is shown in this table:

Structure of the Ordinary Level Paper			
Question	Type	Marks	Time
1	Pictures	35	10–15 minutes
2	Documents	35	10–15 minutes
3	Short answers	60	30 minutes
4	People in History	50	30 minutes

Question 1 – Pictures

1. The pictures in this question come from any part of the course. But the majority of them come from First and Second Year History.
2. Make sure you answer all parts of the question.
3. Keep your answers short – usually one sentence will do.

Question 2 – Documents

1. You will get two documents in this question, again from any part of the course.
2. Read the questions for the first document, then read the document.
3. Read the questions again for the first document, then find the answer in the document.
4. Underline where you think you have found the answer.
5. Use your own words but also make sure you copy parts of the document into your answer.
6. Now do the same for the second document.

Question 3 – Short answers

1. You must answer **10** out of **20** questions.
2. There are **60 marks** going for this question, so you must prepare well for it.
3. If you can answer one or two more, do so. But no more than that.

exam focus

One way of preparing for the short-answer questions is to write answers on all the past examination questions. Then learn your answers. Also use the Glossary at the end of your textbook.

4. If you are asked for **one piece of information**, only give that.

  • *Example*: Explain **one** of these terms . . . .

5. If you are asked for **two pieces of information**, you must give two pieces of information.

  • *Example*: Mention **two** ways in which . . . .

6. Usually **one sentence** will be enough to answer the question.

Question 4 – People in history

1. You are asked to write about a person in history.

2. You select **one person** from Section **A** and **one person** from Section **B**.

3. You are given *Hints* about the person. You should use those Hints but also use other information that you have.

4. You should write **historical information** about that person.

5. Each answer is worth **25 marks**, so it is important to give a full answer to these questions.

6. You should write about one A4 page for your answer.

7. Finally, stick to **historical information** when you are answering *People in History* – forget about the weather! Or how sick you were! Or the bad smell! Or anything like that!

One way of preparing for the *People in History* questions is to write out answers for *People in History* questions from past examination papers. Then learn your answers.

YEAR ONE

How We Find Out
about the Past

1 Historians at Work

- To understand the job of the historian
- To understand the work of the archaeologist

The job of the historian

What is history?

History is the story of the past based on evidence.

What is evidence?

This is the information which proves or disproves the story of the past. Historians get their evidence from **sources**.

What are sources?

1. Historians use primary and secondary sources.
2. They can be written, visual or oral.

Types of sources

1. **Written sources**
   - **Manuscripts** are books written by hand.
   - An **autobiography** is the story of a person's own life.
   - A **biography** is written by a historian about another person's life.
   - A **census** (of population) records information about families, businesses, housing, education.
   - **Newspapers** are another kind of published source.
2. **Visual sources**
   - Photographs, paintings, documentaries
   - Cartoons and drawings
   - Maps
3. **Oral sources**
   - Interviews

What is a primary source?

A primary source comes directly from the time that is being studied.

- *Examples*: a diary, a newspaper

What is a secondary source?

1. A secondary source comes from after the time being studied.
2. Secondary sources are based on primary sources.
   - *Example*: your history textbook

Where are sources stored?

1. An **archive** collects mainly written (documentary) sources.
   - *Example*: The National Archives in Dublin
2. A **museum** collects and stores objects for study and display.
   - *Examples:* The National Museum in Dublin, local museums
3. A **library** stores books.
   - *Examples:* The National Library in Dublin, your local county or city library
4. Some of these sources are stored on microfilm (a small film), microfiche (micro-images reproduced on a flat sheet) or on computer.

What is prehistory?

Prehistory is the history of people before writing was invented.

What is bias?

Historians are biased if they deliberately favour one side over the other.

What is propaganda?

Propaganda is using information to influence people's opinions or to convince people that a particular belief is true.

What is chronology?

Chronology is putting events in order of time (when they happened).

Decade = 10 years

Century = 100 years

An age = a number of decades or centuries

BC = the years before the birth of Christ

AD = the years after the birth of Christ

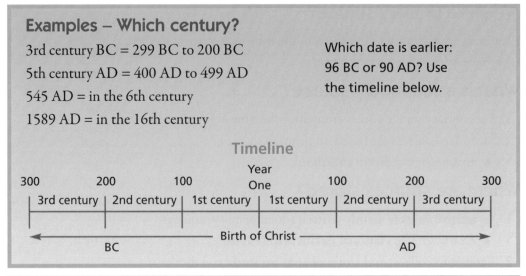

Examples – Which century?

3rd century BC = 299 BC to 200 BC

5th century AD = 400 AD to 499 AD

545 AD = in the 6th century

1589 AD = in the 16th century

Which date is earlier: 96 BC or 90 AD? Use the timeline below.

Timeline

			Year One			
300	200	100		100	200	300
3rd century	2nd century	1st century		1st century	2nd century	3rd century

Birth of Christ

BC   AD

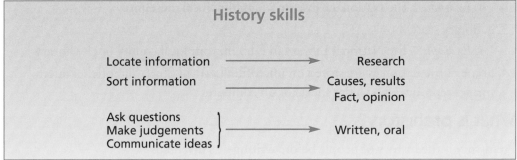

History skills

Locate information ⟶ Research

Sort information ⟶ Causes, results / Fact, opinion

Ask questions / Make judgements / Communicate ideas ⟶ Written, oral

The work of the archaeologist

What is Archaeology?

1. Archaeology is the story of the past from material remains.
2. Material remains are **artefacts** and **buildings**.

What are artefacts?

Artefacts are objects made by people.

- *Examples*: spears, pots, coins and rings

How do archaeologists find sites?

1. **Above ground**
   - Some sites are above ground.
   - *Examples*: castles, the pyramids

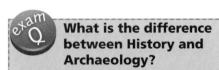

What is the difference between History and Archaeology?

History depends mostly on written sources for evidence, while archaeology depends mostly on objects (artefacts, ruins).

2. **Below ground**
- Some are found by chance when people are ploughing or building.
- *Examples*: The Ardagh Chalice was found when two boys were digging for potatoes and the Terracotta Army was found when people were digging for a well in China.

Stories from history

These are legends or biblical stories.
- *Example*: the story of Troy

Aerial photography

This shows up **crop marks** (patterns in the way crops grow) which indicate that a feature lies under the soil.

Underwater archaeology

This is using sonar, submarines and diving gear to explore sunken wrecks.

What is rescue or salvage archaeology?

This is archaeology undertaken before new roads or buildings are developed.

How do archaeologists excavate sites?

Records – are kept on all finds in computers

Sieves – to sort out artefacts

Diggers – to clear away topsoil

Laboratory – bones, teeth, and skulls are investigated for age and injuries

Survey – to draw an accurate plan of the site

Grid of squares – to accurately record each 'find'

Digging – using shovels, trowels, brushes

Archaeological site and excavation

What instruments do archaeologists use when excavating a site?

Trowels, sieves and brushes are some of the instruments used.

How do archaeologists date objects?

1. **Stratigraphy**: When layers are laid down in the earth, the oldest layers and finds are at the bottom and the youngest layers and finds are at the top.
2. **Tree-ring dating** (also called dendrochronology): Archaeologists can tell when a tree was growing by studying the pattern of rings. The pattern of rings on a piece of wood is compared with the record of tree-ring growth in Ireland, which is held in Queen's University, Belfast.
3. **Carbon-14 dating**: When a plant, person or animal was alive can be worked out by measuring the amount of carbon-14 remaining in the sample of wood, or in the human or animal bone which was found.
4. **Coins and pottery**: Objects found alongside these objects will be from the same age.

What is conservation?

Conservation is the protection and preservation of ancient objects so that they do not decay. This is usually done in a museum.

History, archaeology and tourism

Many of the most popular tourist sites in Ireland are based on history and archaeology.

- *Examples*: Bunratty Castle, Co Clare; Newgrange, Co Meath

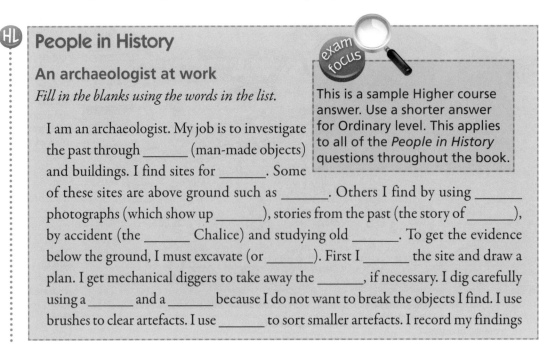

HL People in History

An archaeologist at work
Fill in the blanks using the words in the list.

> **exam focus**
> This is a sample Higher course answer. Use a shorter answer for Ordinary level. This applies to all of the *People in History* questions throughout the book.

I am an archaeologist. My job is to investigate the past through _____ (man-made objects) and buildings. I find sites for _____. Some of these sites are above ground such as _____. Others I find by using _____ photographs (which show up _____), stories from the past (the story of _____), by accident (the _____ Chalice) and studying old _____. To get the evidence below the ground, I must excavate (or _____). First I _____ the site and draw a plan. I get mechanical diggers to take away the _____, if necessary. I dig carefully using a _____ and a _____ because I do not want to break the objects I find. I use brushes to clear artefacts. I use _____ to sort smaller artefacts. I record my findings by _____ them and storing them in plastic bags. I keep the records in a _____. I take photographs of the site and make _____ of the artefacts. I record where I find them. I take the artefacts to a _____. I use the skills of _____ to investigate some of the objects, such as bones and skulls. I have learnt about the shapes of houses from the _____. I will date the objects by using _____ or _____ dating. In _____, I compare timber I find with the record of tree-ring growth in Ireland to work out when the timber was used. _____ dating is based on the amount of carbon left in living objects after they have died. I will put the artefacts into a museum (e.g. the _____) for display. Here they will be _____ (protected and cared for). I have worked on many archaeological sites in Ireland, such as before _____ were built, or before new buildings were built in Dublin and Cork. This is called _____. The work I do helps the growth of the _____ industry in Ireland.

Use your textbook to check your answers when you are finished. (Words can be used more than once)

aerial	dig	National Museum	sieves
Ardagh	drawings	numbering	survey
artefacts	excavation	postholes	topsoil
carbon 14	field-computer	salvage	tourist
castles	laboratory	archaeology	tree-ring dating
conserved	maps	scientists	trowel
crop marks	motorways	shovel	Troy

Past questions on *Historians at Work*

Pictures

1. Picture A shows archaeologists at work on a site. (2005)
   (a) What work is being done by the archaeologist marked X in the picture?
   (b) What do you think the archaeologists have discovered?
   (c) Give one example from the picture of how archaeologists record information.
   (d) Name one method of dating an archaeologist would use to date objects found on a site.

Picture A

Short-Answer Questions

1. What is a secondary source? Give one example.
2. What do historians mean by the term *prehistory*?
3. Explain two of the following terms used by historians: *Bias; Primary source; Archives; Museums.*
4. What is an artefact? Give an example.
5. From your study of history, explain what a primary source is. Give one example.
6. Name two instruments (or tools) an archaeologist would use while excavating a site.
7. Name two methods used by archaeologists to try to date objects they find.
8. Mention two types of primary source a historian can use.
9. Explain the difference between a primary source and a secondary source.
10. The term *census* refers to an official population count. True or False?
11. To which century does the following date belong? AD 1825
12. 'A birth certificate is an example of a secondary source.' True or False?
13. Put X in the box beside the correct answer below.

    An Eyewitness account is an example of which type of source?

    (a) Primary source

    (b) Secondary source
14. Mention one place artefacts are displayed in public.
15. Why do historians prefer to obtain information from more than one source?
16. During an excavation, why are archaeologists very careful with objects that they find?
17. 'A diary is an example of a secondary source.' True or False?

People in History

Ordinary level

1. An archaeologist at work
   - *Hints*: Choosing a site; Excavating a site; Instruments used; Finds and dating

Higher level

1. An archaeologist working on a dig

2 Our Roots in Ancient Civilisation: Ancient Ireland

aims

- To understand how people lived in the Stone Age, Bronze Age and Iron Age
- To understand the life of a monk in an early Irish monastery

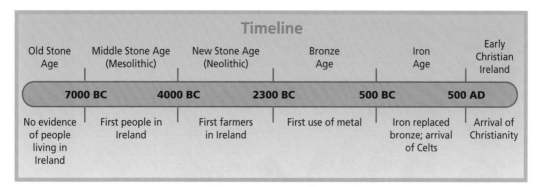

Timeline					
Old Stone Age	Middle Stone Age (Mesolithic)	New Stone Age (Neolithic)	Bronze Age	Iron Age	Early Christian Ireland
	7000 BC	4000 BC	2300 BC	500 BC	500 AD
No evidence of people living in Ireland	First people in Ireland	First farmers in Ireland	First use of metal	Iron replaced bronze; arrival of Celts	Arrival of Christianity

The Mesolithic Period (Middle Stone Age)

What is the Mesolithic Period?

The Mesolithic Period refers to a stage in human history during which people used stone tools and weapons. It is also called the Middle Stone Age.

When did the first people come to Ireland?

The first people came to Ireland in the Mesolithic period (or Middle Stone Age).

How did they get here?

The sea level rose after the Ice Age so it is likely they came by **dugout canoes** or **skin-covered boats** across the narrow sea from Britain.

What do we know about the Mesolithic people?

1. **Houses**: They lived in houses made of light branches covered with skins, grass, leaves or plants. There was a hearth or fireplace in the centre of the house (hut).
2. **Food and family**: These people were **hunter-gatherers** – they hunted boar, duck and pigeon for food; they caught fish and they gathered berries and nuts. They cooked on a **cooking spit**.

3. Mesolithic people were **nomadic** – they moved from one place to another when the food supply ran out.

4. **Work and tools**: Their weapons and tools were made of **stone**.

   - Stone axes were used to cut trees; spears and arrows had sharp flint stones on top; skins were cleaned with **scrapers**; skins were stitched with **bone needles**.

How do we know about Mesolithic people in Ireland?

Examples of Mesolithic sites in Ireland include Mount Sandel, Co Derry, and Lough Boora, Co Offaly. Archaeologists have excavated sites here which showed how Mesolithic people lived. Evidence from **middens** – mounds or heaps of shells, animal bones or other refuse – can be used by archaeologists to study the life of the people.

Mesolithic campsite

Stone axe and arrowhead with flint

The Neolithic Period (New Stone Age)

The first farmers

The Neolithic people were Ireland's **first farmers**.

- They cleared the forest to create small farms.
- They ploughed the fields with wooden ploughs.
- They grew crops such as wheat and barley.
- They domesticated animals such as cattle, sheep, goats and dogs.
- They made permanent settlements.

How do we know about Neolithic people in Ireland?

Examples of Neolithic sites in Ireland include Lough Gur, Co Limerick, the Boyne Valley, Co Meath, and the Céide Fields, Co Mayo.

How did they build their houses?

1. They built rectangular or circular-shaped houses.
2. They built the walls of timber planks or wattle and daub.

What was wattle and daub?

Wattle was interwoven sticks; the sticks were covered by daub (mud).

3. They thatched the roof with straw from wheat or barley.
4. They had a hearth in the middle of the floor, with a cooking spit.

What is a posthole?

It is a hole in the ground which held the posts for the walls of houses.

Work, weapons and tools

1. Neolithic people used stone tools and weapons similar to the Mesolithic people.
2. They were **farmers** so they worked the land, ploughing the small fields, cutting corn, ground the corn on a **saddle stone** (or saddle quern) and used the straw for thatch. They also minded cattle and sheep.
3. They engaged in **spinning** and **weaving** to make cloth from the wool of the sheep.
4. They also hunted and gathered.

How did Neolithic people bury their dead?

1. They buried them in **megalithic** or great stone tombs:
   - **Court cairns**
   - **Portal dolmens**
   - **Passage graves**

What was a court cairn?

2. A court cairn had a semi-circular court (or open space) in front of the entrance leading into a passage and a burial chamber. The tomb was covered with a large mound of stones. Bodies were cremated (burned) in the court and the ashes were placed in pots in the burial chamber.
   - *Example*: Creevykeel court cairn, Co Sligo

Court cairn

What was a portal dolmen?

3. This was a tomb with three large upright stones and a large **capstone** on top. The tomb was covered with a mound of stones.

   - *Example*: Poulnabrone portal dolmen, Co Clare

What was a passage grave?

4. Passage graves had a long passage leading into a burial chamber. Passage graves were sometimes built together in a 'cemetery'. In Newgrange passage grave, the rays of the rising sun on 21 December shine through a **roof box** over the front entrance and reach the burial chamber inside.

   - *Example*: Newgrange, Dowth and Knowth passage graves, in the Boyne Valley, Co Meath

Portal dolmen

Newgrange passage grave

Pottery

Neolithic people made pottery from clay.

- The pottery was used for storing food, for cooking and for burials.

The Bronze Age

What was the Bronze Age?

In the Bronze Age, copper and tin were combined to make bronze. This was the first use of metal. The Stone Age gave way to the Bronze Age.

What was the source of copper and tin?

Copper was mined near Mount Gabriel, Co Cork, and Killarney, Co Kerry.

Tin was imported from mines in Cornwall in England.

What kinds of houses did Bronze Age people live in?

Bronze Age people lived in houses similar to those lived in by Neolithic people.

- They were made of wattle and daub walls, with a thatched roof.
- A timber fence with an earthen bank surrounded the houses, providing protection.

What did Bronze Age people eat?

They ate the same type of foods as Neolithic people.

- Wheat and oats were used to make bread and porridge. Grain was ground on a **saddle stone**. Cattle provided meat and rivers and lakes were a source of fish.
- Cooking was done on bronze **cauldrons** or on cooking spits.

What was a *fulacht fiadh*?

A *fulacht fiadh* was an ancient cooking place.

- A hole was dug in the ground and lined with timber or flat stones. It was filled with water.
- Large stones were heated in a fire and put into the water to bring it to the boil.
- Meat was wrapped in straw and placed in the water until it was cooked.

What work was done?

1. **Farming** was the most important occupation.
2. There were also **craftsmen** who made bronze and gold objects.

Arts and crafts

Gold was used to make fine objects such as lunulae and sun disks, torcs, necklaces and bracelets.

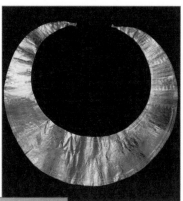

Gold lunula

Gold sun disk

Gold torc

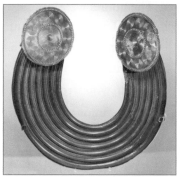

Gold necklace

What were bronze and gold used for?

Objects made of **bronze**: Swords, axes, spearheads, arrowheads

Objects made of **gold**: Lunulae, sun discs, torcs, necklaces

How did Bronze Age people bury their dead?

1. A **cist grave** was a rectangular pit dug in the ground and lined with stone slabs. A single body was buried there in a crouched position. **Grave goods** such as food, arrow heads, beads and pins were placed in the grave as well.

2. A **wedge tomb** was built with large flat stones on the sides and a capstone on top. They were called wedge tombs because they were wedge-shaped. The entrance was wider and higher than the back of the tomb.

3. **Standing stones** were tall stones laid out in a line, in a circle or on their own. They were used for religious ceremonies and to mark burial sites.

The Celts and the Iron Age

Who were the Celts?

1. The Celts lived in southern Germany, Austria and Switzerland.
2. Their language and culture spread to France, Britain and Ireland.
   - The Celtic language and culture, and the use of iron were widespread in Ireland by 300 BC.

What was the Iron Age?

It was a period in which iron was used instead of bronze to make weapons and tools. Bronze and gold were still used for ornaments.

How was Celtic society organised?

1. The Celts divided Ireland into kingdoms or ***tuatha***. A king or *rí* ruled each *tuath*. The king was elected by the royal family (called the ***derbhfine***).

2. The **nobles** were composed of warriors and the **Aos Dána**. The Aos Dána had special skills. They were made up of:
   - **judges**, who knew the Celtic or Brehon laws
   - **druids**, who were the Celtic priests
   - *filí*, who wrote poetry on the history and traditions of the tribe

3. The **commoners** were the farmers who worked the land and herded cattle. Most of the work was done by labourers and slaves (who were captured from other tribes).

How do we know about the Celts?

We have two main sources:

- **Archaeological evidence** – ring forts, weapons, graves
- **Documentary (written) evidence** – Celtic legends such as *An Táin Bó Cúailnge* and Celtic laws known as the Brehon laws

What type of houses did the Celts use?

1. The Celts lived mainly in **ring forts** and *crannógs*.
2. **What was a ring fort?**
   - A **ring fort** was an area enclosed by a circular earthen bank. Farmers built houses of wattle and daub walls with thatched roofs inside in the ring fort.
   - *Examples*: There are examples of ring forts all over Ireland. Place-names with *rath* or *lios* indicated that ring forts were found in the locality (Rathmore, Lismore).
   - Some ring forts had **souterrains** which were underground storage areas, under a house in the ring fort.
3. **What was a *crannóg*?**
   - A *crannóg* was an artificial lake dwelling. Farmers built an artificial island with a house on top of it. Boats were used to travel between the lakeshore and the *crannóg*.
   - *Examples*: There are many examples of the *crannóg* in the lakes of the midlands of Ireland.

Other Celtic settlements

4. **What were hill forts?**
   - Hill forts were surrounded by very large circular earthen banks, similar to ring forts but much wider. They were built on prominent hills and were used mainly for religious ceremonies.
   - *Examples*: The Hill of Tara, Co Meath; Navan Fort, Co Armagh
5. **What were promontory forts?**
   - Promontory forts were built on headlands or cliff edges. They were surrounded by earthen or stone banks. They were used for religious ceremonies.
   - *Example*: Dún Aengus in the Aran Islands

Food

1. The Celts got meat from cattle, sheep and pigs. They cooked the meat on a cooking spit or in a *fulacht fiadh*.
2. They produced milk, butter and cheese from cow's milk. They used wheat and oats to make bread and porridge, and they made ale from barley.
3. The cooking was done by the women, who also did the spinning and the weaving to make cloth.
4. The Celts held **feasts** to celebrate victory in battle. The **hero's portion** was the best portion of the meat and it was given to the bravest warrior.

How did the Celts grind their corn?

They used a **rotary quern** (and not a saddle quern, which had been used by the Neolithic people in Ireland).

Tools and weapons

1. Axes, swords, spear heads and arrow heads were made from iron.
2. Ornaments such as torcs were made from gold or bronze.

Celtic art

This was called *La Tène* art. It consisted of spirals, curved lines and florals.
- *Example*: The Turoe Stone, Co Galway

Celtic religion and burials

1. The Celts **cremated** their dead and placed their ashes in a pot in the ground or in a **cist grave**.
2. They included **grave goods** with the ashes.

What was an ogham stone?

1. **Ogham stones** were standing stones which marked graves or land boundaries.
2. The first form of writing in Ireland was called **ogham** writing. It was a series of lines cut into the side of the ogham stones.

People in History

A farmer in ancient Ireland

Ordinary level example

I am a farmer in the **Neolithic** period (New Stone Age). I am one of Ireland's **first farmers**. The walls of my house are made of **wattle** and **daub** (interwoven sticks and mud) and the roof is **thatched**. In the middle of the floor is a **cooking spit** where our food is cooked. All our tools and weapons are made of **stone**. We use **flint**, which can be broken into sharp pieces to make **arrows** and **spears**. I had to cut down trees with a **stone axe** to clear the ground for fields. I till the fields with a **timber plough**. I grow wheat and barley, which I cut with a **sickle**. Then my wife grinds the grain on a **saddle stone** (a stone with a hollow in which the grain is ground with another stone). I have a few cattle, sheep, pigs and goats. I keep them in small **fields** with stone walls. We also get food from **hunting** and **gathering**

In the *People in History* question (Q. 4), Ordinary level students get hints, and they should use these, but they do not have to confine themselves to the hints. Higher level students do not get hints.

- *Example:* Write about a farmer in ancient Ireland.
  - *(Ordinary level) Hints:* Housing, clothing and food; Farming methods; Arts and crafts; Burial customs

berries. We use the **wool** from the sheep to make **woollen clothes**. We use **pottery** for cooking and storing food. We bury our dead in great stone (megalithic) **tombs**. These are portal dolmens, court cairns and passage graves. We **cremate** the bodies and put the ashes into pots in the tombs.

Higher level example

Fill in the blanks using the words in the list.

I am a farmer in the _____ period (New Stone Age). I am one of Ireland's **first farmers**. I live in Lough _____ (Co Limerick). I have a rectangular-shaped house. The walls are made of _____ and _____ (interwoven sticks and mud) and the roof is **thatched**. Others have their houses made of _____ **planks**. In the middle of the floor is a **cooking** _____ where our food is cooked. All our tools and weapons are made of _____. We use **flint**, which can be broken into sharp pieces to make _____ and **spears**. I had to cut down trees with a **stone** _____ to clear the ground for fields. I till the fields with a _____ and a **timber** _____, pulled by **oxen**. I grow wheat and barley which I cut with a _____. Then my wife grinds the grain on a _____ **stone** (a stone with a hollow in which the grain is ground with another stone). We use the straw for the _____. We make **porridge** and _____ from the grain. I have a few cattle, sheep, pigs and goats. I keep them in small **fields** with stone walls, like the _____ Fields. I kill a pig every winter for meat. But we also get food from _____ and from **gathering** berries. We use the **wool** from the sheep to make woollen clothes through _____ and weaving. We also use **skins**, which we clean with a _____ We use _____ **needles** to sew the skins together. We use _____ for cooking and storing food. We make it by forming coils with the mud. We bury our dead in great stone (_____) **tombs**. These are portal _____, court cairns and _____ graves *[Explain each of these in your answer.]* We _____ the bodies and put the ashes into pots in the tombs.

Use your textbook to check your answers when you are finished. (Words can be used more than once)

arrows	dolmens	plough	stone
axe	Gur	pottery	thatch
bone	hunting	saddle	timber
bread	mattock	scraper	wattle
Céide	megalithic	sickle	
cremate	Neolithic	spinning	
daub	passage	spit	

Early Christian Ireland

The arrival of Christianity

Christianity came to Ireland in the 5th century. St Patrick and other missionaries converted the Celtic people to Christianity.

What are monasteries?

Monasteries are buildings in which monks and priests pray to God.

What was life like in a monastery in Early Christian Ireland?

1. Some monasteries (such as **Clonmacnoise** and **Glendalough**) were large. Others, such as **Skellig Michael** off the Kerry coast, were small and remote.

2. The main buildings in a monastery were:
   - The church
   - The abbot's house
   - The **refectory** (for eating)
   - The **scriptorium** (for copying manuscripts)
   - The **cells** for each of the monks

3. Some of the larger monasteries had **round towers**, which were used as bell towers and for protections from attack.
   - *Examples*: The round towers in Clonmacnoise and in Glendalough

Know one or two of the examples here

Founder	Monastery location
St Enda	Aran islands
St Finian	Clonard, Co Meath
St Brendan	Clonfert, Co Galway
St Ciaran	Clonmacnoise, Co Offaly
St Kevin	Glendalough, Co Wicklow

You should use the information in 'What was life like in a monastery in Early Christian Ireland?', 'What did the monks do?', 'Copying Manuscripts', 'Metalworking' and 'Stone Crosses' to write a *People in History* account on '**A monk in a monastery in Early Christian Ireland**'.

What did the monks do?

1. The monks followed strict rules. They wore long tunics with woollen cloaks, and leather shoes or sandals.
   - Their main activity was prayer.
   - They also worked in the fields to produce food for the monastery.

Copying manuscripts

2. Some monks (scribes) worked in the scriptorium copying manuscripts to create hand-written books.
   - *Examples*: *The Cathach* (a copy of the psalms and the earliest manuscript), the *Book of Kells* (a copy of the Four Gospels now held in Trinity College, Dublin)

3. The monks used **quills** (feathers) to write on **vellum** (calfskin) or **parchment** (sheepskin).

Metalworking

4. Other monks produced silver chalices, crosiers and brooches. They added gold wiring called **filigree** to these.
   - *Examples*: Ardagh Chalice; Derrynaflan Chalice

Ardagh Chalice

Stone crosses

5. Some monks carved high stone crosses which had scenes from the Bible and the lives of saints.
   - *Example*: St Muireadach's High Cross, Monasterboise, Co Louth

Irish monks abroad

6. Some Irish monks went abroad and founded monasteries in Britain and on the Continent.
   - *Examples*: St Columcille went to the remote island of Iona in Scotland; St Columbanus founded monasteries in France and Italy.

Past questions on *Our Roots in Ancient Civilisation: Ancient Ireland*

Pictures

1. Picture A shows Poulnabrone dolmen. (2007)
   - (i) What is the name given to the stone marked **X**?
   - (ii) Why did Stone Age farmers build structures like this?
   - (iii) Give **two** reasons why that period was called the Stone Age.

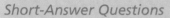

Picture A

Short-Answer Questions

1. Archaeologists sometimes describe the earliest Irish people as *hunter-gatherers*. What is meant by that term?
2. Name **two** advances made by Neolithic people (New Stone Age).
3. What was wattle and daub?
4. Name **two** types of tomb from Neolithic Ireland.
5. Explain two of the following terms as used by archaeologists: *Artefact; Megalith; Midden; Posthole.*
6. Name **two** metal ores used in Ireland during the Bronze Age.

7. What language did the early Christian monks use to write manuscripts such as the *Book of Kells*?

8. Name **two** types of dwellings from Celtic Ireland.

9. Why were cattle important to the Celts?

10. Name one type of metal used by the Celts to make tools and weapons.

11. For what purpose was the *stone quern* used in Celtic Ireland?

12. Explain **two** of the following terms relating to ancient Ireland: *Torc; Fulachta Fiadh; Aos Dána; Ogham.*

13. Explain the meaning of **two** of the following terms: *Souterrain; Fulacht Fiadh; Tánaiste; Derbhfine.*

14. Mention **two** effects of the coming of Christianity to Ireland.

15. Name **one** Early Irish monastery and **one** monk associated with that monastery.

16. What was the purpose of the round tower in the early Christian monastery?

People in History

Ordinary level

1. A person living in Ireland during the Stone Age **or** the Bronze Age **or** the Iron Age
   - *Hints*: Housing, clothing and food; Farming methods; Arts and crafts; Burial customs

Higher level

1. A person living in ancient (pre-Christian) Ireland

2. A farmer in ancient (pre-Christian) Ireland

3. A monk in an early Irish monastery

Long-Answer Questions (for Higher level)

1. Give **two** reasons why megalithic tombs can be a good source of information about life in the Stone Age.

2. From the following, identify **two** important archaeological sites associated with life in Ireland during the Stone Age: *Céide Fields; Jerpoint; Wood Quay; Dowth.*

3. From what two metals was bronze made?

4. Explain two of the following terms related to ancient Ireland: *Dolmen; Druid; Tuath.*

5. Write an account on two of the following aspects of life in Celtic Ireland:
   (a) Food and clothing
   (b) Housing
   (c) Work, art and craft

3 Our Roots in Ancient Civilisation: Ancient Rome

The Roman Empire

1. In Roman legend, Rome was founded by Romulus.
2. Rome actually grew from villages on the hills around the River Tiber.
3. Rome conquered all the land around the Mediterranean Sea. Its empire stretched north to **Hadrian's Wall** between Scotland and England.

The Roman Empire

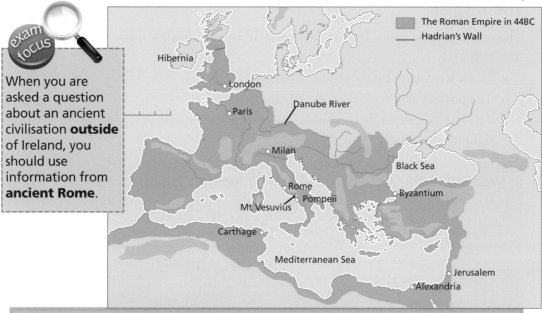

The Roman Empire in 44BC
Hadrian's Wall

Hibernia
London
Paris
Danube River
Milan
Black Sea
Rome
Pompeii
Byzantium
Mt Vesuvius
Carthage
Mediterranean Sea
Jerusalem
Alexandria

How do we know about ancient Rome?

There are two main sources:

● **Archaeological evidence**: Coins, buildings, ruins of Pompeii and Herculaneum
● **Documentary evidence**: The writings of Roman authors such as Cicero and Tacitus

Roman towns

1. Romans built new towns on a **grid pattern**, surrounded by walls.
2. The main buildings were:
   ● The Forum or marketplace
   ● The amphitheatre for gladiatorial contests
   ● The public baths

What happened in Pompeii in 79 AD?

Mount Vesuvius erupted and covered the town of Pompeii. The ruins of the town have been excavated to show what life was like in a Roman town.

Roman houses

1. Well-off Romans (patricians) lived in a private house (called a *domus*), which was surrounded by walls. The houses had:
   - an *atrium* – an open courtyard with a pool in the middle
   - a *peristylium* – a garden with statues of the gods
   - a kitchen and bedrooms round the atrium
2. The inside walls were covered in **murals** (wall paintings) and the floors with **mosaics** (scenes made from small pieces of glass or pottery).

The *Insulae*

The poorer classes (plebs) lived in *insulae* (apartment blocks), which were four to six storeys tall.

- There were shops on the ground floor.
- The poorest families lived in the top floor.
- The residents depended on public toilets and on the public fountains because there was no water supply in the *insulae*.

What was the source of water in Roman towns?

Water was supplied to Romans towns via the **aqueducts** – channels for carrying water.

People in History

A person living in ancient Rome

Higher level example

I am a general living in ancient Rome. Rome rules over a great **empire** which controls all the land around the Mediterranean Sea, Gaul (France) and Britannia as far north as **Hadrian's Wall**. I am in charge of many **legions** (a legion is 5,000 soldiers), which are divided into **centuries** (groups of 100 soldiers). It is our victories which maintain the power of the Roman Empire. When I am away on campaigns I have to live in temporary and permanent **camps**. Our soldiers are equipped with swords, javelins, shields and helmets.

This is a sample **Higher course** answer. Use a shorter answer for Ordinary level.

Stick to the 'history' when writing *People in History* answers!

The city of Rome has a population of about 1 million people. The most important buildings are located in the **Forum**. These are the courts, temples and government buildings. I live in a private house called a *domus*. The centre room in the *domus* is called the *atrium* and there is a pool there. There is also an enclosed garden called the *peristylium*. Many of the rooms have **mosaics** (designs with tiles) on the floor while the walls have **murals** (paintings). Near us are *insulae* (apartment blocks) which are rented to poorer Romans. We have a *villa* in the countryside with a large farm and we go there during the hot summer.

I am head of the family and my wife is in charge of the household and directs the work of the slaves. I wear a **tunic** with a *toga* over it when I go to the Senate to discuss government business. My wife wears a *stola*. My sons are in secondary school preparing for a life in politics or the army. My daughter is learning how to run a household because she is now 14 and ready for marriage. Her marriage to the son of a rich Roman merchant has already been arranged.

I often go to the **public baths** where there are three types of baths – the cold, hot and warm. Here I meet and discuss business with other important city leaders. I like going to chariot races held in the **Circus Maximus** and gladiator contests held in the **Colosseum**. I also like to see plays in the **open-air theatres**.

Food and drink

1. Poorer families depended on bread or a kind of porridge made from wheat and barley.
2. The government also gave out free grain to poorer people because there was so much poverty. This was called the **dole**.
3. Richer Romans had three meals a day, including the *cena* – the main meal – in the evening, after the baths. Slaves served the food as the men and women lay on couches and faced into a table.

Education

1. Poorer children did not learn to read and write.
2. Richer children went to primary school at age 7, where they learnt to write on wax tablets.
3. **Boys** went to secondary school, where they studied history, philosophy, geometry and the writings of the Greek and Latin authors. Some received training in public speaking for use in politics.
4. Richer **girls** ended their education at primary school because they were often married off at an early age – say 14.

What language did the ancient Romans speak?

Latin was the language of ancient Romans.

Leisure and entertainment

1. **Gladiators** were slaves who had to fight each other or wild animals in an amphitheatre, such as the **Colosseum** in Rome. They used swords, nets, tridents (three-pronged pikes), shields and daggers. They often fought to the death.

What is the Colosseum?

The **Colosseum** is an amphitheatre built in the centre of Rome. It was the largest ever built in the Roman Empire and could hold 50,000 spectators.

2. Chariot racing was held in the **Circus Maximus**, which could hold 250,000 people. Four teams (called Red, Green, Blue and White) raced seven times around a central spine. Champion charioteers had large followings.
3. Plays were held in **open-air theatres** in daylight. Actors wore masks.
4. Romans went to the **baths** each day in the early afternoon. There were about 1,000 private baths and 11 public ones, e.g. the Baths of Caracalla.
   - The baths had a warm room, a hot room and a cold room. Romans rubbed oil into the body to clean themselves. This was scraped off with a *strigil*.
   - Women had their own baths.

Romans at work

1. **Farming** was the most important occupation in ancient Rome. Slaves did most of the work on the farms, and everywhere else.
2. Richer Romans became generals or senators (politicians).
3. Poorer Romans worked as craftsmen such as bakers, glassworkers or carpenters in their own workshops.
4. Many people worked for the government as tax collectors or in the Roman army.

The Roman army

1. The army was divided into legions (groups of about 5,000 soldiers) and centuries (groups of 100 soldiers).
2. Some soldiers lived in permanent forts along the border of the empire.
3. Soldiers went on long, fast marches and built temporary camps at night.

Julius Caesar was a great Roman general and leader who conquered Gaul (France) and invaded Britain.

4. They used swords, shields, helmets and javelins.

5. Discipline was strict.

Slaves

1. Most of the work on farms and in towns was done by slaves who were owned by Roman citizens or by the government. They were bought and sold at markets.

2. Slaves sometimes rebelled against harsh treatment. The most serious rebellion was led by **Spartacus**. It took the Roman authorities two years to crush the rebel army of about 90,000 slaves.

Roman art and architecture

1. The Romans used pillars, rounded arches and domes in their buildings.

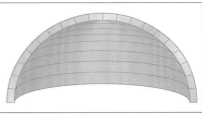
A dome

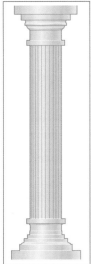
A roman pillar

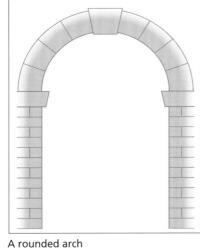
A rounded arch

2. Inside some building there were **murals** (wall paintings) and **mosaics** (scenes made from small pieces of glass or pottery) on the floors.

What are frescoes?

The Romans decorated the walls of their homes with **murals** or wall paintings. These are called **frescoes** – paintings done on wet plaster.

3. The style of Roman (and Greek) art and architecture is described as 'classical'.

The **classical style** of Greek and Roman art, architecture and literature (writing) was later copied during the Renaissance in Italy in the 15th and 16th centuries.

Religion

Religion was important to the ancient Romans, who celebrated many religious festivals. They worshipped many gods and goddesses.

The Romans used bronze and marble to make statues of gods and goddesses.

Some Roman Gods and Goddesses	
Jupiter	Father of the Gods
Neptune	God of the Sea
Mars	God of War
Venus	Goddess of Love

Funerals and burial customs

1. Some Romans believed that their spirit was carried across the **River Styx** to the underworld by **Charon**, the ferryman. They placed a **coin** in the mouth of the dead person to pay the ferryman.
2. Other Romans wanted to be remembered with death masks and inscriptions on tombs.
3. When **rich Romans** died, they were dressed in a *toga* for their funeral. They were carried in a procession of relatives, musicians and mourners before they were cremated. Their ashes were placed in urns (pottery jars) and buried in cemeteries outside the town or city walls.
4. **Poorer Romans** also had processions. They were then cremated and their ashes were buried in simple graves.

Christian burials

5. Christians buried their dead in the **catacombs** (underground tunnels and passages). They were not cremated. Christians believed they were leaving earth to be with God in heaven.

What was the place of Christianity in ancient Rome?

Christianity spread from Palestine to Rome. Christians refused to follow the state gods of Rome so they were persecuted. Christianity became the state religion after the Emperor Constantine was converted to the religion.

The decline of the Roman Empire

The Roman Empire collapsed at the end of the 5th century AD. It was weakened by

- Civil wars
- High taxes and high prices
- Attacks from barbarian tribes

What were the achievements of the Roman Empire?

1. Towns and cities

- Many cities owe their origins to Roman builders and planners – for example, London, Paris and Lyons.

2. Architecture and sculpture

St Peter's Basilica in Rome

- Roman-style architecture and sculpture was copied by people in the Renaissance (15th- and 16th-century Italy) – for example, St Peter's Basilica in Rome.
- Many modern government buildings and churches followed the Roman style –for example, the White House in Washington, D.C.

3. Language

- Many modern languages such as French, Italian, Portuguese and Spanish are based on Latin, the language of the Romans.
- English contains many words derived from Latin. (For example, the word *aquarium* comes from the Latin word *aqua* (meaning *water*), and prefix *semi-* (as in *semi-final*) comes from the Latin word *semi* (meaning *half*).

4. Christianity

- The bishop of Rome became the Pope, or leader, of the Roman Catholic Church.

Past questions on *Our Roots in Ancient Civilisation: Ancient Rome*

People in History

Ordinary level

1. A person living in an ancient civilisation **outside** of Ireland
   - *Hints*: Housing; Clothing and food; Arts and crafts; Burial customs

Higher level

1. A person living in a **named** ancient civilisation **outside** of Ireland
2. A young person in a **named** ancient civilisation **outside** of Ireland

Long-Answer Questions (for Higher level)

1. (i)   Name **two** achievements of a **named** civilisation **outside** of Ireland.
   (ii) Explain how information about this civilisation was discovered.
   (iii) Write an account of **two** of the following aspects of the **named** ancient civilisations:
      (a) Burial customs and religion
      (b) Food and clothing
      (c) Arts, crafts and work

2. Select an ancient civilisation **outside** of Ireland that you have studied and answer the questions which follow. (Please write the name of the ancient civilisation that you have selected at the top of your account.)
   (i)   Name **one** famous person associated with the civilisation that you have chosen.
   (ii) Describe the house that a rich person lived in during the civilisation.
   (iii) Write an account of **two** of the following during that civilisation:
      (a) Food and clothing
      (b) Work, arts and crafts
      (c) Burial customs
   (iv) In your opinion, what were the main achievements of that civilisation?

4 Medieval Society: Castle, Church and City

- To understand what life was like in castles and in manors
- To understand what life was like in towns and cities
- To understand the life of a monk in a medieval monastery

What were the Middle Ages?

The terms *Middle Ages* or *medieval times* covers the centuries from about 5th century to 15th century.

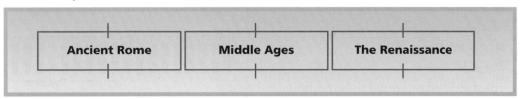

| Ancient Rome | Middle Ages | The Renaissance |

How do we know about the Middle Ages?

The key sources are:

- **Archaeological evidence** – ruins of castles, excavations in towns
- **Documentary evidence** – the **Bayeux Tapestry**, which is an account of the Norman invasion of England, and the **Domesday Book**, which lists land ownership in England after the invasion of the Normans

A section of Bayeux Tapestry

Who were the Normans?

The Normans came from Normandy in France. Led by William the Conqueror, they conquered Britain in 1066. One hundred years later, they invaded Ireland and conquered many parts of it. They brought their laws and way of life to Ireland.

What was the feudal system?

The feudal system (or feudalism) was the system which controlled land ownership and defence in the Middle Ages.

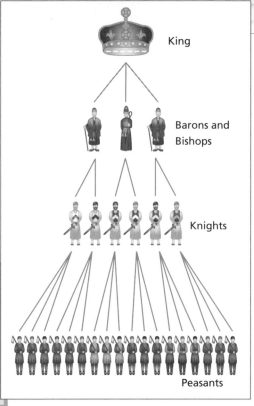

- The king owned all the land.
- He granted land to **bishops** and **barons**. They promised to fight for the king and provide him with knights.
- They granted land to the **knights**. The knights promised to fight for their lords and obey them.
- The knights gave land to the **peasants** who worked some days for the lord in order to pay their rent.

What is a fief and what is a vassal?

Fief = the land which was handed over by the king or lord

Vassal = the lord or knight who received the land and promised to be faithful

The feudal system

Medieval castles

1. Kings and lords built castles to defend their land, to provide a place to live and to protect local people.

Motte and bailey castles

2. The first castles were motte and bailey castles, which were relatively easy to build.

   - A **motte** was a mound of earth on which a timber fence and a keep (or tower) were built.
   - A **bailey** was a courtyard attached to the motte.

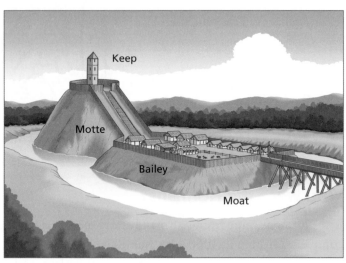

Motte and bailey

   - *Example*: The timber of motte and bailey castles rotted so all that is left is the mound (motte) – Knockgraffon Motte, near Cahir, Co Tipperary

Stone castles

3. Stone castles replaced the motte and bailey castles because they were stronger.
   - *Examples*: Trim Castle, Co Meath; Carrickfergus Castle, Co Antrim

4. The castle's **defensive features** included a curtain wall, moat, battlements, towers (turrets), drawbridge, portcullis, outer bailey, inner bailey, keep, workshops and stables.

Explain in a sentence how each of these features helped in the defence of a castle: curtain wall, moat, battlements, towers (turrets), drawbridge, portcullis, outer bailey, inner bailey, keep, workshops, stables.

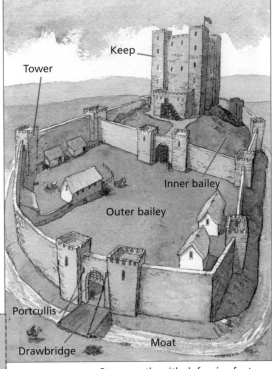

Stone castle with defensive features

5. Those who wished to **attack** stone castles used scaling ladders, throwing rocks, siege towers, archers, battering ram and undermining the wall.

Explain in a sentence how each of these helped in the attack of a castle: scaling ladders, throwing rocks, siege towers, archers, battering ram, undermining the wall.

Stone castle from outside showing attack and weapons of attack

People in History

The lord/lady of the castle: A lord living in the Middle Ages (medieval times)

Fill in the blanks using the words in the list. (Words can be used more than once)

I am a **baron** living in a castle. I got land (called a _____) from the **king**. I became his _____ and I promised to fight for him. This is called the **feudal system** or _____. I also rent land to lesser lords called _____. I control the lands of a _____. I help the king control the country. I hold court and settle disputes. I enjoy **hunting** and _____ with other lords and knights. I sometimes organise **tournaments** and _____ so that knights can practise their fighting. I used to live in a **motte and** _____ castle made of _____. When it burned down I built a **stone castle**, which provides a stronger defence. The outer wall of my castle is surrounded by a _____ and I have a _____ and _____ in case of attack. The castle is very difficult to capture. When the castle was under siege, the attackers used _____ **ladders, siege** _____ and **battering** _____, but they failed in their assault. Inside the walls is the **bailey** or _____ with stables, huts for servants and a forge. The most important building in my castle is the _____. Even if my enemies broke through the walls of the castle, we are well protected in the _____. The **door** is above ground with steep steps. We have a **narrow** _____ **staircase** in the keep, which will make it difficult for attackers to take over the building. My family live in the keep and we have _____ in the **great hall** for visiting nobles. **Tapestries** hang from the walls and entertainment is provided by _____ and **musicians**. The servants of the castle are organised by my wife, the **lady** of the castle. My marriage to the daughter of another lord was arranged. Her family had to pay a _____ to me. When I die, my eldest son will succeed me as lord of the castle.

Use your textbook to check your answers when you are finished.

bailey	fief	manor	timber
courtyard	hawking	moat	towers
dowry	jesters	portcullis	vassal
drawbridge	jousts	rams	
feasts	keep	scaling	
feudalism	knights	spiral	

People in History

A knight in the Middle Ages

Fill in the blanks using the words in the list. (Words can be used more than once)

I am a **knight** in the Middle Ages. I am from a _____ family who came to conquer Ireland. I went through _____ **stages** before I became a knight. I became a _____ when I was 7 years old. I went to live in another lord's castle and I helped the _____ of the castle. I became a _____ when I was 14 years old. I helped my lord dress for _____ (combats with other knights). I practised with _____, swords and shields. I became a _____ when I was 21 years old. I _____ all night before the ceremony. In the ceremony, I was _____ a knight as I knelt before my lord and he placed a _____ on my shoulder. I took **vows of** _____ to be loyal, to help the poor and to protect women and children. I practise in _____ and **jousts**. I wear a suit of _____ and chain mail. I wear the _____ of my family on my shield. This tells everybody who I am. I also have a **helmet** with a _____ to protect my eyes. My weapons are a lance, a sword and a _____. I got land (**fief**) from a **baron** – I'm his _____. I am loyal to my lord and I will be ready to go into battle if he needs me. This is called _____. I live in a village in a _____ **house** with a wall and a moat. I will build a _____ **house** soon because this is stronger – more like a castle. I control the land around, which I rent to peasants (_____). They work three _____ fields, but they also have to harvest crops for me as part of the rent.

Use your textbook to check your answers when you are finished.

armour	jousts	open	three
battle axe	knight	page	tournaments
chivalry	Lady	prayed	tower
crest	lances	serfs	vassal
dubbed	manor	squire	visor
feudalism	Norman	sword	

The medieval manor

Knights were given **manors**.

- The medieval manor was the village and the land around it. The knights kept some of the land for their own private use – this was called the demesne.
- The land around the village was divided into **three large open fields**. Peasants were given land in each field, and the land was divided into **strips**.

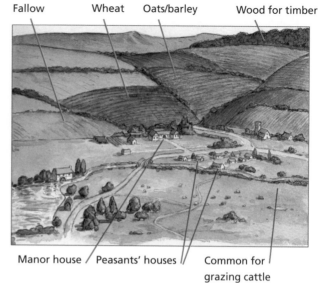

Fallow   Wheat   Oats/barley   Wood for timber

Manor house / Peasants' houses /   Common for grazing cattle

A medieval village with a three-field system

People in History

A peasant in a medieval manor

Fill in the blanks using the words in the list. (Words can be used more than once)

I am a peasant in a medieval manor. The manor is our _____ and the land around. It is controlled by the lord who lives in the _____ **house** (a stone house with a wall and a moat). I am a _____ so I am not free. I have to ask my lord's permission to leave the manor. I live in a house made of _____ and _____ **walls** (interwoven sticks and mud) and a thatched roof. We have little **furniture**, only a few _____ and a table. I eat _____ for my breakfast, bread and cheese for lunch and thick _____ (or pottage) for dinner. I rarely have _____. My wife works hard to feed the chickens and bake bread. Around my village, there are three large, **open** _____. I **rent** land from the _____. My land is divided into _____ in each of the fields, so that I get a mixture of good and bad land. I grow _____ in one, oats in the other and I leave the third _____ (unused) so that it can recover for the next year's growing. All the peasants in the village help each other at _____ time. I graze my cattle and sheep in the _____ and I gather wood in the forest. I work six days a week. Sometimes I have to fish in the river or hunt in the woods for food. But I would be in trouble if I was caught poaching by the _____, who is in charge of the lord's land. I have to do extra work on the **lord's land** such as _____, sowing and harvesting. I have to grind corn in the **lord's** _____. I also have to pay _____ (one-tenth of my produce) to the parish priest for his upkeep.

Some people in my village are _____ . But the only way I can become a _____ is to get away from the village for a year and a day without being caught.

Use your textbook to check your answers when you are finished.

bailiff	freemen	ploughing	tithe
common	harvest	porridge	village
daub	lord	serf	wattle
fallow	manor	soup	wheat
fields	meat	stools	
freeman	mill	strips	

Tower houses

Tower houses later replaced manor houses because they were safer; they were like the keep of a castle.

- *Examples*: Bunratty Castle, Co Clare; Blarney Castle, Co Cork; Ross Castle, Co Kerry

Medieval cities and towns

Towns and cities in Ireland were founded by the Vikings and Normans. They were founded along the coast, at river crossings, along routes and near castles or monasteries.

- *Examples*: **Viking towns** – Dublin, Cork, Waterford, Limerick; **Norman towns** – Athenry, Galway, Athlone, Nenagh

2–3 storey buildings

Narrow streets

The features of a medieval town

People in History

A merchant in a medieval city

I am a merchant in a medieval town. I trade in **woollen** cloth. I travel throughout France to buy the cloth. I sell it to **shops** and at **markets** and **fairs**. The bad state of the roads, the dangers of being robbed, the extortions I have to face, and the system of fines and tolls which landowners force me to pay before letting me pass through their land, all cause me and my fellow merchants great trouble. I am a member of the **merchant's guild**, which controls the way in which trade is conducted in the towns. Our **guild** regulates prices, quality and weights and measures. Our guild has an agreement with the local **lord** which has reduced our **taxes**. We also **stop merchants** who are not members of our guild from trading. The guild also takes **care** of the burial of its deceased members. Each guild has a **patron saint**, celebrates religious festivals together, and puts on religious plays. We compete with other guilds on **festival days**. The members of the merchant guilds are very important members of the medieval town. Our members take part in running the **corporation** (or town council). One of our members was mayor of the town last year and I was elected to the council. Our power has increased and we are wealthier and of higher social status than the members of the craft guilds such as the carpenters. I live in a fine **stone house** which is better than the **wattle and daub houses** of the poorer people or the timber frame houses of the craftsmen. My **town** is very crowded and its streets are narrow and dirty. There is a **wall** around the town with gates to control entry. They are locked at night and a **curfew** is imposed on people in the town. We have to put out fires in our houses then. But our town is prosperous because we have a **charter** from the king to trade and levy taxes. In the market square is the **guildhall** where we hold our meetings and which shows how powerful we are.

People in History

A craftsman in the Middle Ages

Fill in the blanks using the words in the list. (Words can be used more than once)

I am a craftsman in a medieval town. I am a **shoemaker**. I became an _____ when I was 14 years old and I started to learn my trade. I was trained by a _____ **craftsman**. I lived with the _____ family. I slept and worked in the _____. Here we made and sold shoes. The master had a _____ of a shoe over the door. The shops of other tradesmen, such as tailors and bakers, have signs to show the purpose of their workshops. Working conditions were tough as an _____; I worked very hard, but my master punished me sometimes. I became a _____ after seven years. This meant that I was free to work for anyone and I was paid by the _____. I passed a special test set by the guild and I made my own _____. Because of this I became a master craftsman. Now I have my own workshop and apprentices. I am a member of the shoemaker's _____, which sets standards for our shoes. The _____ is an organisation which also decides who can become a craftsman. As well as this, it sets the _____ of goods. All the other crafts have guilds as well. Sometimes **bad craftsmen** or **cheating** _____ have been **punished** by dragging them around town with their bad products tied around their necks. There are other shoemakers along our **street**, so people call the street _____ Street. Other streets are called after other trades, e.g. Baker Street. My **town** is very crowded and has streets that are _____ and dirty. There is a narrow _____ around the town with gates to control entry. They are locked at night and a _____ is imposed on the town. We have to put out _____ in our houses then. But our town is prosperous because we have a _____ from the king to trade and levy _____

Use your textbook to check your answers when you are finished.

apprentice	day	master	shopkeepers
apprentice	fires	master's	sign
Brogue	guild	masterpiece	taxes
charter	guild	narrow	wall
curfew	journeyman	price	workshop

Church and monastery architecture

1. **Church architecture – Romanesque**
   - The features of Romanesque churches included rounded arches, square towers, thick walls and thick pillars.
   - *Example*: Cormac's Chapel, Cashel, Co Tipperary

2. **Church architecture – Gothic**
   - The features of Gothic churches included spires, buttresses, flying buttresses, rose windows and lancet windows.
   - *Examples*: Christ Church Cathedral, Dublin; St Patrick's Cathedral, Dublin; St Canice's Cathedral, Kilkenny

Square tower

Thick walls

Rounded arches   A Romanesque church

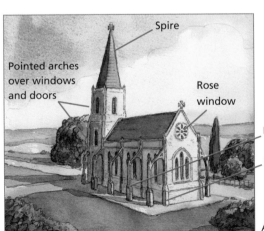

Spire

Pointed arches over windows and doors

Rose window

Flying buttress

Buttress

A Gothic church

   - *Examples* of medieval monasteries include Mellifont, Co Louth, Jerpoint, Co Kilkenny and Holy Cross, Co Tipperary.

3. Monastery architecture

A medieval monastery typically included a church, a refectory, a dormitory, a chapter house, a scriptorium and a cloister.

Church   Chapter house

Refectory

Cloister

Dormitory

Scriptorium

A medieval monastery

People in History

A monk in a medieval monastery

Fill in the blanks using the words in the list. (Words can be used more than once)

I am a monk in a medieval monastery. I joined the **Benedictines** as a _____. I learned the rule of **St** _____ and I helped with work in the monastery. The monastery is surrounded by a _____. We have a _____ which faces east–west, a _____ (a covered walkway where we pray), a _____ (for meals), a _____ **room** and an _____ **house**. We have large fields around the monastery. The _____ (head of the monastery) was happy with my progress so I became a monk. I had part of my head shaved in a _____ and I took _____ **vows:** _____ – I had to give up all my possessions, _____ – I had to promise that I would not marry or have children, _____ – I had to promise to obey the _____ (the head of the monastery). My day is organised around _____ and **work**. All the monks come together to pray _____ **times a day.** We all wear _____ and leather sandals. We meet every morning in the _____ **room.** The _____ gives us our jobs for the day there. I copy _____ in the _____ most days. I use a quill (a pointed feather) and ink. The books we copy are stories from the _____. Other monks work in the fields or take care of the sick or distribute food to the poor. We eat all our meals in the _____ in _____. A passage from the Bible is read as we eat. We all sleep in the _____. New orders have been founded, such as the _____ and the **Dominicans** because some people think that our monasteries have become too rich.

Use your textbook to check your answers when you are finished.

abbot	church	novice	seven
abbot	cloister	obedience	three
Benedict	dormitory	poverty	tonsure
Bible	Franciscans	prayer	wall
chapter	habits	refectory	
chastity	manuscripts	scriptorium	

The decline of the Middle Ages

What was the Black Death?

- The Black Death was a **plague** which spread across Europe in the middle of the 14th century. It was spread by **fleas** on black rats.
- About one-quarter to one-third of the people in Ireland and in Europe died from the plague. Some thought it was a punishment from God for their sins. It led to the decline of the Middle Ages.

Picture A1

Past questions on *Medieval Society: Castle, Church and City*

Pictures

1. Picture A1 is an artist's impression of a medieval manor house; A2 shows a map of a medieval manor.
   (i) From picture **A1**, identify **one** defensive feature of the manor house.
   (ii) Explain the purpose of the common marked **X** in picture **A2**.
   (iii) Picture **A2** shows the three-field or open-field system of farming. Mention **two** disadvantages of this system.

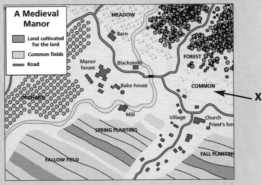

Picture A2

Short-Answer Questions

1. List **two** important effects of the coming of the Normans to Ireland.
2. During the Middle Ages, in which part of the castle did the lord and lady live?
3. Name **two** defensive features of a Norman castle.
4. Explain two of the following features of a castle during the Middle Ages: *Keep; Moat; Portcullis; Turret.*
5. Name **two** stages in the training of a knight.
6. During the Middle Ages, what was chivalry?
7. In medieval times, what was jousting?
8. Explain **two** of the following terms relating to a medieval manor: *Demesne; Serf; Tithe; Pottage.*
9. Explain **one** of the following terms from the Middle Ages: *Charter; Curfew; Pillory.*
10. Mention **two** dangers faced by people who lived in towns during the Middle Ages.

11. Name **two** stages in the training of a medieval craftsman.
12. What was the role of the guild in a medieval town?
13. Give **one** major characteristic of Gothic architecture.
14. Name **two** services provided by monasteries to local communities in the Middle Ages.
15. During the Middle Ages, name **two** orders of monks or friars.
16. Explain the purpose of **one** of the following buildings in a medieval monastery: *Chapter house; Cloisters; Refectory.*
17. During the Middle Ages, what was the Black Death?

People in History

Ordinary level

1. A knight in a castle during the Middle Ages
    - *Hints*: Training; Clothes and weapons; Daily life in the castle; Tournaments and jousts
2. A monk in a medieval monastery
    - *Hints*: Reasons for becoming a monk; Main building; Daily life; Serving the local people
3. A craftsman living in a medieval town
    - *Hints*: Training; Working life; Life in the town; Entertainment

Higher level

1. The lord **or** lady of a medieval castle
2. A serf in a medieval manor

Long-Answer Questions (for Higher level)

1.
    (i)   Explain **two** of the following: *Sanctuary; Abbot; Title; Cloister.*
    (ii) Mention **three** ways in which medieval castles were defended.
    (iii) What were the problems faced by town dwellers in the Middle Ages?
    (iv) Write an account of the life and training of a craftsman in a medieval town

2.
    (i)   During the Middle Ages, what was *chivalry*?
    (ii) Mention two dangers faced by people living in towns during the Middle Ages.
    (iii) Explain three of the following terms relating to castles during the Middle Ages: *Turret; Moat; Keep; Portcullis; Bailey.*
    (iv) Outline the main stages in the training of a craftsman in a medieval town.
    (v)   Write an account of the life of a serf in a medieval manor.

5 ⬡ The Renaissance

aims
- To understand differences between medieval and Renaissance art
- To learn the lives of key Renaissance people

What was the Renaissance?

The Renaissance was the revival or rebirth of interest in the learning of ancient Greece and Rome. It began in Italy in the 14th century, mainly in the city of Florence, and spread to other European countries.

What does 'Renaissance' mean?
The word *Renaissance* means revival or rebirth.

What were the causes of the Renaissance in Italy?

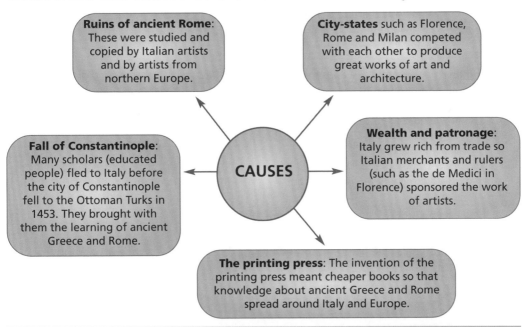

Ruins of ancient Rome: These were studied and copied by Italian artists and by artists from northern Europe.

City-states such as Florence, Rome and Milan competed with each other to produce great works of art and architecture.

Fall of Constantinople: Many scholars (educated people) fled to Italy before the city of Constantinople fell to the Ottoman Turks in 1453. They brought with them the learning of ancient Greece and Rome.

CAUSES

Wealth and patronage: Italy grew rich from trade so Italian merchants and rulers (such as the de Medici in Florence) sponsored the work of artists.

The printing press: The invention of the printing press meant cheaper books so that knowledge about ancient Greece and Rome spread around Italy and Europe.

How do we know about the Renaissance?
Key sources are:
- **Art and architecture**, such as the paintings, sculptures and buildings of the Renaissance
- **Documentary evidence**, such as the notebooks of Leonardo da Vinci and Vasari's *Lives of the Artists*

What was Humanism?

Humanism was a revived interest in the work of ancient Greece and Rome.

Changes in art and architecture

Painting

Medieval painting	Renaissance painting
 *Maesta* by Cimabue	 The *Alba Madonna* by Raphael
<ul><li>Religious message only</li><li>Painted wood panels</li><li>Lifeless people</li><li>No variety in colour</li><li>No depth (perspective)</li></ul>	<ul><li>Perspective (depth)</li><li>Renaissance-style clothes</li><li>Realistic people</li><li>Variety of colours</li></ul>
Themes <ul><li>Religious message only – scenes from the Bible and the lives of saints</li></ul>	**Themes** <ul><li>Renaissance artists painted many different themes – religious themes, portraits of leaders and their wives, nature and landscape</li></ul>
Materials <ul><li>Egg yolk with powdered colours, which dried quickly so changes could not be made</li></ul>	**Materials** <ul><li>Oil with colours so that the paint dried more slowly and artists could vary colours and shading; increased use of canvas</li></ul>
Perspective <ul><li>Two-dimensional – the paintings lacked depth</li></ul>	**Perspective** <ul><li>Three-dimensional – the paintings had depth</li></ul>

What is a fresco?

A fresco is a painting done on **damp plaster** so that the painting became part of the plaster.

- *Example*: Michelangelo's ceiling of the Sistine Chapel

Sculpture

Medieval sculpture
- Religious themes
- Lacking in feeling
- Part of a church or cathedral

Renaissance sculpture
- People were more realistic and lifelike

Architecture

Medieval architecture
- Gothic-style architecture

Renaissance architecture
- Roman-style architecture (also called classical architecture)

Pointed arches over windows and doors

Spire

(a)
(b)

(a) Flying buttress and
(b) buttresses

Gothic

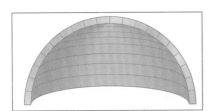

Dome

Column

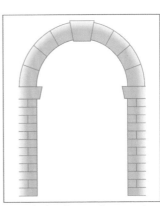

Rounded arch over doors and windows

Rennaissance

Renaissance lives: Lorenzo de Medici and patronage

1. The de Medici family ruled Florence. They were great **patrons of the arts**.
2. Lorenzo de Medici was known as 'the Magnificent'.
   - He supported artists such as Leonardo da Vinci and Michelangelo.
   - He collected manuscripts in a private library.
   - He set up a school of sculpture to train young sculptors, including Michelangelo.

Who were patrons of the arts?

These were wealthy merchants or rulers who paid artists to paint pictures, make sculptures or design buildings. The Popes, including Julius II, were also patrons.

People in History

A printer during the Renaissance: Gutenberg and the printing press

Johann Gutenberg, who was born in Mainz, Germany, was the inventor of the printing press. Before his invention, books were either **hand-written** (manuscripts) or were printed on hand-carved wooden blocks. Gutenberg used his skill as a goldsmith to invent **moveable metal type**. These were individual metal letters which could be used and reused. He also invented the **printing press**, which was an invention based on the wine presses used in his area.

A printing press

Gutenberg's **first book** was the Bible in Latin. This was known as the **42-line Bible** because it had 42 lines on each page in Gothic type, or letters. The letters of each word and line were composed on a stick (like a Scrabble stick). The words for each page were put together into a frame. The frame was placed in the printing press. Then the letters were inked. A double page was placed on top of the letters. The press was brought down on top of the paper.

The use of **paper** was much cheaper than vellum or parchment, which was used for medieval manuscripts. Decorations were hand-painted on the pages afterwards. All the pages of the Bible were brought together and bound as a book.

Gutenberg was a very good printer, but he was a **bad businessman**. A year after printing the 42-line Bible, he was expelled from the business by his partners. But his printing press spread to other parts of Europe. Aldus Manutius in Venice and William Caxton in London became important printers.

Gutenberg's invention of the printing press had very important **results**. There was now a plentiful supply of books, which meant books became cheaper. Education became more important as people wanted to read and write and literacy spread. New ideas from

HL

the Renaissance about art, architecture, science and medicine spread widely throughout Europe. These new ideas led to the Age of Exploration and the Reformation. Gutenberg's invention of the printing press meant that knowledge was not confined to a small number of people but was spread widely. Later developments such as newspapers, magazines and textbooks show how important Gutenberg's invention was.

People in History

Leonardo da Vinci

1. Leonardo da Vinci was born near Florence. He was apprenticed to Master Verrocchio.
2. He went to work for the ruler of Milan, designing fortifications.
3. He painted *The Virgin of the Rocks* on canvas. He used a **sfumato** style in his painting.
4. Da Vinci painted *The Last Supper* on a dining room wall of a monastery in Milan. It was not a true fresco because da Vinci used oil painting.
5. He kept **notebooks** containing his ideas and studies.
6. He studied **astronomy**, **geology** and **engineering**. He also studied human anatomy by dissecting dead bodies.
7. He designed **machines** such as a helicopter and a tank.
8. He painted the *Mona Lisa* in Florence.
9. He died in France.

What is sfumato?

Sfumato is a painting technique which Leonardo used to blur the outlines of figures and blend them into their surroundings.

- *Example*: Leonardo's painting the *Mona Lisa*

People in History

A named Renaissance artist: Michelangelo
Fill in the blanks using the words in the list. (Words can be used more than once)

Michelangelo was born near _____ in Italy. At this time the _____ – the revival of interest in the _____ of ancient Greece and Rome – was spreading in Italy. He became an _____ to Master **Verrochio**. He learnt how to mix colours and to paint _____ (wall paintings done on wet plaster). He was also very interested in _____. Michelangelo was invited to the school of sculpture set up by **Lorenzo** _____, leader of Florence. Lorenzo became a _____ of

Michelangelo. After his training, Michelangelo went to Rome. Here he sculpted the _____, a sculpture showing the dead Jesus in his mother's arms. Michelangelo cut his name along a band in this sculpture: 'I, Michelangelo, sculptor.' Later he sculptured _____ in Florence. This was cut from _____ marble and was a huge sculpture of _____, the biblical figure who killed Goliath. This was placed in the square in Florence to show off the glory of the city. Pope _____ asked Michelangelo to paint the _____ of the **Sistine** _____ in Rome. Michelangelo worked on this _____ for four years. This showed scenes from the _____ from the creation of the world to the Flood. He also painted the _____, another fresco, behind the altar of the Sistine Chapel. This showed God in judgement, sending people to heaven or hell. Parts of the _____ figures in this were later painted over. Before he died he designed the _____ of St Peter's Church in Rome. He was buried first in Rome, but his body was later taken back for burial in Florence. Michelangelo showed he was a gifted painter, sculptor and _____.

Use your textbook to check your answers when you are finished.

apprentice	*David*	frescoes	*Pietà*
architect	David	Julius II	Renaissance
Bible	de Medici	*Last Judgement*	sculpture
Carrara	Dome	learning	
ceiling	Florence	nude	
Chapel	fresco	patron	

exam focus

When the exam question says, 'A **named** Renaissance artist/ sculptor/scientist', always begin by naming the person you are writing about. For example, you could start with this simple statement:

'Michelangelo was a _____.'

People in History

A named Renaissance artist from outside of Italy: Albrecht Dürer

Albrecht **Dürer** was a German artist. The ideas of the **Renaissance** spread to Germany through the printing press, which was invented in Germany. He was born in **Nuremberg**, where his father was a **goldsmith**. He learnt about **engraving** (picture-printing) in his father's workshop. When he was 13, Dürer drew a **self-portrait**. Then he became an **apprentice** to the chief painter in his town. After finishing his training, he travelled to

Italy to study the methods of making paintings and engravings there and to meet with other artists. On his return, he set up his own workshop in Nuremberg. Soon afterward he was appointed as court painter to the court of **Emperor Maximilian**, leader of the Holy Roman Empire, who became Dürer's patron.

Dürer liked to paint self-portraits, portraits and studies of animals and plants. He painted **self-portraits** because he wanted to be remembered. Dürer's **portraits** were realistic because he liked to reveal the character of the person he was painting. He was most famous for his **engravings**. These are prints made from wood or copper onto which he cut the pictures. His prints were distributed and sold widely, making him famous and wealthy. He engraved *The Four Horsemen of the Apocalypse* and *Knight, Death and the Devil*. He also did an engraving of *Saint Jerome in His Study*. Dürer believed he was as good a painter as he was an engraver, but some people said his engraving was better.

He painted plants and animals in great detail. His *The Great Piece of Turf* shows a clump of grass and his *Young Hare* is very detailed and lifelike. He always signed his name 'AD' at the bottom of his paintings. He died after catching a fever while observing a stranded whale in Holland. After his death, German painting declined because of the **influence** of the **Protestant Reformation**, which did not like displays of art in churches, in contrast to the Catholic Church, which continued to encourage religious paintings and sculptures.

> **exam focus**
>
> - When you are asked to write about an artist from **outside** of Italy, use Dürer.
> - Be careful **not** to use **Rembrandt** as a named Renaissance artist from **outside** of Italy. He painted in the 17th century and so he may not be regarded as a Renaissance painter.

People in History

A named Renaissance scientist: Galileo

Galileo was a Renaissance **scientist** who was born in **Pisa**, Italy. He first studied **medicine** at the University of Pisa, but his interest soon changed to **mathematics** and **science**. He proposed the **pendulum clock** after observing the chandeliers swinging in Pisa Cathedral. He concluded that the swing took the same time whether it was long or short.

Galileo became a **professor of mathematics** in Padua University. He believed he could apply mathematics to the study of the world. One of his discoveries was the **theory of the speed of falling bodies**. He said that solid objects all fall at the same speed. Before this insight, people believed that heavier objects fell faster than lighter objects. Many people believed that he dropped objects from the **Leaning Tower of Pisa** to prove his point, but there is no proof of this.

Galileo invented his own **telescope** to study the universe. His important astronomical discoveries include observing the four moons of **Jupiter**, the mountains and craters on the moon, and sunspots.

Galileo used his observations to support the idea that the **Sun**, not the Earth, was the centre of the universe. This idea was first put forward by **Copernicus**, a Polish astronomer. Prior to this most people followed the ancient Greeks who thought that the Earth was the centre of the universe.

When Galileo supported this new idea he got into trouble with the **Catholic Church**. He was summoned to Rome to appear before the **Court of Inquisition**, a church court. Galileo was told he could not support the idea of a sun-centred universe. He was forced to **deny** what he believed under threat of torture. He was placed under **house arrest** in his house in Florence, where he now lived. He continued to work until his death at age 77, though he went blind.

Galileo is called the **Father of Modern Science** because his ideas were based on scientific methods of close observation and experimentation. His ideas were added to by other scientists: **Kepler**, a German scientist, showed that the Earth went around the Sun in an elliptical path, not a circular path, as Galileo believed; **Newton**, an English scientist, discovered the laws of gravity based on Galileo's ideas about the speed of falling objects.

What happened to medicine during the Renaissance?

Several important developments occurred in medicine during the Renaissance:

- The human body began to be studied in detail.
- **Vesalius** wrote *On the Structure of the Human Body*, which reported observations made during dissections of the body. He believed that medicine should be based on **observation** and he corrected many of the old medical ideas handed down from the Greeks.
- An Englishman, William Harvey, discovered that **blood** circulated around the body.

People in History

A named Renaissance writer: Shakespeare

Shakespeare was a **Renaissance writer** of plays and poetry. He was born in Stratford-on-Avon and later went to live in London but left his wife, Anne Hathaway, and his children behind him. He became an **actor** and **writer of plays** with the King's Men, a theatre company. They performed in the **Globe Theatre**, which was an open-air theatre on the banks of the River Thames. Plays were performed in the afternoon, not at night, because there was no artificial lighting for night-time performances. Sometimes Shakespeare performed roles in his own plays, such as when he played the Ghost in *Hamlet*.

Shakespeare wrote **38 plays** which were performed before Queen Elizabeth and King James as well as at the Globe. His plays made him rich and famous; he owned property in both London and Stratford. His plays had many interesting characters, from kings and queens to rogues. They displayed a wide range of emotions from love and ambition to jealousy and selfishness. Shakespeare took his ideas from classical (Greek and Roman) literature as well as the history of England.

His plays included **tragedies** such as *Hamlet, Romeo and Juliet* and *Macbeth*; his **comedies** included *The Merchant of Venice* and his **histories** included *Henry V* and *Julius Caesar*. Shakespeare also wrote poems and sonnets (14-line poems).

There was no stage scenery in the Globe Theatre, so Shakespeare had to put the time and place of the action into the words of the actors. **Women** were not allowed to act, so young boys whose voices had not yet broken played female parts. The audiences took part in the plays by cheering, booing or throwing spoiled fruit if they did not like a play.

Towards the end of his life, Shakespeare returned to **Stratford**, where he died at age 52. His plays contributed to the use of the vernacular language (the language of the people) rather than Latin, which was the language of learning during the Middle Ages.

What were the results of the Renaissance?

1. **The printing press** led to increased education and literacy. It also spread new ideas.
2. The Renaissance fostered a **questioning spirit** in which old ideas were no longer accepted without question.
3. This questioning spirit led to the **Age of Exploration**, the **Reformation** and to new scientific discoveries.
4. The result was **new knowledge** in geography, science, medicine and astronomy.
5. There were also new developments in **painting**, **sculpture** and **architecture**. These included perspective, sfumato and classical architecture.

> **exam focus**
>
> Use examples from what happened **during** the Renaissance to write more on the **results** or **influence** of the Renaissance e.g. the work of artists, scientists and writers.

exam Q
Write an account of the **main developments** in two of the following areas during the Renaissance: (a) Architecture (b) Science and medicine (c) Sculpture (d) Printing (see p. 62).

Summary of Main Developments during the Renaissance	
Art	Different to medieval painting; many themes – religious, legends, portraits; lifelike people; perspective – 3-dimensional (3D); new materials – oil, canvas; fresco painting ● *Examples*: Leonardo da Vinci – *The Last Supper*, the *Mona Lisa*; Michelangelo – ceiling of the Sistine Chapel, *The Last Judgement* – both frescoes; Dürer – the northern Renaissance
Architecture	Different to medieval architecture; Roman-style (classical) with rounded arches, domes, Greek and Roman columns ● *Examples*: Tiempetto; St Peter's Basilica, Rome; Florence Cathedral
Sculpture	Different to medieval sculpture; lifelike people, sculptures of rulers as well as religious figures ● *Example*: Michelangelo's *Pietà* (religious), *David*
Printing	Invented by **Gutenberg**, moveable metallic type (letters) and printing press; replaced manuscripts (hand-written books); first book printed – 42-line Bible; more and cheaper books; spread of education and literacy; printing helped cause the Reformation – Luther's 95 Theses were printed and spread over Germany
Science and medicine	New ideas – **Copernicus** – Sun centre of universe; backed up by **Galileo** – used telescope – also discovered four moons of Jupiter; craters on the Moon; speed of falling bodies; brought before Inquisition; **Vesalius**, *On the Structure of the Human Body* – dissections lead to a better understanding of workings of the body; **Harvey** – circulation of the blood

Past questions on *The Renaissance*

Picture A

Pictures

1. Picture A is a painting called the *Adoration of the Magi* by Botticelli
   (i) From the painting, give **two** pieces of evidence to show that this is a Renaissance painting.
   (ii) Apart from Botticelli, name **one** Renaissance painter and **two** of his works.

Short-Answer Questions

1. Give **two** reasons why the Renaissance began in Italy.
2. Give **two** reasons why the printing press was important during the Renaissance period.

3. Why were patrons so important during the Renaissance?
4. Name **one** patron of artists during the Renaissance.
5. Name **two** features of Renaissance architecture.
6. Name **one** Renaissance painter from **outside** of Italy and **one** of that painter's works.
7. Name **one** Renaissance sculptor and **one** of his works.
8. Mention the name of **one** Renaissance writer and **one** work by that writer.
9. Explain **two** of the following terms relating to the Renaissance: *Fresco; Sfumato; Perspective; Humanism.*
10. Mention **two** developments in science or medicine during the Renaissance.
11. Mention **one** scientific theory or discovery associated with Copernicus or Galileo.

People in History

Ordinary level

1. A named Renaissance artist
   - *Hints*: Early life and training; Patrons; New techniques of painting; Principal works

Higher level

1. A **named** Renaissance artist from **outside** of Italy
2. A **named** Renaissance painter or sculptor

Long-Answer Questions (for Higher level)

1. (i) Why were patrons so important during the Renaissance?
   (ii) Name **two** important patrons of the arts in Italy during the Renaissance.
   (iii) Mention **three** changes that took place in painting during the Renaissance.
   (iv) Write an account of the main developments in **two** of the following areas during the Renaissance: (a) Architecture (b) Science and medicine (c) Sculpture (d) Painting.
2. (i) Give **two** reasons why the invention of the printing press is regarded as one of the most important developments of the Renaissance.
   (ii) Mention **four** changes that took place in painting during the Renaissance.
   (iii) Write an account of the main developments in **two** of the following areas during the Renaissance: (a) Architecture (b) Science (c) Sculpture.
   (iv) Write an account on **one** Renaissance writer or artist **who was not from Italy**.

YEAR TWO

Studies of Change

Topics of study

Ordinary level

Students studying this syllabus at **Ordinary level** may concentrate on the Special Studies:

- Columbus **OR** Magellan
- Martin Luther **OR** John Calvin
- Munster **OR** Ulster Plantation
- George Washington **OR** Robespierre **OR** Wolfe Tone
- Contrasting Lifestyles c. 1850: Industrial England and Rural Ireland

Higher level

Students studying the syllabus at **Higher level** will study all of the topics.

6 The Age of Exploration

What was the Age of Exploration?

In the 15th and 16th centuries, Europeans began to explore other parts of the world. This is called the Age of Exploration or the Age of Discovery.

What were the causes of the Age of Exploration?

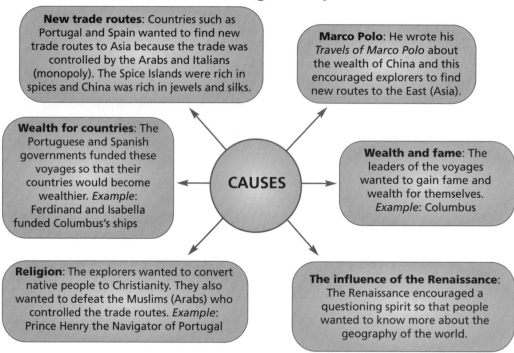

New trade routes: Countries such as Portugal and Spain wanted to find new trade routes to Asia because the trade was controlled by the Arabs and Italians (monopoly). The Spice Islands were rich in spices and China was rich in jewels and silks.

Marco Polo: He wrote his *Travels of Marco Polo* about the wealth of China and this encouraged explorers to find new routes to the East (Asia).

Wealth for countries: The Portuguese and Spanish governments funded these voyages so that their countries would become wealthier. *Example*: Ferdinand and Isabella funded Columbus's ships

CAUSES

Wealth and fame: The leaders of the voyages wanted to gain fame and wealth for themselves. *Example*: Columbus

Religion: The explorers wanted to convert native people to Christianity. They also wanted to defeat the Muslims (Arabs) who controlled the trade routes. *Example*: Prince Henry the Navigator of Portugal

The influence of the Renaissance: The Renaissance encouraged a questioning spirit so that people wanted to know more about the geography of the world.

What made the voyages of exploration possible?

Improvements in ships and navigation

1. **New ships:** A new ship, the **caravel**, was developed which could sail on longer voyages. It had a lateen sail (to sail against the wind), square sails (to sail with the wind) and rudders for steering. It was clinker-built (the boards overlapped) which made it stronger.

2. **Compasses**: These were used to find direction.

3. **Latitude**: Latitude (north and south of the equator) was worked out using a **quadrant** or an **astrolabe**.

Compass

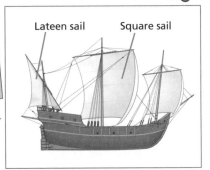

Lateen sail   Square sail

Caravel

4. **Maps**: **Portolan charts** showed places along the coast joined by straight lines. Newer maps were developed to include the new discoveries.

5. **Speed**: A log and line was used to work out the speed of the ship in knots (nautical miles).

6. **Depth**: A lead and line was used to work out the depth of the water along the coast.

7. **Logbook**: The Logbook kept a record of all the events of the voyage so it was used again in later voyages.

Quadrant

The Portuguese voyages

Why did the Portuguese explore?

1. The Portuguese drove the Muslims from their own country and heard of gold mines in Africa.

2. The Portuguese believed they could join forces with a Christian king, Prester John, to attack the Muslims in Africa.

3. The Portuguese wanted to profit from trade with Africa.

Who was Prince Henry the Navigator?

4. The Portuguese voyages were organised by **Prince Henry the Navigator**. He founded a school for navigation at **Sagres** where mapmakers, shipbuilders and astronomers met to plan voyages along the coast of Africa.

5. Prince Henry sent ships along the coast of Africa. A **stone pillar** (*padrão*) was erected at the end of each voyage. The Portuguese discovered the Azores and the Canary Islands.

What did Diaz achieve?

6. Diaz sailed three ships along the coast of Africa as far as the Orange River. Here he was blown by a storm further southwards.

7. When Diaz turned eastwards he discovered he had rounded the southern tip of Africa. He called this the Cape of Storms, but the king of Portugal later called it the **Cape of Good Hope**.

What did da Gama achieve?

8. Da Gama sailed four ships, including his flagship, the *São Gabriel* from Lisbon. He sailed southwards into the Atlantic Ocean and away from the coast of Africa in order to avoid northerly winds and currents.

9. Da Gama rounded the Cape of Good Hope and sailed to **Calicut in India** with the help of an Arab pilot. He was the first European to reach India.

Portuguese trade

10. The Portuguese later defeated the Arabs and controlled the **trade** from the Spice Islands.

What were the Spice Islands?

These were islands in south-east Asia which produced spices which were desired by Europeans to flavour and preserve food.

What were the results of the Portuguese voyages?

1. Portugal grew prosperous on trade from Africa, India and the Spice Islands.

2. The Portuguese empire included countries in Africa – Angola, Mozambique – and Asia.

3. The Portuguese language and culture and the Catholic religion spread to these countries.

4. Portugal also got part of South America – Brazil – under the terms of the Treaty of Tordesillas, which divided the lands discovered during the Age of Exploration between Portugal and Spain.

Special study – A voyage of exploration: The first voyage of Christopher Columbus

Why did Columbus explore?

1. Columbus believed the earth was smaller than it actually is.

2. He believed that the world was round and that if he sailed westwards, he would reach Cathay (China) and Cipango (Japan).

3. He also wanted to convert native people to Catholicism.

4. He wanted to become famous and wealthy.

Who gave him help?

5. Columbus asked Portugal, England and France for support for his voyage of exploration, but they refused.

> **exam focus**
>
> You can use the story of Columbus's first voyage to answer the *People in History* question on 'a **named leader** of a voyage of discovery during the Age of Exploration' or 'a **sailor** on a voyage of discovery during the Age of Exploration'.

6. Instead, Columbus was helped by **Ferdinand** and **Isabella**, king and queen of Spain. They provided him with three ships, the *Santa María*, the *Niña* and the *Pinta*.

7. He was promised that he would become the governor of the lands he would discover, as well as getting the title Admiral of the Ocean Sea.

What happened on his voyage?

8. In 1492, Columbus sailed from **Palos**, in the south of Spain, with a crew of about 90 sailors, mostly from the local area. Some sailors were experienced; others sought adventure, fame and riches. He headed for the Canary Islands, where he carried out repairs and took on fresh water and supplies.

9. Columbus sailed westwards, helped by a following wind – the **trade winds**. He kept two **logbooks** – one in which he recorded the correct distances the ships were travelling, and one in which he recorded shorter distances so as not to alarm his crew. They were frightened about travelling so far away from the normal sea routes.

10. When the sailors got anxious, he promised he would return to Spain if they did not see land within a few days.

What did he discover?

11. Shortly after, the *Pinta* fired a cannon shot to signal sight of land.

12. Columbus landed on **San Salvador** in the Bahama Islands.

13. He later explored **Cuba** and **Hispaniola**. Columbus thought he had found Cipango (Japan), but he couldn't find the great cities mentioned by Marco Polo.

14. The *Santa María* ran aground and he constructed a fort with its timbers. He set sail for Spain, leaving behind 40 men in the fort.

15. He took with him gold, pineapples and six Indians. He was praised by Ferdinand and Isabella when he got home.

What were the results of his voyage?

16. Columbus went on later voyages and discovered more islands as well as the coast of South America. He still thought he had discovered the **Indies**.

17. Instead, he had discovered a new continent which was eventually named 'America' after another explorer, **Amerigo Vespucci**, who realised that a new continent had been discovered.

> **exam focus**
>
> You are only allowed 2 marks for **background information**. So when you are writing about Columbus's voyage of discovery, keep the background information brief. *Example*: 'Columbus was an Italian sailor who sailed for Spain. He believed the world was round and that if he sailed west, he would reach Cipango (Japan) and the Spice Islands...'

18. Spain brought **settlers** to these lands, spread the Spanish culture and language and the Catholic religion. Gold and silver were sent back. As a result, Spain grew rich and powerful.

19. The Pope got Spain and Portugal to agree to the **Treaty of Tordesillas** in which they divided the newly discovered lands between them. Land to the west of the **line of**

Tordesillas belonged to Spain; land to the east belonged to Portugal. This meant that most of South America became Spanish but Brazil became Portuguese.

What is the New World?

The New World refers to North and South America, as opposed to the Old World, which was Europe, Asia and Africa.

People in History

A sailor on a named voyage of discovery during the Age of Exploration

I was a sailor on **Columbus's** first voyage of discovery. I lived in **Palos**, where Columbus began his voyage. I was an **experienced** sailor but others were freemen who came along with promises of fame and riches and 'gold-covered' houses. In all, there were about **90** of us on the three ships which Columbus got from **Ferdinand and Isabella**, the king and queen of Spain. I sailed on the *Santa María* which was the flagship, and the others were the *Niña* and the *Pinta*. The *Santa María* was about 18 metres long and it had a **lateen sail** and two square sails.

Columbus believed that the world was **round**, that it was **smaller** than it really is and that if he sailed **westwards** he would reach Cipango (Japan) and Cathay (China). He wanted to discover the riches described by **Marco Polo** in his book of travels. He was promised by Ferdinand and Isabella that he would become the **governor** of all he discovered and would get the title **'Admiral of the Ocean Sea'**.

We first sailed for the **Canary Islands** to take on board fresh water and food. This was our last stop before we sailed out into the Atlantic Ocean. As we headed westwards, we were helped by the **trade winds** and were able to sail about 100 miles a day.

Conditions on board were rough. Our food was dry and salted. We were given one hot meal a day, which was cooked in the **firebox** on deck. We also got wine or water.

As we sailed on, we were afraid that if we went too far we would not be able to get back. But Columbus kept two **logbooks** – one recorded the true distance we travelled, the other one recorded a shorter distance. We were told the shorter distance. Very soon we forced him to promise to turn back if land was not discovered within a few days. But soon after, the *Pinta* fired a shot – the signal that its crew had sighted land. I was with Columbus as we landed on this new island, which Columbus called **San Salvador**.

We next sailed to **Cuba** and **Hispaniola**, where the *Santa María* ran aground. Columbus believed that these islands were islands off the coast of Asia. We returned to Spain and Columbus was given a great welcome by Ferdinand and Isabella. We brought back gold, pineapples, parrots and six natives, whom Columbus called **Indians**.

Columbus did not realise it, but he had discovered a new continent which was later named 'America' after Amerigo Vespucci. Columbus's voyage led to greater Spanish conquests, the division of the New World between Spain and Portugal by the Treaty of Tordesillas, the spread of Spanish culture, language and religion and the growth of Spanish power.

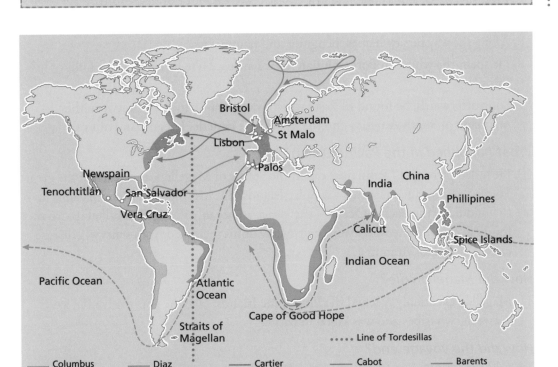

Voyages of exploration

Magellan's voyage around the world

Who was Magellan?

1. Ferdinand Magellan was a Portuguese captain who sailed for Spain.

Who gave him help?

2. Magellan proposed to **King Charles V** of Spain that the Spice Islands were in the Spanish half of the world. He promised he would find a new route there by sailing south around the newly discovered continent of America.

3. He believed that there was a strait – *El Paso* – which would take him into the great South Sea which the Spanish had seen from Panama.

4. Charles gave five ships to Magellan and made him governor of all the lands he would discover, and promised him 5 per cent of the profits of the voyage.

Where did he sail?

5. Magellan sailed from **Seville** with the ships, including the flagship, *Trinidad*.

6. He sailed to the **Canary Islands** to get fresh supplies of water and food. He crossed the Atlantic Ocean and sailed down the coast of South America looking for El Paso.

> Use **examples** from what happened during the Age of Exploration to write more on its results.

7. Along the way he saw llamas, penguins and hammocks.

8. He spent the winter in **Port St Julian** in Argentina. Here he cleaned the hulls of his ships.

9. Soon afterwards, he found El Paso, which was a strait which ran between the mainland of South America and the island of **Tierra del Fuego** (land of fire).

What happened in the Pacific Ocean?

10. He sailed through El Paso, now called the **Straits of Magellan**, and reached the great South Sea. He sailed towards the Spice Islands. But his ships experienced calms in the middle of the **Pacific Ocean** – the 'peaceful ocean', as Magellan called it – so the food ran out and the water went bad. Many of his men died from **scurvy** (a disease caused by lack of vitamin C).

How did Magellan die?

11. Magellan eventually reached the **Philippine Islands**. Here he got involved in a war between two tribes and was killed in battle.

How did the voyage end?

12. Sebastian **del Cano** took command and reached the Spice Islands. He then sailed the last remaining ship, the *Victoria*, round the coast of Africa back to Spain. Only 18 sailors survived the voyage.

13. Magellan's voyage proved the **earth was round**. But it also proved the Spice Islands were in the Portuguese half of the world.

The Spanish conquest of the New World

Cortés and the Aztecs

1. Cortés conquered the **Aztecs** in Mexico.

2. The Spanish colony of New Spain was set up on the remains of the Aztec Empire.

Who were the *conquistadores*?

They were the Spanish adventurers who conquered parts of the New World for Spain.

People in History

A native of a land discovered by Europeans during the Age of Exploration

I am an **Aztec**, a native of Mexico. My ruler was **Montezuma** and we lived in the city of **Tenochtitlan**. This was a city in the middle of a lake with canals and temples. It was connected to the mainland by **causeways**. We ruled over other tribes in our area and we offered **sacrifices** to the gods of captured enemy tribesmen.

We believed that one day our god, **Quetzalcoatl**, would return to us. When the Spaniards, led by **Cortés**, landed in Mexico, our emperor, Montezuma, thought he was the god returning and went out to greet him. We thought they were six-legged and two-headed gods. Little did we know that Cortés was a **soldier** and **adventurer** and that they were *conquistadores* who wanted to conquer our land and find **gold** and **silver**. The Spaniards were welcomed to our city but soon they got greedy for gold. We began fighting the Spaniards and they were lucky to escape, but we killed our emperor for helping them.

Cortés and the Spaniards then formed an army of 100,000 men by getting help from neighbouring **tribes**. They did not like us Aztecs because of the heavy taxes and slavery we imposed on them as well as our practice of sacrificing their men to our gods. Cortés and his army surrounded and captured our city, Tenochtitlan. The city was **destroyed** and thousands of our tribe were killed. The Spaniards made **slaves** of us and I am working in the mines while others are working the fields. They are rebuilding our city and calling it **Mexico City**. The Spaniards have brought cattle, plants, ploughs and hundreds of **priests** to establish a new colony, which they call **New Spain**. Cortés has been made **governor** of New Spain. The Spanish language and culture is everywhere and our language and religion have been destroyed.

Pizarro and the Incas

3. Pizarro conquered the **Incas** in Peru.
4. The Spaniards discovered great **silver mines** there. The silver was mined by native people and sent across the seas to Spain.

What were the results of the Age of Exploration?

On Europe	On the New World
1. Rise of Empires: Some European countries such as Portugal, Spain and England created great empires (see map).	**1. Decay of Empires:** The Aztec empire in Mexico and the Inca empire in Peru collapsed. Natives were used as slaves, and many died from European diseases.

On Europe contd.

2. **Mediterranean Sea/Atlantic Ocean:** The Mediterranean Sea declined in importance and the Atlantic became the great trading ocean between the empires and the mother countries.

   - Italian cities such as **Genoa** and **Venice** declined and Atlantic cities such as London, Amsterdam and Seville grew.

3. **New foods to Europe:** Tea, potatoes, sugar and turkeys are examples of the new foods brought from America. Tobacco was also introduced to Europe.

4. **Geographical knowledge:** Europeans developed new maps and all the main parts of the world were explored. The old ideas Europeans had about the world were shown to be wrong.

5. **Conflicts between European powers:** The Treaty of Tordesillas was agreed to prevent conflict between Spain and Portugal. England raided Spanish ships transporting gold from the New World and this led to war between the two, including the launching of the **Spanish Armada** against England. England fought France in the **Seven Years' War** for control of North America. Conflicts over the scramble for colonies in Africa in the 19th century contributed to the causes of World War I.

On the New World contd.

2. **Slavery:** Shortages of native workers to work on European plantations in the Americas led to slaves being brought from Africa.

3. **Spread of Christianity:** Spain and Portugal spread the Catholic religion, and Britain and Holland spread Protestant religions in the areas they conquered.

4. **European culture:** European culture, language and architecture spread to the colonies while native culture declined. European culture was spread by the millions of migrants (planters, settlers) who came from Europe to live in the new colonies.

exam focus

Use **examples** from what happened during the Age of Exploration to write more on its results.

exam Q

Past questions on *The Age of Exploration*

Pictures

1. Picture A is an artist's impression of the court of Prince Henry the Navigator.
   (i) From picture A, identify **one** aid to navigation which made voyages of discovery possible during the 15th and 16th centuries.
   (ii) What name is given to the type of boat marked X?

X

Picture A

(iii) Mention **two** features of this boat which made it faster and stronger than other sailing ships of its time.

Short-Answer Questions

1. Name and explain one instrument of navigation used during the Age of Exploration.
2. Give two dangers feared by sailors during the Age of Exploration.
3. Mention **two** developments in boatbuilding or navigation which made sea voyages possible during the 15th and 16th centuries.
4. During the Age of Exploration, what was a *Caravel*?
5. During the Age of Exploration, give **two** reasons why rulers were prepared to sponsor voyages.
6. For what purpose were **two** of the following used during the Age of Exploration?
   Portolan charts; Astrolabe; Log and Line; Caravels.
7. Name the country that discovered the sea route to India during the Age of Exploration.
8. Name **one** explorer and name **one** place or sea route discovered by that explorer.
9. During the Age of Exploration, who were the *conquistadores*?

People in History

Ordinary level

1. A **named** explorer who led a voyage of exploration
   - *Hints*: Reasons for the voyage; Preparations for the voyage; Conditions for the crew on the voyage; Results of the voyage

Higher level

1. A **named** leader on a voyage during the Age of Exploration
2. A sailor on a voyage of discovery during the Age of Exploration
3. A native of a land discovered by Europeans during the Age of Exploration

Sources Question (for Higher level)

Source D

Privileges Granted by Their Catholic Majesties FERDINAND and ISABELLA to Columbus, 30th of April 1492.

You, *Christopher Columbus*, with some of our vessels (ships) and men, are commanded to discover and subdue some Islands and Continent in the ocean ... Therefore it is but just and reasonable, that since you expose yourself to such danger to serve us, you should be rewarded for it.

Our will is, that you, *Christopher Columbus*, shall be our Admiral, Viceroy, and Governor in the Islands and Continent you discover and conquer ... and that for the future, your sons and successors may call themselves Dons, Admirals, Viceroys, and

Governors of them; and that you may freely decide all causes, civil and criminal, as you shall think fit in justice, and that you have power to punish offenders.

A. Source D
   (i)   What command was given to Columbus?
   (ii) What rewards did the king and queen grant Columbus?
   (iii) Why were rulers such as Ferdinand and Isabella of Spain willing to sponsor voyages of exploration?
   (iv) Mention **two** dangers faced by sailors on voyages such as these.
   (v)   Name **two** instruments which helped sailors to navigate while at sea during the Age of Exploration.

B. Source E
   (i)   Columbus returned to Spain with some inhabitants of the land he discovered (marked **X**). Why did Columbus call these men *Indians*?

   (ii) Name **two** new products brought from the New World to Europe by explorers or traders.
   (iii) Suggest **two** effects which voyages of exploration had on the native people of the New World.

Source E: Christopher Columbus returns to the Spanish court, 1493.

C. Write an account of **one** of the following topics:
   (i)   Achievements of the Portuguese voyages of exploration.
   (ii) The conflict between European powers as a result of the voyages of exploration.
   (iii) The Spanish conquest of either Mexico **or** Peru.

Long-Answer Questions (for Higher level)
   (i)   Give **two** reasons why rulers were prepared to sponsor voyages of exploration.
   (ii) Give **one** reason why the development of the caravel helped to make possible voyages of discovery.
   (iii) Name **two** instruments that helped sailors to navigate while at sea during the Age of Exploration.
   (iv) Write an account of Portugal's contribution to the Age of Exploration.
   (v)   'Europe benefited, while the newly discovered lands and their peoples were exploited terribly.' Do you agree? Write an account explaining your answer.

The Reformation

aims

- To understand the causes of the Reformation
- To know the role played by Martin Luther and John Calvin in the Reformation
- To understand the role of the Catholic Counter-Reformation

What was the Reformation?

The Reformation began in Germany as a protest against abuses in the Catholic Church. It led to the establishment of the Protestant churches.

What were the causes of the Reformation?

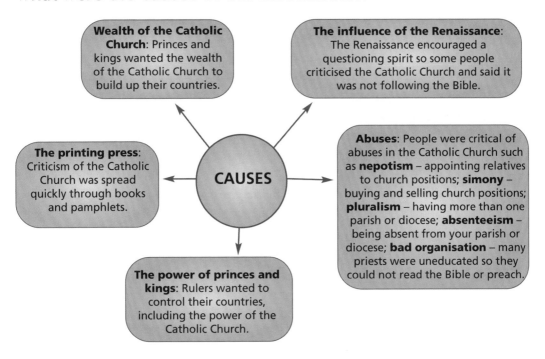

Wealth of the Catholic Church: Princes and kings wanted the wealth of the Catholic Church to build up their countries.

The influence of the Renaissance: The Renaissance encouraged a questioning spirit so some people criticised the Catholic Church and said it was not following the Bible.

The printing press: Criticism of the Catholic Church was spread quickly through books and pamphlets.

CAUSES

Abuses: People were critical of abuses in the Catholic Church such as **nepotism** – appointing relatives to church positions; **simony** – buying and selling church positions; **pluralism** – having more than one parish or diocese; **absenteeism** – being absent from your parish or diocese; **bad organisation** – many priests were uneducated so they could not read the Bible or preach.

The power of princes and kings: Rulers wanted to control their countries, including the power of the Catholic Church.

Where did the Reformation begin?

The Reformation started in Germany in the early 16th century. Martin Luther criticised the Catholic Church.

Special study – The life of a reformer: Martin Luther

People in History

A follower of a named religious reformer during the Reformation

I am a follower of **Martin Luther**, who began the Reformation in Germany. Luther was an **Augustinian** monk who was **Professor of Theology** at Wittenberg University. He was worried about **salvation** (going to heaven), but he read in the Bible that 'the just man shall live by faith alone'. He said that **only faith in God** would allow a person to get to heaven.

He criticised John **Tetzel** for preaching indulgences. Luther wrote his **95 Theses** in Latin and pinned them on the church door at **Wittenberg**. He wanted scholars to discuss his views. But very soon his theses were translated into **German**, printed and distributed all over Germany. I was one of the many Germans who agreed with Luther because we did not want to pay money to Rome and because our priests were ignorant.

The **Pope** took action against Luther. He ordered Luther to meet **Cardinal Cajetan**, but he couldn't persuade Luther to change his ideas. Luther then debated with a theologian, **John Eck**, but again Luther did not change his mind. Then the Pope sent Luther a **papal bull** (letter) ordering him to withdraw his teachings or else be **excommunicated** (banned from sacraments). I saw Luther publicly burning the papal letter; the Pope excommunicated him.

The emperor, **Charles V**, called the **Diet of Worms** – a meeting of the princes of the empire. Luther was promised he would not be harmed, so he attended the meeting. He refused to change his views. Charles V then issued the **Edict of Worms** to arrest Luther. But **Frederick the Wise**, the ruler of Saxony, took Luther and hid him in Wartburg Castle so that he would be safe. Here he spent the next year translating the **New Testament** into German so that ordinary Germans could read the Bible.

Luther's ideas got support from other **princes**. They protested to the emperor that they wanted to practise their own religion so they became known as **Protestants**. Some of Luther's followers (with Luther's approval) wrote out the **Confession of Augsburg**, which was a statement of Lutheran beliefs, but it was rejected by the emperor. Luther died in 1546 before the divisions between Catholic and Protestant princes broke into war.

Calvin's Reformation in Geneva

People in History

A follower of a named religious reformer during the Reformation

I am a follower of **John Calvin**, who founded the **Calvinist Church** in Geneva. Calvin was born in **France**, but because he converted to Protestantism he had to leave. He went to **Basel** in Switzerland and wrote *The Institutes of the Christian Religion*, which stated his beliefs. He was invited to **Geneva** to set up a new church.

I joined his church in Geneva because I supported his beliefs. I believe in **predestination**, the view that God has selected those who go to heaven and to hell. I am one of the **elect** who is going to heaven. I think that the **Bible** is the only source for the teachings of Christ. In our church there are **two sacraments**, baptism and the Eucharist.

Calvin believed that Geneva was the **City of God** and that Rome was the **City of the Devil** because that was where the Pope lived.

Our church in Geneva is very **well organised**. We have **pastors** who preach and conduct services in the vernacular. I am a **teacher** and we are in charge of the schools because we believe everyone must be educated in order to be able to read the Bible. There are also **deacons** who take care of the sick and elderly. But it is the **Elders** who are in charge. They encourage people to spy on others and they enforce the rules.

Calvin's rules are **strict**. No drunkenness is tolerated, but Calvin was forced to re-open taverns when he closed them. Songs and dances were banned and vulgar singing is punished with piercing the tongue of the singer. Card and dice playing are banned; we must all dress plainly, with no frills. Anyone breaking these rules is **punished** severely, even by death at the stake.

Calvin's religion is **spreading** to other countries. Our school system in Geneva is very good and missionaries are trained in university. In **France**, there are one million Calvinists who are called **Huguenots**. John **Knox** took the Calvinist religion to Scotland, where Calvinists are called **Presbyterians**. Calvinists in England are called **Puritans**, but some of them have immigrated to America to practise their religion freely. We all follow Calvin loyally because we believe he will lead us to heaven.

Religious Differences						
	Finding out about God	Salvation	Sacraments	Clergy	Head of the Church	Church services
Catholic beliefs	The Bible and the teachings of the Church	Faith and good works	Seven sacraments	Clergy were specially educated; clergy cannot marry	The Pope	Mass in Latin
Luther's beliefs	The Bible	By faith alone	Two sacraments – Baptism and Eucharist	Any Christian can be a clergy-man; clergy can marry	Princes and kings	In the vernacular
Calvin's beliefs	The Bible	Predestin-ation	Two sacraments – Baptism and Eucharist	Any Christian can be a clergy-man; clergy can marry	Lay rulers – the elders	In the vernacular

The Reformation in England and Ireland

1. **Henry VIII** wanted to annul his marriage with **Catherine of Aragon** and to marry **Anne Boleyn**. But the Catholic Church would not allow him.
   - He appointed Thomas **Cranmer** as Archbishop of Canterbury; Cranmer gave Henry a divorce. Henry then married Anne Boleyn.
2. Henry passed the **Act of Supremacy**, which made him Supreme Head of the Church of England. The **Oath of Supremacy** had to be taken to recognise Henry as head of the Church. Those who did not take the Oath, including Thomas More, Lord Chancellor of England, were beheaded.
3. Henry closed the **monasteries** and confiscated their lands. He said they were badly run, and that they were still loyal to the Pope.
4. Henry introduced the **Bible in English** but he wanted to keep **Catholic services**.
5. Protestantism was developed fully under **Edward VI**. The **Book of Common Prayer**, which included Protestant prayers, was introduced.
6. **Queen Mary** restored Catholicism as the main religion of England, but she did not re-open the monasteries.
7. **Queen Elizabeth** established the **Church of England** (or Anglican Church) with herself as Supreme Governor of the Church. She made the Church of England the official religion of England.

Results of the English Reformation

1. The king/queen became head of the Church.
2. Parliament became more powerful because the Tudor rulers needed to pass laws through parliament.
3. England was united behind the Crown when Catholic Spain attacked with its Armada.
4. The monasteries were closed.

The Reformation in Ireland

The Tudors introduced the same religious changes in Ireland as they did in England. But they failed to convert Ireland to Protestantism. **Why?**
- Irish Catholics rejected Protestantism because they saw it as part of England's plan to control the country.
- Irish was the main language of the people, while the new religion was linked to the spread of the English language.
- Irish Catholics resisted the closure of the monasteries.

The Catholic Counter-Reformation

The Catholic Counter-Reformation refers to the efforts of the Catholic Church to reform itself and to stop the spread of Protestantism.

The Council of Trent

The Council of Trent was a council of the cardinals and bishops to reform the Catholic Church.

Work of the Council of Trent	
Faith (beliefs)	Discipline (rules)
• Faith and good works were necessary for salvation • The word of God was found in the Bible and the teachings of the Church • Seven sacraments • Priests were special people; they could not marry	• Simony, nepotism, pluralism banned • Catholics must be taught from a catechism (a book with questions and answers about the Church's teachings • Images of Christ, Mary and saints to be placed in churches

Results of the Council of Trent

1. The Catholic religion became the most important Christian religion in Europe.
2. There were greater divisions between Catholics and Protestants in Europe.

Religious orders: Ignatius Loyola and the Jesuits

1. The **Jesuits** (Society of Jesus) was a religious order founded by **Ignatius Loyola**.
   - He wrote the *Spiritual Exercises* as a guide to train his followers.
   - He was an ex-soldier, so the Jesuits were organised like an **army** with a governor-general at their head and they followed strict discipline.
2. **The work of the Jesuits**
   - The Jesuits spread the Catholic religion through preaching and deeds of charity.
   - They founded schools and colleges to teach the sons of nobles and merchants – the future leaders.
   - They became missionaries to Ireland, India, Japan and other countries.
   - Their work maintained Catholicism in Ireland, Poland and Austria.

Who was Francis Xavier?

Francis Xavier was a famous Jesuit missionary who travelled to India and Japan.

The Court of Inquisition

1. The Inquisition was a court of the Catholic Church which tried people accused of **heresy** (beliefs contrary to the Catholic Church).
   - It was mainly active in Spain and Italy.
   - It used torture to get people to confess.
   - Accused people had to prove their innocence.

- Punishments included: wearing a San Benito (a special garment), whipping or burning at the stake.

2. The result of the work of the Inquisition was that Protestantism was crushed in Spain and Italy.

What were the results of the Reformation?

1. Europe was **divided** between Catholic and Protestant countries.
   - Catholic = Spain, Italy, Ireland
   - Protestant = England, Scotland, Holland, Norway

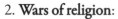

2. **Wars of religion**:
   - Civil wars in England, France and Germany

'Effects' = 'Results' = 'Impact'

   - War between Spain and England in which Spain attacked with its Armada
   - The Thirty Years War, which involved Sweden, Denmark, states of Germany, Austria and other countries

3. **Intolerance and Persecution**:
   - Catholics and Protestants persecuted each other.

4. **Art and architecture**:
   - Protestant churches followed a plain style.
   - Catholic churches were richly decorated.

When you are writing about the **effects or results** of the Reformation, you don't have to confine yourself to the immediate effects. You can mention effects up to the present day. You can also include the results of the individual reformers, such as Luther or Calvin.

5. **Education**:
   - Protestant churches wanted everybody to be able to read the Bible.

Past Questions on *The Reformation*

Short-Answer Questions

1. Give **two** reasons why many people thought the Catholic Church was in need of reform around 1500.
2. Name **one** religious reformer from **outside** of Germany **and** one of his beliefs.
3. What was the main result of the Diet of Worms in 1521?
4. Mention **two** ways in which the Catholic Church tried to stop the spread of the Protestant religions during the 16th century.
5. Describe **one** important effect of the Reformation on Ireland.
6. How did the Catholic Church change as a result of the Reformation?
7. During the period of the Reformation and Counter-Reformation, what was the Inquisition?
8. Mention **two** decisions made at the Council of Trent (1545–1563).
9. Mention **one** contribution made by Ignatius Loyola to the Catholic Counter-Reformation.
10. Give **two** consequences of the Reformation in Europe during the period 1517 to 1648.

People in History

Ordinary level

1. A **named** religious reformer at the time of the Reformation
    *   *Hints*: Early life; Reasons for becoming a reformer; Main beliefs in his religion; Results of his work

Higher level

1. A named religious reformer at the time of the Reformation

Source Questions (for Higher level)

Source E

Excerpts from Martin Luther's 95 Theses, October 31, 1517

36. Any truly repentant Christian has a right to full remission of penalty and guilt, even without indulgence letters.

47. Christians are to be taught that the buying of indulgences is a matter of free choice, not commanded.

49. Christians are to be taught that papal indulgences are useful only if they do not put their trust in them, but very harmful if they lose their fear of God because of them.

53. They are the enemies of Christ and the pope who forbid altogether the preaching of the Word of God in some churches in order that indulgences may be preached in others.

54. Injury is done to the Word of God when, in the same sermon, an equal or larger amount of time is devoted to indulgences than to the Word.

62. The true treasure of the church is the most holy gospel of the glory and grace of God.

(Source: Internet Medieval Sourcebook. www.fordham.edu/halsall/sbook.htm)

A. Source D

(i)   What was a Papal Bull?

(ii) Why is Luther burning this Papal Bull?

(iii) What happened to Luther as a result of this action?

B. Source E

Study the excerpts from the 95 Theses and answer the following questions:

(i)   To what does a truly repentant Christian have a right?

(ii) What is the true treasure of the Church?

Source D:
Martin Luther burning a Papal Bull in Wittenberg, 10 December 1520

(iii) From the theses shown above, is Luther totally against the sale of indulgences? Explain your answer.

(iv) Why do you think that the Pope became alarmed by the theses? Give **two** reasons for your answer.

C. 'The Reformation changed the face of Europe.'

Write about **one** of the following topics:

(i)   The impact of the Reformation on Ireland.

(ii) Religious wars in Europe.

(iii) The Counter-Reformation.

Long Answers (Higher level)

(i)   Explain **two** of the following: *Heresy; Nepotism; Simony; Pluralism.*

(ii) What did the Peace of Augsburg decide?

(iii) Describe one important effect of the Reformation on Ireland.

(iv) Write an account of **two** of the following: *Calvin's church in Geneva; Henry VIII and the Reformation in England; Ignatius Loyola and the Jesuits.*

8 Plantations in Ireland

aims
- To understand the background to the plantations
- To give a brief outline of some plantations
- To undertake special study of the Plantation of Ulster
- To know the impact of the plantations in Ireland

How was Ireland ruled around 1500?

1. The **king** of England was Lord of Ireland but he had little power.
2. The **Pale** was the only part of Ireland where the king's officials had power. The Pale stretched around Dublin, from Dundalk in the north to Dalkey in the south.

What was English common law?

This was the law of the English. Under common law, the eldest son became the new lord.

3. **The Anglo-Irish lords**: These were descendant of the Anglo-Normans. By 1500 they were largely independent of the English Crown. They used English common law and sometimes Gaelic Brehon law.
   - *Examples*: The Fitzgeralds of Kildare and the Fitzgeralds of Desmond (Munster)

What was Brehon law?

This was Gaelic law. Under Brehon law, the chief (or *taoiseach*) was elected from the *derbhfine* (royal family).

4. **The Gaelic Irish lords**: These were native Irish lords who followed Brehon law. They ruled their own kingdoms.
   - *Examples*: The O'Neills of Tyrone, O'Donnells of Donegal, McCarthys of Cork

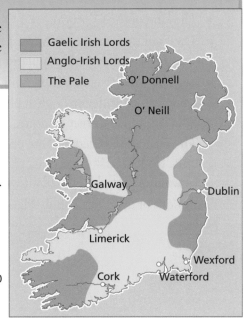

Map of Ireland in 1500

What efforts were made to conquer Ireland by the Tudors?

1. The Tudor kings and queens of England wanted to conquer Ireland because they
   - wanted to protect England from attack by France and Spain
   - wanted to introduce the Protestant religion to Ireland
   - thought English culture was superior to Gaelic culture
2. The Tudors tried to conquer Ireland by
   - military **conquest**
   - **surrender and regrant**
     - This was where Gaelic and Anglo-Irish lords surrendered their land to the king – when the lords promised to use English law, the king regranted the land to the lords and gave them English titles.
3. Both of these methods failed so a new policy was tried. This was called **plantation**.

What was plantation?

- Land was confiscated from rebellious chiefs and lords.
- The land was given to loyal settlers or planters.
- The planters would use English law, language and customs.

The Plantation of Laois-Offaly

1. The policy was first tried in the Plantation of Laois-Offaly.

What ruler established the Plantation of Laois-Offaly?
It was Queen Mary.

- The land of the O'Moores and O'Connors was confiscated in Laois and Offaly.
- The English government wanted to impose English law, protect the Pale, and control the native Irish population.
- Queen's County (Laois) and King's County (Offaly) were created.
- Land was set aside for English planters, and poorer land along the Shannon was reserved for loyal Irish planters.
- The plantation failed because only 80 planters were granted land; no planters came from England so Gaelic planters were given land; the O'Moores and O'Connors attacked the planters.

2. The lessons of the Laois-Offaly Plantation were used in the next plantation, Munster.

The Plantation of Munster

1. **Causes**: The Fitzgeralds of Desmond, led by **James Fitzmaurice Fitzgerald**, rose twice against English rule in Munster. But both rebellions were defeated.
   - The land of the Fitzgeralds was confiscated.

2. **Aims of the Plantation**: The English government wanted to strengthen Munster against a Spanish invasion. It wanted to spread English language, culture and the Protestant religion.

3. **Plan of Plantation**: The confiscated land was **surveyed** and **mapped**.
   - The land was divided into estates of 4,000, 6,000, 8,000 and 12,000 acres.
   - The planters who got land were called **undertakers** because they undertook to carry out certain conditions.
     - They would bring in English farmers and craftsmen.
     - They would pay rent to the Crown.
     - They would defend themselves after seven years.

Who was Sir Walter Raleigh?

One of the most famous undertakers was Sir Walter Raleigh, who received 42,000 acres around Youghal, Co Cork. He was reputed to have brought the first potatoes from America to Ireland.

Success of the Plantation

- **New towns** were developed such as Bandon and Mallow in Co Cork, Lismore in Co Waterford and Killarney in Co Kerry.
- **New family names** such as Browne, Carew and Denny came to Ireland.
- **New farming methods** were used – there was an increase in tillage, and new breeds of cattle and sheep were introduced.
- **Trade** prospered as timber, wool and hides (leather) were exported through Youghal and Cork.
- But not enough English planters were attracted to Munster, so undertakers had to rent land to the Gaelic Irish and the Anglo-Irish.
- During the **Nine Years War** (1594–1603), many planters went back to England. After the war was over, **new planters**, such as Richard Boyle, Earl of Cork, took over some of the land. A wealthy Protestant landowning minority developed.

Special Study – The Plantation of Ulster

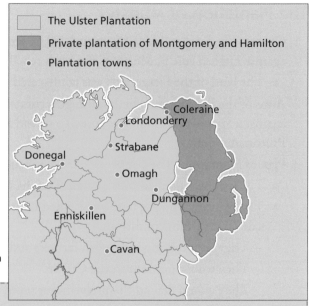

The Ulster Plantation

Legend:
- ☐ The Ulster Plantation
- ■ Private plantation of Montgomery and Hamilton
- • Plantation towns

Map towns: Coleraine, Londonderry, Strabane, Donegal, Omagh, Dungannon, Enniskillen, Cavan

People in History

A native Irish person who lost land during a named plantation in Ireland

I am a native Irish person who lost land during the Plantation of Ulster. I am a member of the **O'Neill clan** in Co Tyrone and our chief, **Hugh O'Neill**, was defeated at the end of the Nine Years War in the **Battle of Kinsale**. After he left Ireland in the **Flight of the Earls** our land was **confiscated**. The land of Co Tyrone and five other counties has now been planted by **King James I**. He surveyed and mapped the land first. The **surveyors** had to be protected by soldiers because those of us who lost land would have attacked them. The land was then divided between **Church** land and **Crown** land, and this land was used for the plantation. In Co Tyrone, they built **new towns** such as Omagh and Strabane. These towns have squares in the middle with wide streets and a Protestant church. Our land was given to **undertakers** (those who promised to carry out certain conditions) and **servitors** (who were government officials or soldiers owed money from the Nine Years War) or **loyal Irish**. Those who got 1,000 acres had to build a **bawn**, those with 1,500 acres had to build a **bawn and stone house** and those who got 2,000 acres had to build a **bawn and a stone castle**. The planters are Protestants – either Presbyterians from Scotland or members of the Church of England. They brought with them farmers who will rent the land from them. But since they are short of farmers, some of the Gaelic Irish are being allowed to rent land from servitors and loyal Irish. They will have to get used to **new farming methods** with more tillage and less cattle raising. Some members of our clan have taken to the hills and the forests and are attacking the planters.

People in History

A planter during a named plantation in Ireland

Fill in the blanks using the words in the list. (Words can be used more than once)

I am a planter in the Ulster Plantation organised by King _____ I. I am a _____ from Scotland who was granted land in Co Tyrone. I am an _____ who has promised to carry out certain conditions. Other planters such as _____ (English soldiers and officials owed money after the Nine Years War) and loyal Irish were given land here and in _____ other counties. I agree with the aims of King _____ in relation to the plantation. He wants to create a loyal and _____ population and to get money for the _____ from the rents. Our land was _____ beforehand and divided into crown land and _____ land. The crown land was used for the plantation and for _____ and schools. As an _____, I am not allowed to have _____ tenants but my rent is lower than the rent paid by servitors and the loyal Irish. I have 1,500 acres so I must also build a _____ (enclosure) and a stone house for defence. Those with 1,000 acres need only build a _____, but those given 2,000 acres must build a _____ and a stone _____ My land is near the town of Omagh, which is a planned settlement with a _____, wide streets, a church and a school. Not far away from me is Co _____, which has been given by the king to companies of London merchants to plant. It looks like the Ulster Plantation is a great success because _____ law, language and culture have been strengthened in this area. We are also loyal to the king, and the Protestant religion is strong with both members of the Church of _____ as well as Presbyterians here. Some of the Gaelic Irish have taken to the _____ and forests and are attacking some of the planters. This doesn't look good for the future, but already we are making Ulster _____ with better roads, new farming methods and better trade.

Use your textbook to check your answers when you are finished.

bawn	English	Londonderry	square
castle	five	Presbyterian	surveyed
church	Gaelic	prosperous	towns
Crown	hills	Protestant	undertaker
England	James	servitors	

The Cromwellian Plantation

1. Cromwell conquered a rebellion which broke out in Ireland.
2. He **confiscated** the land of the rebels.
   - In the Act of Settlement, rebel landowners lost all their land.
   - Those who could not prove their loyalty were transplanted to Connacht.
   - These were Catholic landowners.
   - But Catholic tenants were left in their places.
3. Sir William Petty organised the **Down Survey** to survey all the confiscated land.
   - The land was divided among **adventurers** who provided money to pay for Cromwell's army and soldiers.
4. Cromwell's plantation **resulted** in the transfer of land from Catholic landowners to Protestant landowners.
   - They were landlords now to Catholic tenants.
   - Some Catholic landowners who lost their land took to the hills to become outlaws or Tories.
   - For the next 200 years power and wealth in Ireland remained in the hands of Protestants.

What were the overall results of the Plantations?

1. **Political**: Conflict arose between Catholics and Protestants over land and religion. Protestants controlled most of the power through the **Penal Laws**, which forbade Catholics from owning land, voting or holding government positions. The conflict between Catholics and Protestants continued during the 19th and 20th centuries. They contributed to the **Troubles** in Northern Ireland at the end of the 20th century.

'Effects' = 'Results' = 'Impact'

2. **Religious**: The planters were Protestants, but they were in a minority in Ireland. The majority of the Protestants were confined to Northern Ireland, especially Antrim, Down and north Armagh. The land was now mainly owned by Protestants, while Catholics rented the land from them. In the 19th century, the Catholic tenants led a campaign which led to the Protestant landlords selling the land to the tenants.
   - The plantations failed to crush the Catholic religion.

When you are writing about the **effects or results** of the plantations, you don't have to confine yourself to the immediate effects. You can mention effects up to the present day. You can also include the results of the individual plantations, such as Laois-Offaly, Munster, Ulster and the Cromwellian Plantation.

3. **Cultural**: The culture and language of Gaelic Ireland

declined. English language and culture became more widespread. English common law became the law of Ireland. New farming methods, which depended more on tillage, were introduced. New towns were built.

Past questions on *Plantations in Ireland*

Short-Answer Questions

1. During the plantations in Ireland, explain a major difference between the Gaelic and the English systems of land ownership.
2. Name **two** British rulers who ordered plantations to be carried out in Ireland.
3. Give **two** results of any named plantation from Ireland in the 16th or 17th century.

People in History

Ordinary level

1. A settler who received land during one of the plantations in Ireland during the 16th or 17th century
   - *Hints*: Name of the area planted; Rules for settlers; New ways of life introduced by the settlers; Relationship with the native Irish
2. A Gaelic landowner who lost land during one of the plantations in Ireland during the 16th or 17th century
   - *Hints*: Name of the plantation; Reasons why the land was planted; Relations with the new owners; Results of this plantation

Higher level

1. A settler who received land during a **named** plantation in Ireland during the 16th or 17th century
2. A planter who settled on a **named** Irish plantation

Source Questions (Higher level)

Source D

Advice given to Henry VIII by Thomas Howard, Earl of Surrey, in 1521 on the conquest of Ireland.

In my poor opinion, this land shall never be brought to good order except by conquest and in this manner:

First, provide the army, which your Grace will have there, with money until conquest be perfected.

Secondly, provide the army with food, ordnance, artillery and all other stuff that must be needed in the building of strong fortresses.

Thirdly, unless your Grace send inhabitants, of your own subjects, to inhabit such land as shall be won, all your efforts should be but wastefully spent.

For if this country's people are allowed to inhabit the land, undoubtedly they would return to their old ill-rooted customs.

(Source: Peter Berresford Ellis, *Eyewitness to Irish History*, pp. 51–53)

Source E

Source F

A. Source D

  (i) Mention **one** resource the king is advised to give the army.

  (ii) Why do you think it was necessary to build *strong fortresses*?

  (iii) Suggest **two** Gaelic customs that King Henry VIII might consider 'ill-rooted'.

  (iv) Name **one** British ruler **and** the plantation which he/she carried out in Ireland.

B. Sources E and F

Plantation towns

  (i) From source **E**, give **one** piece of evidence to suggest that the town was well developed and wealthy.

  (ii) From source **F**, identify **two** features which provide evidence that it was a plantation town.

C. Name **one** of the plantations which you have studied and write about the effects of that plantation on **two** of the following:

  (i) Religion

  (ii) Political control

  (iii) Language and customs

Long Answers (Higher level)

(i) Give **two** reasons why English rulers adopted a policy of plantation in Ireland.

(ii) (a) Name **one** plantation you have studied and name the English ruler who carried out that plantation.

     (b) Mention **one** type of people who received land in that plantation.

     (c) Mention **one** condition under which these planters received land.

(iii) Write on the main consequences (results) of plantations in Ireland under **each** of **two** of the following headings: (a) Religion (b) Politics (c) Culture *(Note: your answer may include both immediate and long-term results.)*

9 The Political Revolutions

aims
- To understand the background of each of the revolutions
- To have an overall understanding of each revolution
- To make a special study of one revolutionary
- To understand the impact of the revolutions

The American War of Independence

What was the American War of Independence?

1. It was a war between Great Britain and 13 British colonies in North America, and it became a global war between several European great powers.

2. It is also known as the American Revolutionary War.

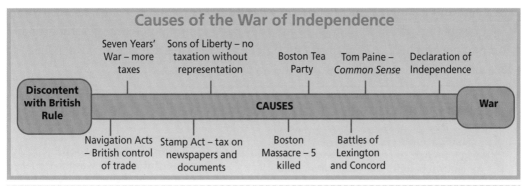

Causes of the War of Independence

People in History

A supporter of the government describes how revolution broke out in America

I am a supporter of the government in the disagreements between the Americans and the British government. There are **thirteen colonies** in America ruled by Britain. I live in Boston, which is the main city in one of the colonies called Massachusetts.

The Americans are complaining that their trade is controlled by the **Navigation Acts** – which state that American sugar and cotton can only be sold to England. Instead of selling the goods to Britain, the Americans are smuggling them out, which is breaking the law. The Americans are also objecting to paying extra **taxes**. I don't know why, because the British government is only asking the Americans to cover some of the cost of the **Seven Years' War** in which they defeated the French and protected the Americans. The Americans are also objecting to paying for their own defence.

The government had to pass the **Stamp Act**, which was a tax on newspapers and legal documents. The Americans objected by tarring and feathering stamp officials and by burning stamps. They even came up with a slogan, '**No Taxation without Representation**', because they said they should not have to pay taxes if they were not represented in Westminster.

Britain had to impose taxes on **tea**. People in Boston especially resented this. They tarred and feathered customs officials. Some threw stones at British soldiers in Boston and the soldiers opened fire, killing five people. This is known as the **Boston Massacre**. Then some Bostonians dressed as Indians and raided ships carrying tea for the East India Company. They threw 342 boxes of tea into Boston harbour. I think the British government was correct in closing down Boston port after this so-called **Boston Tea Party**.

The Americans and the British government are drifting closer to war, or revolution, as the Americans call it. British troops were ambushed as they tried to capture weapons and ammunition in **Concord**. Paul **Revere** had ridden through the night to alert people. The first shots were fired in **Lexington** and there were no weapons in Concord when the British got there.

That troublemaker Tom Paine is encouraging the Americans to rebel and go for complete independence in his book, ***Common Sense***. Now there is a Continental Congress being held in Philadelphia and they have appointed **George Washington** as commander-in-chief of a Continental Army. The Americans have also issued a **Declaration of Independence**. Surely, the revolution has broken out.

What were the causes of the American War of Independence?

Navigation Acts: Britain used the Navigation Acts to control American trade for its own benefit. The Acts stated that American products such as sugar, cotton and tobacco could only be sold to England. Americans smuggled these goods and this led to clashes with the English.

No Taxation without Representation: This was the slogan of the Sons of Liberty, who said Britain should not tax America when Americans were not represented in Parliament in London.

Tom Paine: Tom Paine wrote *Common Sense*, which encouraged the Americans to fight for complete independence from Britain.

CAUSES

More taxation: Britain wanted the Americans to pay for the Seven Years' War and for its own defence. Britain imposed the Stamp Act, which said newspapers and legal documents must be taxed. The Americans rioted against this, burnt the stamps and attacked the stamp officials.

Boston Massacre: In Boston, British troops killed five people who were protesting about taxes on tea.

Lexington and Concord: British troops marched from Boston to Concord to try to capture an American store of arms and ammunition. Paul Revere rode through the night to warn people so there was no arms and ammunition when the British arrived. The British were attacked at Lexington on the way there and ambushed at Concord on the way back. These were the first shots of the American War of Independence.

Boston Tea Party: Americans dressed as Indians raided ships in Boston harbour and threw 342 crates of tea into the water. The British government closed the port and imposed martial (military) law.

Progress of the War

Major Events in the American War of Independence

- **1770** Boston Massacre
- **1775** Washington appointed commander-in-chief of Continental Army
- **1776** Washington's victory at Trenton
- **1777** Washington's victory at Princeton
- **1777–78** Washington wintered at Valley Forge

(Timeline: 1770 — 1775 — 1783)

- **1773** Boston Tea Party
- **1775** Battles of Lexington and Concord
- **1776** Declaration of Independence
- **1777** Battle of Saratoga
- **1781** Washington's victory at the Battle of Yorktown
- **1783** The Treaty of Versailles

1. George **Washington** was appointed as **Commander-in-chief** of the Continental (American) Army.

2. The **Continental Congress** (a meeting of the representatives of the 13 colonies) passed the Declaration of Independence on 4 July 1776. The Declaration of Independence marked the final break from Britain.

3. The British defeated the Americans at **Bunker Hill** in Boston, even though they suffered huge losses.

4. Washington's invasion of British-controlled Canada failed.

5. New York City fell to the British.

6. Washington retreated to Pennsylvania, but he won surprise victories at **Trenton** and **Princeton**.

7. The American general Gates won a huge victory over the British army at the **Battle of Saratoga**. This resulted in France (and, later, Spain and Holland) joining the war on the side of the Americans. The French provided men and ships for America.

8. The British captured **Philadelphia**, the capital of the American colonies.

9. Washington spent the winter of 1777–78 in **Valley Forge**, near Philadelphia. With the help of a German officer, Baron von Steuben, he formed a well-trained army.

10. Washington won the **Battle of Yorktown**. He surrounded a British army on land while the French navy surrounded it by sea.

11. In 1783 the British government recognised the independence of America in the **Treaty of Versailles**.

Special study – The life of a revolutionary: George Washington

People in History

The life of a revolutionary: George Washington

Fill in the blanks using the words in the list. (Words can be used more than once)

George Washington owned a _____ **plantation** in Mount Vernon, Virginia. He gained experience in war during the **Seven Years' War** against the French. He represented Virginia in the _____ **Congress**, which appointed him _____ **-in-chief** of the Continental (American) Army to oppose Britain. As commander-in-chief, he faced a number of **problems**: his army was made up of _____ soldiers who often went home to farm. On the other hand, the British army was more experienced and disciplined. Washington began with success in taking _____, but he soon lost **New York**. His first important success was his surprise attack on the British at _____. He crossed the icy Delaware River on Christmas Day and caught the British by surprise as they celebrated. Washington next defeated the British at _____. He also sent some of his troops to help General Gates defeat the British at _____. This was a **turning point** in the war because now the _____ began to help the Americans. However, during the winter of 1777/78, Washington had to retreat to _____, about 20 miles from Philadelphia, which was under British control. In _____, Washington's men suffered from cold and starvation and many returned home. But Washington stayed there and he got Baron **von** _____, a Prussian officer, to train the soldiers, making them into a disciplined army. Washington's army continued to fight over the next few years. In 1781, Washington surrounded the British army under _____ at _____. Washington was helped by the _____ navy, which cut off supplies to the British from the sea. The British were forced to surrender. A couple of years later, America got its independence at the Treaty of _____. After the war, Washington headed the **Constitutional Convention**, which drew up the American _____. He then served eight years as _____ of the United States of America. When he died at his home in Mount Vernon, he was regarded as '**the** _____ **of the United States**'.

Use your textbook to check your answers when you are finished.

Boston	Father	Saratoga	Versailles
commander	French	Steuben	Yorktown
Constitution	part-time	tobacco	
Continental	president	Trenton	
Cornwallis	Princeton	Valley Forge	

What were the results of the American War of Independence?

1. George Washington was president of the Constitutional Convention which drew up the **American Constitution**.
2. Washington became the **first president** of the United States of America.
3. The USA began as **13 states**, but it later expanded to **50 states**. (America later bought some land from the French and the Russians, and America took over other land when it defeated Mexico in war.)
4. America became the **most powerful country** in the world during the 20th century.
5. The American Revolution inspired the **French** to overthrow their king in the French Revolution in 1789.
6. The ideas of the Declaration of Independence and the American Constitution were followed in other countries, such as **Ireland**. This led to the Rising of 1798 and the Volunteer movement in Ireland.

The French Revolution

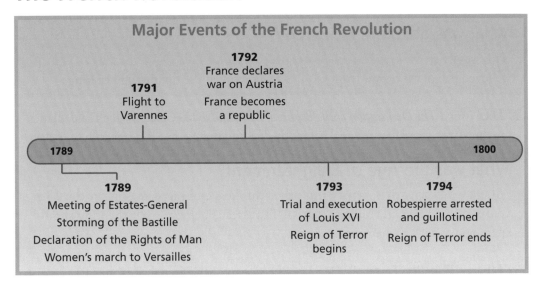

Major Events of the French Revolution

1791
Flight to Varennes

1792
France declares war on Austria
France becomes a republic

1789 — 1800

1789
Meeting of Estates-General
Storming of the Bastille
Declaration of the Rights of Man
Women's march to Versailles

1793
Trial and execution of Louis XVI
Reign of Terror begins

1794
Robespierre arrested and guillotined
Reign of Terror ends

What were the causes of the French Revolution?

Peasants and middle classes: The peasants and middle classes were the Third Estate. They paid taxes to run the country. The peasants paid taxes to the clergy and nobility.

Absolute monarchy: The French people thought King Louis XVI was too powerful. People also did not like his wife, Marie Antoinette.

Nobility and clergy: These were known as the First Estate (clergy) and the Second Estate (nobility). The nobility and clergy did not pay taxes. The nobles had complete power over their peasants (farmers).

CAUSES

The American War of Independence: Some French leaders wanted to follow the example of America, which got rid of its all-powerful rulers. France helped America in the War of Independence and now France was nearly bankrupt. The king needed to raise taxes.

Age of Enlightenment: French thinkers wanted the king to share power with parliament.

The Fall of the Bastille: People in Paris suffered from bread shortages and high prices. They attacked the Bastille – a large prison fortress – because they thought it stored arms. The Bastille was captured on 14 July and this sparked off the French Revolution.

The meeting of the Estates-General: The king called the Estates-General (or parliament) together to pass more taxes. The Third Estate wanted all three estates to meet as one, but the First and Second Estates wanted to vote separately. Eventually, the Third Estate got its way and they formed the Constituent Assembly (later called the National Assembly).

Progress of the Revolution

1. The National Assembly abolished the privileges of the nobility and the clergy.

What was absolute monarchy?

This was when the king had full power over everyone. Louis XVI, the king of France, believed he got his power from God. This was called the **divine right of kings**.

2. They issued *The Declaration of the Rights of Man and of the Citizen*, which said all men are born free, that all were equal before the law and that people had freedom of speech.

What was the Age of Enlightenment?

An era when scientists, artists and other thinkers embraced reason. In the 18th century, some French thinkers (such as Rousseau) believed that the king should share power with parliament.

3. **'Liberty, Equality, Fraternity'** became the slogan of the French Revolution.

What is the meaning of 'Liberty, Equality, Fraternity'?

Liberty – All people should be free

Equality – All people are equal

Fraternity – All people are brothers

4. The market women and fishwives of Paris marched to the Palace of Versailles and forced the king and queen to live in Paris.

5. King Louis was plotting with his brother-in-law, the emperor of Austria. He attempted to leave France secretly, but he was recognised and brought back to Paris.

6. War broke out between France and Austria and later Prussia.

7. The *sans-culottes* (working-class people in Paris) were still suspicious that the king was plotting against the Revolution, so they put him and his family in prison.

8. France was declared a republic in 1792. Evidence of the king's plotting was found and he was executed by guillotine. His wife was executed later.

9. **Reign of Terror**: France faced many problems. The revolutionary leaders set up a Committee of Public Safety to run the country. The president of the Committee was **Robespierre**.

People in History

A named revolutionary in France: Robespierre

Maximilien Robespierre was a **French** revolutionary leader. He was trained as a **lawyer** and elected to the **Third Estate**. He favoured all three Estates meeting as one. He supported the **ideas** of the revolution – '**Liberty**, **Equality**, **Fraternity**'. After King Louis XVI tried to organise help from outside of France, Robespierre **voted for** the execution of the king. Robespierre was a member of the **Jacobins**, a political group in revolutionary France. As France was faced with more and more trouble, Robespierre believed that **strong government** and a **reign of terror** were needed to save the revolution.

France was in **danger** from war as Britain, Holland and Spain joined Austria and Prussia against the revolution. The **Committee of Public Safety** was set up to overcome the dangers and its **president** was Robespierre.

Apart from the war, Robespierre and the Committee faced dangers from **opposition** to the revolution from nobles and **rebellion** in different parts of France. Robespierre decided that violence and terror were the only ways to save the revolution.

He brought in the **Law of Suspects**, which punished anyone thought to be against the revolution. About 2,500 people were killed in Paris and over 16,000 in the rest of France, many by the **guillotine**, the new symbol of the Reign of Terror.

Robespierre put down the **rebellions** in different parts of France with great cruelty, including 30,000 killed in Lyons.

To fight the war, Robespierre organised **mass enlistment** in the French army. There were over 1 million soldiers in the French army, much larger than the other armies. The French army saved the revolution from defeat.

Then Robespierre brought in the **Law of Maximum** which controlled rising prices by putting a maximum price on many goods.

Robespierre and the Committee succeeded in overcoming the problems they faced, but they did this by using methods which were very harsh.

Once the revolution was no longer in danger, people expected that Robespierre would ease off the harsh measures. But he didn't, so many people, including the *sans-culottes*, turned against him. They thought he had too much power. He was shouted down when he spoke in the Assembly. He was later arrested and tried. He was **guillotined** and over a hundred of his supporters were also executed.

What were the results of the French Revolution?

1. **Napoleon** took control of France after the Reign of Terror. He established the Napoleonic Code, which influenced the laws of continental Europe.
2. The **ideas** of the French Revolution – 'Liberty, Equality and Fraternity' – spread to other countries. These ideas influenced the development of the modern world as people wanted greater freedom and equality.
3. **Ireland** was influenced by the ideas of the French Revolution. The United Irishmen was founded to spread the ideas of revolutionary France. **Wolfe Tone** got the French government to help the United Irishmen rebel against the British government in Ireland.
4. **Abolition of Slavery**: Slavery was abolished in France by the revolutionary leaders.
5. **Middle-class power**: The middle classes got more power in France as the clergy and nobility lost much of their power.
6. **Metric system**: The French introduced the metric system, which spread to the rest of Europe.

Ireland in the Age of Revolutions

What were the causes of revolution in Ireland?

Catholic and Presbyterian discontent: The Penal Laws were used by the Protestant Ascendancy to control the Catholics and Presbyterians. Even though some of the laws were repealed (abolished), Catholics and Presbyterians were still banned from parliament. They also paid one-tenth of their crops to support the Anglican clergy.

The power of the Protestant Ascendancy: The Protestant Ascendancy controlled the land and power in Ireland, even though they were only 15% of the population.

CAUSES

The influence of the American and French Revolutions: The victory of the Americans over the British encouraged some people to think that the Irish parliament could get more power. The ideas of the French Revolution were popular in Belfast and they led to the founding of the United Irishmen.

Poverty in the countryside: The population rose rapidly in the 18th century, so farms were subdivided. This made families worse off. Groups like the Whiteboys were formed to protest against rents and tithes.

What was the Protestant Ascendancy?

These were members of the Church of Ireland (Anglican Church) who controlled the land and held power in Ireland.

Who were the United Irishmen?

The United Irishmen was a group founded in Belfast to unite all religions and to reduce English power in Ireland. Later they planned a rebellion in Ireland.

People in History

A named revolutionary leader in Ireland: Wolfe Tone

Fill in the blanks using the words in the list. (Words can be used more than once)

Wolfe Tone was born in Dublin. He became a _____ but preferred politics to law. He supported the principles of the _____ Revolution, 'Liberty, _____, Fraternity'. He attended the inaugural meeting of the **Society of the _____ Irishmen** in Belfast. He wanted parliament to be reformed in order to give a greater say to the people. He also said that English control of Irish affairs should be ended. Tone was a member of the **Catholic delegation** to London which achieved _____ **for Catholics**. But Tone was bitterly disappointed that Catholics could still not become _____ of _____ nor hold high positions of power.

Tone wrote a report for a French spy in Ireland, William _____. When _____ was caught and executed, Tone was allowed go to _____. From there he travelled to France to get help from the revolutionary government of France, which was at _____ with Britain. He persuaded the French government that if the French invaded Ireland, Catholics and _____ would rise up in support of them. Tone was on the **French fleet** led by _____ which sailed to _____ **Bay**, but it had to turn back due to storms. Tone was bitterly disappointed.

Tone was in France when the main actions of the _____ **Rebellion** took place around Dublin, in Wexford, in Ulster and in Connacht. But he still persuaded the French government to send more troops to Ireland. He was on board one of the French ships which were captured off the _____ coast.

Tone was taken to Dublin, tried for _____ and found guilty. He wanted to be shot like a soldier. When this was refused, he committed _____. Tone became known as the **Father of Irish _____** because his ideas provided inspiration for later revolutionary leaders, such as the Young _____, the Fenians and the leaders of the

1916 Rising. He wanted to create an Irish _____ based on the unity of all Irishmen, Catholic, Protestant or Dissenter.

Use your textbook to check your answers when you are finished.

1798	French	Presbyterians	United
America	Hoche	reforms	war
Bantry	Irelanders	republic	
barrister	Jackson	Republicanism	
Donegal	members	suicide	
Equality	parliament	treason	

What happened during the Rising of 1798?

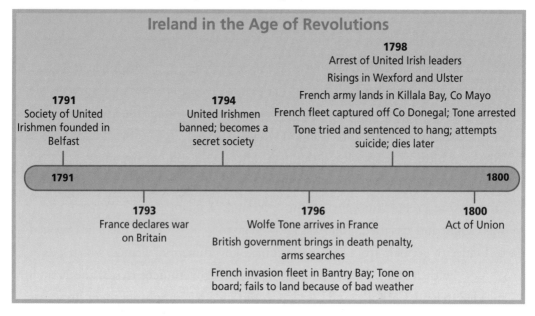

Ireland in the Age of Revolutions

1791
Society of United Irishmen founded in Belfast

1793
France declares war on Britain

1794
United Irishmen banned; becomes a secret society

1796
Wolfe Tone arrives in France
British government brings in death penalty, arms searches
French invasion fleet in Bantry Bay; Tone on board; fails to land because of bad weather

1798
Arrest of United Irish leaders
Risings in Wexford and Ulster
French army lands in Killala Bay, Co Mayo
French fleet captured off Co Donegal; Tone arrested
Tone tried and sentenced to hang; attempts suicide; dies later

1800
Act of Union

1791 ———————————————————— 1800

1. The United Irishmen planned a rising. But the British government knew about the plans through information provided by **spies**.
2. The **leaders** of the United Irishmen, including Lord Edward Fitzgerald, were arrested.
3. The Rising went ahead in Dublin, Kildare and Meath where the **mail coaches** were attacked. But the attacks were easily put down.
4. In **Wexford**, Father John Murphy and Bagenal Harvey defeated yeomanry (part-time soldiers) and militia (full-time soldiers) at **Oulart Hill**; they captured **Enniscorthy** and Wexford town.
5. 200 Protestants were burned in a barn and 100 were killed in Wexford town.
6. The rebel groups were defeated at New Ross and Arklow as they tried to move out of Wexford. Then they were defeated in a major battle at **Vinegar Hill**.

7. A Rising in **Ulster** was also defeated, and the leaders, Henry Joy McCracken and Henry Munro, were executed.

8. French troops led by General **Humbert** landed in Killala, Co Mayo. They defeated the British at the **Races of Castlebar**. But they were beaten in Ballinamuck, Co Longford.

9. When Tone arrived in Donegal with a French fleet, he was captured. He was tried for treason, found guilty and sentenced to death. But he committed suicide instead.

10. The **Rising of 1798** was defeated because of poor organisation, stronger government forces, spies and insufficient French help.

What were the results of the 1798 Rising?

1. 30,000 people died.

2. There were **bitter divisions** between Catholics and Protestants.

3. The **Act of Union** was passed in 1800 to abolish the parliament in Dublin and to send members of the Irish parliament and Lords to represent Ireland in the parliament in Westminster.

'Effects' = 'Results' = 'Impact'

4. **Robert Emmet** was influenced by the United Irishmen. He attempted a failed rebellion in Dublin in 1803. He was arrested and executed.

5. Wolfe Tone was regarded as the **Father of Irish Republicanism**. His ideas that Britain was the never-ending source of trouble in Ireland and that Protestants and Catholics should be united influenced later leaders. His example inspired later rebellions, such as the Rising of 1867 and the 1916 Rising.

What were the overall results of the Age of Revolutions?

1. The power of the **monarchy** was reduced.

2. **Democracy** grew as more people were given the right to vote and the power of parliament increased.

3. **Greater equality**: Some leaders demanded more equality for everybody. Some favoured socialism – the belief that wealth should be spread evenly.

4. **The example of the USA**: The USA won its independence from the stronger power of Britain; this encouraged other countries to try to gain independence.

When you are writing about the **effects or results** of the revolutions, you don't have to confine yourself to the immediate effects; you can mention **effects up to the present day**. You can also **include the results** of the individual revolutions, such as the American, French and Irish.

5. **Violence**: The use of violence and revolution in winning political power became more common.

6. **Armies**: France owed its survival to conscription (compulsory enlistment of men into the army). Now other countries followed its example and armies grew much larger and war became more destructive.

Past questions on *The Political Revolutions*

Short-Answer Questions

1. Choose one of the revolutions (America **or** France **or** Ireland) from the period 1771–1815, and give **two** causes of that revolution: *Country; Cause 1; Cause 2.*

2. Give **two** causes of the American Revolution.

3. In relation to one of the revolutions in America, France or Ireland during the 18th century, name a **leader** of that revolution and one of his **aims**.

4. Put the following events in the correct order *(please start with the earliest)*: *French Revolution; The 1798 Rebellion; The American War of Independence.*

5. Explain one of the following terms from the Age of Revolutions: *Boston Tea Party; Guillotine; United Irishmen.*

6. What was the Reign of Terror in France in the 1790s?

7. Which Irish county was the scene of the most intense rebel activity during the 1798 Rising?

People in History

Ordinary level

1. A **named** revolutionary leader (in France, Ireland or America) during the Age of Revolutions, 1770–1815
   - *Hints*: Early life; Reasons for supporting the revolution; Main events during the revolution; Later life and death

Higher level

1. A **named** leader involved in a revolution (America, France or Ireland) during the period 1770–1815

2. A supporter of a named revolutionary leader during the period 1770–1803

Source Questions (Higher level)

Source D

The execution of French king Louis XVI (London Times, 25th January, 1793)

About half past nine, the king arrived at the place of execution. Louis mounted the scaffold calmly, the trumpets sounding and drums beating during the whole time. He made a sign of wishing to speak to the multitude, the drums ceased, and Louis spoke these few words. *I die innocent; I pardon my enemies.* His executioners then laid hold of him and, an instant after, his head was separated from his body.

Since the king's execution, a general consternation has prevailed throughout Paris; the Sans Culottes are the only persons that rejoice. The honest citizens, safe within their houses, could not suppress their heartfelt grief, and mourned in private with their families the murder of their much-loved Sovereign.

The Republican tyrants of France have murdered their king without even the shadow of justice, and of course they cannot expect friendship with any civilised part of the world. The vengeance of Europe will now rapidly fall on them.

Source E:
Wolfe Tone and the French attempt to land at Bantry Bay, December 1796. (Source: www.napoleon-series.org)

Source F

Extract from a speech by Wolfe Tone, 1798

From my earliest youth, I have regarded the connection between Ireland and Great Britain as the curse of the Irish nation; felt convinced that, whilst it lasted, this country could never be free or happy. I determined to apply all the powers, which my individual efforts could move, in order to separate the two countries. That Ireland was not able, of herself, to throw off the yoke, I knew. I therefore sought for aid, wherever it was to be found. Under the flag of the French Republic, I sought to save and liberate my own country.

A. Source D

   (i) *'The king met his death bravely.'*
      Give **one** piece of evidence from the newspaper article to support this view.

   (ii) According to the article, who were the only persons to rejoice following the king's execution?

   (iii) Was the writer a supporter **or** an opponent of the king's execution? Give **one** piece of evidence from the source to explain your answer.

B. Source E and Source F

   (i) Why did the fleet sent by the French in 1796, shown in Source E, fail to land?

   (ii) In source F, what does Wolfe Tone consider to be the 'curse of the Irish nation'?

   (iii) Give **two** reasons why Wolfe Tone sought military help from the French.

C. Write an account of **one** of the following topics:

   (i) Causes of the American War of Independence.

   (ii) The Reign of Terror in France, September 1793 to July 1794.

   (iii) Reasons for the failure of the 1798 Rebellion in Ireland.

HL

Long-Answer Questions (Higher level)

(i)   Mention **two** causes of the American War of Independence.

(ii) Give **two** reasons why the Americans defeated the British during the War of Independence.

(iii) Explain the influence of the American Revolution on events in France during the late 18th century.

(iv) Write an account of **two** of the following:

   (a) The 'Reign of Terror' during the French Revolution.

   (b) The consequences of the French Revolution.

   (c) The main events during the 1798 Rebellion.

   (d) The results of the 1798 Rebellion in Ireland.

10 From Farm to Factory

aims
- To understand the causes of the Agricultural and Industrial Revolutions
- To understand the impact of changes in agriculture, transport and so forth
- To make a special study of social conditions in Industrial Britain
- To make a special study of social conditions in Ireland at the same time

Social change: From farm to factory

Agricultural and Industrial Revolution

From the middle of the 18th century onwards, Britain went through an Agricultural and Industrial Revolution.

- In the **Agricultural Revolution**, changes in farming methods resulted in more food being produced.
- In the **Industrial Revolution**, goods such as clothes were now made in **factories**, instead of in houses in **domestic industry**.

What were the causes of the Industrial Revolution?

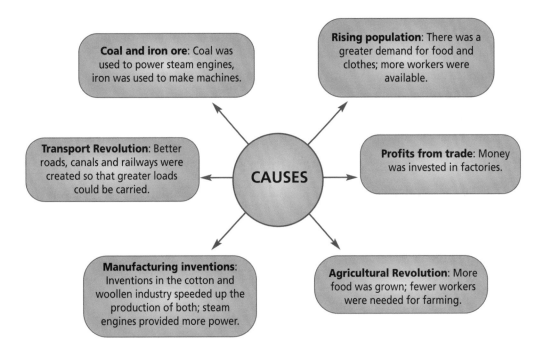

Coal and iron ore: Coal was used to power steam engines, iron was used to make machines.

Rising population: There was a greater demand for food and clothes; more workers were available.

Transport Revolution: Better roads, canals and railways were created so that greater loads could be carried.

CAUSES

Profits from trade: Money was invested in factories.

Manufacturing inventions: Inventions in the cotton and woollen industry speeded up the production of both; steam engines provided more power.

Agricultural Revolution: More food was grown; fewer workers were needed for farming.

What was the Agricultural Revolution?

The Agricultural Revolution consisted of changes made to the system and methods of farming, which resulted in more food being produced.

What was enclosure?

Since the Middle Ages, the three-field (or open-field) system was used in Britain. This system had many **faults**. All this changed during the Agricultural Revolution. The fields were now enclosed so that the three open fields and the common land were divided into farms surrounded by fences and hedges. This was called **enclosure**.

Weaknesses of the Old System (the three-field system)	Strengths of the New System (enclosure)
• One-third of the land was not used each year. • Weeds spread easily. • No machinery was used. • Cattle and sheep were sparse.	• All the land was used. • Farmers could control their own land. • Good farmers could introduce new methods and machinery. • More food was produced for the cities.

New methods of farming

1. **Norfolk Crop Rotation: Charles Townshend** developed this system.
   - Turnips and clover were now grown (as well as wheat and barley) so that all the land was used every year.
   - Turnips were fed to the cattle in winter.
2. **Selective breeding: Robert Bakewell** introduced new breeding techniques so that cattle and sheep produced **more meat**.
3. **New machinery: Jethro Tull** invented the **seed drill**. This scattered seed evenly and the resulting crops were easier to weed.
   - **Cyrus McCormick** invented the **reaper**, which enabled the faster harvesting of corn.
4. **Arthur Young** wrote about the new methods and encouraged farmers to use them.

What was the Transport Revolution?

1. The older methods of transport were slow and expensive, and the loads that could be carried were small.
2. **Roads: Thomas Telford** and **John McAdam** introduced new road surfaces, which improved the roads.
   - **Turnpike trusts** were companies which took over sections of roads, introduced toll gates (turnpikes) and tolls and used the money to maintain the roads.
3. **Canals: James Brindley** built the first canal to carry coal from Worsley to Manchester.
   - Aqueducts, tunnels and locks were used in the **Canal Age** – larger loads could now be carried.

4. **Railways**: **Richard Trevithick** designed the first small steam engine on wheels.
   - The first **goods train** ran between **Stockton** and **Darlington**. The train was designed by **George Stephenson**.
   - The first **passenger line** ran between Manchester and Liverpool. George and Robert Stephenson's *Rocket* won a competition to run along the line.
   - Railways spread rapidly all over Britain – trains were a faster, cheaper and more comfortable form of transport. Trains led to the decline of coaches and canals.

5. **Manufacturing inventions**: New spinning and weaving machines were invented; they speeded up the making of cotton and woollen cloth.

Inventions in the Cotton and Woollen Industry	
Spinning inventions (more thread could be made)	**Weaving inventions (more cloth could be made)**
• James Hargreaves – Spinning Jenny • Richard Arkwright – Water frame • Samuel Crompton – Spinning mule	• John Kay – Flying shuttle • Edmund Cartwright – Power loom

6. **Steam power**: The steam engine was the most important invention of the Industrial Revolution.
   - **Thomas Newcomen** used steam engines to pump water out of mines.
   - **James Watt** added a fly-wheel so that his engine could be used to power machines in factories.

7. **Other changes**: Coal was used instead of charcoal for smelting iron.
   - **Abraham Darby** used **coke** (baked coal) for smelting iron ore.
   - **Henry Cort** invented **puddling and rolling**, which improved the quality of iron.
   - **Henry Bessemer** invented the **Bessemer Converter**, which lessened the cost of producing steel.

What were the effects of the manufacturing inventions?

1. The factory system took over from the domestic system.
2. The growth of factories led to the growth of cities.

What was the Great Exhibition?

This was a huge display of the goods and changes made during the Agricultural and Industrial Revolutions in Britain. It was held in London in the middle of the 19th century.

Where were the main centres of growth during the Industrial Revolution in Britain?

The main centres of growth were around the **coalfields** – Manchester, Liverpool, Birmingham, Leeds, Glasgow

Special study – Contrasting lifestyles c. 1850: Industrial England and rural Ireland

How bad were working conditions in the factories?

People in History

A factory worker during the Industrial Revolution

I am a factory worker in a **cotton factory** in Manchester. Our factory is five storeys tall and has small windows. The floors are full of **machines** for spinning (**Crompton's spinning mule**) and weaving (**Cartwright's power loom**) cotton. They are powered by a huge **steam engine** designed by James **Watt**. The noise in the factory is deafening and it is very hot. We will be **fined** if we open a window because the owner doesn't want the threads to dry out, which would cause them to break. I am one of the **few men** working in the factory – I am a **mechanic** working on machines and other men are **supervisors**. Most of the workers are **women and children**, who are much cheaper to hire than men. I get over £1.50 a week because I'm a **skilled craftsman** who trained for seven years as an **apprentice**. Women get only 35p a week and children half that. They are treated badly by the supervisors, who often beat the children for falling asleep or talking. The supervisors also force the women to work hard. **Accidents** are common as women get their hair and clothes caught in machines and children get caught under them. The factory owner doesn't care because he is only concerned about earning **profits**.

We all live close to the factory in **small houses** built by the factory owner. We are close to the factory so that the factory **siren** can wake us up each morning. We pay him rent, but the houses are often wet and cold and we have no indoor toilets or piped water. Others can't afford what I can, so they live in single rooms with little or no furniture. Many of our neighbours have died from various diseases such as **TB** and **cholera**.

There is talk about **improvements**. The trade unions have called for better working conditions, government commissions have reported in their **Blue Books** how bad conditions are and there are proposals to pass laws which will reduce working hours and send children to school.

How bad were working conditions in the mines?

People in History

A miner during the Industrial Revolution

I am a miner in a **coal mine** during the Industrial Revolution. I live in a coal town where all the workers work in the mine. Our job is very important because coal is used to **power steam engines** in factories and trains, in **furnaces** used for smelting iron ore, in **gas lighting** and in **chemical manufacture**.

I began working in the mine as a **trapper** at age five. I sat in the cold and damp as I opened and closed trapdoors to let wagons through. I got paid 2p a day for 12 hours' work. When I got older, I became a **haulier** – I had to carry large baskets of coal on my back. My job was to fill five tubs of coal a day. This meant I had to make 20 trips with my basket. Other boys and girls around my age also worked here. **Women** also carried coal. Some had to pull small wagons by tying a belt around their waist and passing a chain between their legs. They had to crawl on their hands and feet. Even pregnant women worked like this until the day their children were born – some of them were stillborn.

I am now old enough to be a miner at the **coalface** and use hammers and pickaxes to break the coal. **Accidents** are very common – other miners have died as a result of falling down shafts, being drowned in the mines or falling stones or coal.

One of the big **dangers** is poisonous or explosive gases. We use **ventilation shafts** and **trapdoors** to blow out these gases from the mine. We also take song birds down with us into the mines. When the birds stop singing, we know there are dangerous gases present. Rats also give us warning when they all run off together. Humphrey **Davy** has invented a **safety lamp** which will stop explosions caused by naked flames in lamps. We also use **Newcomen's** and **Watt's** steam engines to pump water out of deep mines. Some of the older miners suffer from miner's lung, so they are short of breath.

The **Mines Act** has been passed. This means that women and children under age 10 cannot work underground in the mines. This will improve conditions for them. Maybe other laws will be passed to help us all.

How bad were living conditions in the cities?

1. The houses of working-class people were grouped together as **slums**.
2. There was no piped water supply or indoor toilets.
3. There were open sewers at the end of the streets.
4. Diseases such as cholera and typhus spread quickly.
   - *Examples*: Manchester, Liverpool and Birmingham

Why did the cities grow?

Cities grew because more people were born in the cities; people migrated from the countryside for work; people emigrated from Ireland to the cities.

How were improvements made in working and living conditions?

The pressure to make improvements in working and living conditions came from three main sources:

- **Government reports** (Blue Books), which showed how bad conditions were
- **Trade unions**, which demanded improved conditions for workers
- Some factory owners, such as **Robert Owen**, and members of parliament, such as **Lord Shaftesbury**, who campaigned for improvements

What improvements were made to working and living conditions?

1. **Factory Acts and Mines Acts**
   - The Factory Acts and Mines Acts reduced the number of hours people had to work.
   - Inspectors were also appointed to enforce the rules.

Factory Acts and Mines Act	
1833 Factory Act	Children under 9 were not allowed to work; 9 to 13 year olds – maximum of 9 hours work, 2 hours of school; inspectors appointed to enforce the law
1836	Registration of births, deaths and marriages
1842 Mines Act	Women and children under 10 years old not allowed to work underground in the mines

Who was Robert Owen?

Owen owned a cotton factory in New Lanark in Scotland. He provided good working and living conditions for his workers. He asked parliament to bring in factory reform.

2. **Public Health**
   - **Edwin Chadwick** published *The Sanitary Condition of the Labouring Population*, which showed how bad living conditions were. This led to the passing of the **Public Health Act**, which set up Boards of Health. Their job was to clean streets, increase piped water supplies and build sewers.

3. Medicine

Discoveries in medicine improved the health of people.

- James Simpson used **chloroform** as an anaesthetic to lessen pain.
- Joseph Lister insisted on **cleanliness** to cut down on the spread of disease.
- Edward Jenner **vaccinated** people with cowpox to prevent them from getting smallpox.

How did life for the rich and the poor differ?

Poor	Rich
Food	
The poor lived close to starvation level. • Bread, cheese, porridge, potatoes	The rich had a plentiful supply of food. • Fish, beef, soup, ham
Education	
Working-class children usually did not go to school. Some went to Sunday School run by religious groups.	There were private tutors for rich children. Boys went to public schools, such as Eton and Harrow. Middle class boys went to grammar schools.
Leisure	
Working-class people had very little time for leisure; free time was spent in taverns (pubs). Later on, there were allowed half-days on Saturday – soccer matches.	The rich had more time and money for leisure; continental trips for the rich. Trains allowed skilled workers and members of the middle class to take day trips.
Cock-fighting, bull-baiting, prize-fighting and cricket were popular sports. Sports became more organised later in 19th century and developed rules and competitions.	

Rural Ireland in the 1840s

Overview

1. Ireland was a mainly **agricultural** country in the 1840s.
2. **Landlords:** There were 20,000 landlords. Some landlords were **absentees** (living in Dublin or England).
3. The landlords rented land to tenants who paid rent twice a year to the landlord's agent.
4. **Tenants: Large farmers** rented over 30 acres. They hired labourers to work on the farm. They lived in two-storey houses.
   - **Small farmers** – rented between 5 and 15 acres; they lived in thatched cottages; they depended on the potato as their main food.

5. **Cottiers**: These were labourers who rented a small plot of land – up to an acre – from a farmer; in return, they worked for the farmer to pay off the rent. They lived in one-room cabins.

6. **Landless labourers**: These were very badly off; they lived in mud cabins on the edge of towns; they depended on the potato for their food.
   - **Spailpeens** were wandering labourers who travelled around looking for work.

7. **Poverty and the workhouse**: Poor people went to the workhouse for help. The British government set up Poor Law Unions (areas), each of which had a workhouse. Families were split up and conditions were bad in the workhouses.

What were the causes of the Great Famine, 1845–50?

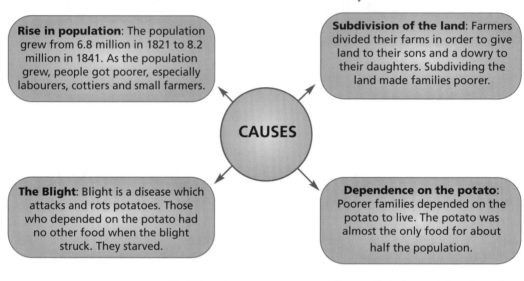

Rise in population: The population grew from 6.8 million in 1821 to 8.2 million in 1841. As the population grew, people got poorer, especially labourers, cottiers and small farmers.

Subdivision of the land: Farmers divided their farms in order to give land to their sons and a dowry to their daughters. Subdividing the land made families poorer.

CAUSES

The Blight: Blight is a disease which attacks and rots potatoes. Those who depended on the potato had no other food when the blight struck. They starved.

Dependence on the potato: Poorer families depended on the potato to live. The potato was almost the only food for about half the population.

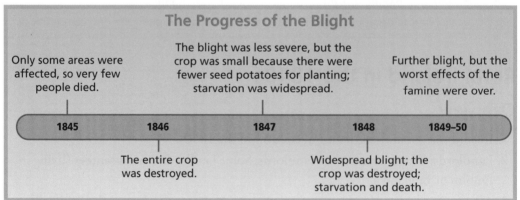

The Progress of the Blight

Only some areas were affected, so very few people died.

The blight was less severe, but the crop was small because there were fewer seed potatoes for planting; starvation was widespread.

Further blight, but the worst effects of the famine were over.

| 1845 | 1846 | 1847 | 1848 | 1849–50 |

The entire crop was destroyed.

Widespread blight; the crop was destroyed; starvation and death.

What help did famine victims get?

1. **Indian corn**: The prime minister, Sir Robert Peel, imported £100,000 worth of Indian corn (maize). The corn was sold through government depots. Some people called it Peel's Brimstone because it was hard to eat.

2. **Public works**: People were paid to work on roads and piers.

3. **Laissez-faire**: A new government led by Lord Jon Russell believed in *laissez-faire* – the view that if governments interfered in the economy, it would make matters worse. The government stopped buying corn, but expanded the public works schemes.

4. **Soup kitchens**: These were first set up by the **Quakers** (or Society of Friends). Soup was cooked in large boilers and given to the poor.

   - The government then passed the **Soup Kitchen Act** to set up their own soup kitchens. Three million people were fed in the soup kitchens, but then the government closed them down and said people had to get help through the workhouses.

5. **Workhouses**: There were over 200,000 people in the workhouses, so they were very overcrowded and disease spread quickly.

6. **Disease**: People died from typhus and relapsing fever. More died from diseases, which were spread in crowded workhouses and towns, than from starvation. Disease affected rich and poor alike.

Where did people emigrate to?

1. People left for Britain, America and Canada. 250,000 left in 1847. Some were helped by landlords; others sent one family member to work and to send money home to pay for other family members.

2. Many people sailed in '**coffin ships**' – ships in very poor condition where disease spread. Some sank on the way.

People in History

A tenant living in Ireland, c. 1850

I am a tenant in Ireland in 1850. I rent **30 acres** of land from a landlord and I pay rent twice a year. I live in a two-storey house with a slated roof. We hire **labourers** to help with the farm work and **servants** to do housework. One son will inherit the farm, another is a priest, another is a lawyer. Our daughters are married off to sons of other large farmers.

We have escaped the worst of the **famine**, which began five years ago. A disease attacked the **potato crop** in Wexford and spread to other parts of the country. In the next year the disease was much worse and most of the potato crop was destroyed. This meant the small farmers, cottiers and labourers had no food and so many of them starved to death. Others were so weak they fell sick and died. But we grew wheat and barley, which we sold to pay the rent; we also had vegetables and cattle, sheep and pigs, so when the potato crop failed we still had food. The famine is not so bad around us in Leinster, but the stories we hear from Connacht and west Cork are terrible.

Some of the small farmers and labourers had to get help. The British government brought in **Indian corn**, which could be bought at depots, but it was difficult to eat so the people called it **Peel's Brimstone**. A much better idea was **soup kitchens**, which the

Quakers set up and which the government also set up. Some of the worst off had to go to **workhouses**, which became very overcrowded and spread disease. Others worked on the **public works**, breaking stones for the roads, but this was very hard work. The government was following the idea of *laissez-faire*, which meant that they would not interfere in the economy for fear they would make matters worse.

Over 1 million people **died** in the last five years, and over 1 million **emigrated** to Britain and the USA. Many **villages** have been devastated. The **emigration** will continue after the famine, so the population will continue to fall. Smaller farmers are ending the practice of **subdivision** (dividing farms between the sons), but that means other sons will have to emigrate or stay single. The areas worst hit by the famine in the west of Ireland continue to see their population decline. These are the areas where **Irish** was mainly spoken, so the Irish language has also declined. There is great bitterness amongst the people about Britain. Many people **blame** the British government for not doing enough to help the famine victims. This bitterness will last for many years.

People in History

A person who left a small farm in Ireland to work in a Lancashire cotton mill, c. 1850

Fill in the blanks using the words in the list. (Words can be used more than once)

I rented a small farm in the West of Ireland. I lived on _____ and milk and I grew _____ to pay my rent to the landlord. But the _____ struck and the potatoes rotted. This was the Great Famine, when many people died from starvation and as many more _____ from Ireland.

I could not pay my rent, so I had to get food for myself and my family from _____ set up by the Quakers. Some of my neighbours had to go to the _____, where the males and females were separated. Conditions in _____ were very bad and some people died from disease.

I saved some money working on government _____ schemes building roads. I used this money to pay for my passage to England. I am now working in a _____ cotton mill and I intend to save money to bring over my family. But the conditions here are very difficult. The building is large, _____ storeys tall and has small windows, and the machines are very noisy. These machines spin _____ and weave _____ cloth. Each morning the _____ of the factory wakes us up for work. I have to work long hours for low pay – I get _____ a week, while women earn 35p and children 18p.

Most of the workers are women and children, but I am employed as a _____.
Other men are employed as _____. We are fined if we are late for work. We are
also fined for whistling, singing or talking or if we _____ a window. The
windows must be kept closed because the factory owner wants to keep the air
_____ so that the threads do not snap. If they did, the machines could break.
Very often I have to force the children to work and to beat them if necessary. The
children have to crawl under the machines if they break down and some have been
injured. Women also get injured if their _____ or hair get caught in the
machines. Many people in England buy the cotton cloth and some of it is exported
to _____.

Use your textbook to check your answers when you are finished.

80p	India	potatoes	workhouse
blight	Lancashire	public works	workhouses
clothes	mechanics	siren	
cotton	moist	soup kitchens	
emigrated	oats	supervisor	
five	open	thread	

What were the results of the Great Famine?

1. **Fall in population**: The population fell by 2 million – 1 million emigrated and 1 million died from starvation and disease.
   - The cottiers and labourers were worst hit; so also was the west of Ireland.
   - The population continued to fall after the famine due to emigration.
2. **Subdivision ended**: Dividing up the farms between members of the family ended; instead, the farms were given to the eldest son and others emigrated.
3. **Decline of the Irish language**: The Irish-speaking areas in the west and south-west of Ireland were worst hit by death and emigration. After the famine, families learnt English for emigration.
4. **Politics**: Bitterness against England grew because people blamed the British government for the famine. Emigrants helped later groups such as the Fenians, the leaders of the 1916 Rising and the IRA work against the British government.

Past questions on *From Farm to Factory*

Short-Answer Questions

1. Give **one** reason why the Industrial Revolution began in Britain.
2. Give **two** factors that made the Agricultural Revolution possible.
3. Mention **one** disadvantage of the open-field system of farming in Britain before the Agricultural Revolution.
4. Mention **two** consequences of enclosure during the Agricultural Revolution.
5. Explain **one** way the Agricultural Revolution contributed to the Industrial Revolution.
6. Mention **two** effects of the Transport Revolution on Britain.
7. During the Transport Revolution, what were *turnpike trusts*?
8. Explain why the 1830s and 1840s in Britain are sometimes known as the *railway age*.
9. Name **two** important inventions during the Industrial Revolution in Britain.
10. What contribution was made to the Industrial Revolution by **one** of the following: *James Hargreaves; George Stephenson; John McAdam?*
11. What was Peel's Brimstone?
12. Explain **one** of the following terms relating to the Irish Famine of the 1840s: *Blight; Soup kitchens; Coffin ships.*
13. Mention **one** action taken by the British government to deal with the Great Famine of the 1840s.
14. Give **two** consequences for Ireland of the Great Famine of the 1840s.

People in History

Ordinary level

1. A worker in a factory or a mine in Industrial England around 1850
   - *Hints*: Working conditions; Life in a city; Pastimes and hobbies; Changes in lifestyle
2. A factory owner or mine owner in England around 1850
   - *Hints*: Running the business; Living conditions; Health and diet; Pastimes and entertainment

Higher level

1. A factory/mine owner during the Industrial Revolution in Britain, c. 1850
2. A mine or factory worker during the Industrial Revolution
3. A farm labourer during the Agricultural Revolution
4. A landlord in Ireland around the year 1850

Source Questions (Higher level)

Source D

*The following are **two** accounts of conditions for the poor in Ireland around 1840.*

Account 1

There are no means of finding out exactly the number of persons who were dependent on potatoes for their support, but it must have formed a large portion of the population of all the western counties, and was not inconsiderable even in the eastern counties of Leinster and Ulster. Perhaps it may be estimated at 2,000,000.

Account 2

The hovels which the poor people were building as I passed, solely by their own efforts, were of the most miserable description; their walls were formed, in several instances, by the backs of fences; the floors sunk in ditches; the height scarcely enough for a man to stand upright; a few pieces of grass sods the only covering; and these extending only partially over the thing called a roof; the elderly people miserably clothed; the children all but naked.

(Source: Stephen J. Campbell, *The Great Irish Famine: Words and Images from the Famine Museum, Strokestown Park, County Roscommon*, p. 18)

A. Study source D, accounts of conditions in Ireland around 1840.

   (i)   From Account 1, how many people does the author believe were dependent on the potato about 1840?

   (ii) Do you think the author of Account 2 is shocked by what he has seen? Give **one** piece of evidence from the account to support your answer.

   (iii) Explain **three** of the following terms relating to life in Ireland around 1840: *Cottier; Conacre; Lazybeds; Middleman; Eviction.*

B. Source E is a map showing the population decline in Ireland between 1841 and 1851.

   (i)   From Source E, name **one** part of the country that experienced:

     (a) a rise in population during this period **and**

     (b) a fall in population greater than 30% during this period.

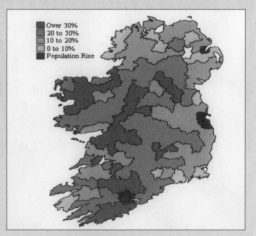

Over 30%
20 to 30%
10 to 20%
0 to 10%
Population Rise

Source E:
The decline in population in Ireland between 1841 and 1851. (Source: R.D. Edwards and T.D. Williams, eds, *The Great Famine: Studies in Irish History, 1845–1852*)

(ii) What measures were taken during the 1840s to help victims of the Famine in Ireland?

C. (i) 'The Industrial Revolution in Britain had a major impact on people's lives.' In the light of the above statement, write an account of the effects of the Industrial Revolution on **one** of the following aspects of everyday life in Britain:

    (a) Housing and diet

    (b) Health and leisure activities

    (c) Education

Long Answers (Higher level)

(i) Mention **two** advantages of the new land enclosure during the Agricultural Revolution.

(ii) **New developments and inventions:**

Match each item in column A, (1)–(6) with its corresponding item in column B, (a)–(f).

You do not need to write out the full text in your answer book, just the correct number and letter.

Column A	Column B
1. Charles Townshend	(a) Spinning Jenny
2. Robert Bakewell	(b) Coke for smelting iron ore
3. James Hargreaves	(c) Selective breeding
4. John Kay	(d) Steam engine improvements
5. James Watt	(e) Norfolk rotation of crops
6. Abraham Darby	(f) 'Flying Shuttle'

(iii) Write an account of **two** of the following:

    (a) Reasons why the Industrial Revolution began in Britain.

    (b) Living conditions for workers in industrial towns.

    (c) Improvements in transport during the Industrial Revolution.

YEAR THREE

Understanding the Modern World

Topics of study

Ordinary level

Students studying this syllabus at **Ordinary level** will study the following topics:

- Political Developments in 20th-century Ireland **OR** Social Change in 20th-century Ireland
- International Relations in the 20th Century – Peace and War in Europe **OR** The Rise of the Superpowers **OR** Moves towards European Unity **OR** African and Asian Nationalism

Higher level

Students studying this syllabus at **Higher level** will study all of the topics:

- Political Developments in 20th-century Ireland
- Social Change in 20th-century Ireland
- International Relations in the 20th Century – Peace and War in Europe AND The Rise of the Superpowers OR Moves towards European Unity OR African and Asian Nationalism

11 Political Developments in 20th-century Ireland

aims
- To understand the differences between nationalists and unionists
- To follow the steps to Irish independence
- To understand political developments under Cumann na nGaedheal and Fianna Fáil
- To assess the impact of World War II, north and south
- To understand political developments in southern Ireland, up to 1985
- To understand political developments in Northern Ireland, up to 1985

Towards an independent Ireland, 1900–22

Political groups in early-20th-century Ireland

1. Ireland was ruled directly from London. Irish members of parliament (MPs) sat in parliament in Westminster. The Lord Lieutenant represented the king of England in Ireland.

2. There were two main political groups:
   - **Nationalists** wanted some form of self-government with a parliament in Dublin.
   - **Unionists** wanted to maintain the Union with Britain.

Nationalists

3. The **Home Rule Party** (also called the **Irish Parliamentary Party**) was the largest nationalist group. It was led by **John Redmond**.
   - Home Rulers wanted a parliament in Dublin to deal with internal Irish affairs.
   - The parliament in London would deal with external affairs.

4. The **Irish Republican Brotherhood** (IRB) was a secret revolutionary organisation.
   - The IRB wanted **complete independence** from Britain.
   - They wanted to establish a **republic**. They wanted to use **physical force** to achieve their aims.

5. **Sinn Féin** was founded by **Arthur Griffith**.
   - Sinn Féin wanted a **dual monarchy** for Britain and Ireland. They wanted to develop **Irish industry** by using tariffs (customs duties) to protect new industry.

Unionists

6. The **Unionist Party** was led by **Edward Carson** and **James Craig**.
   Unionists were **opposed** to Home Rule.
   - They said 'Home Rule is Rome Rule' – that Catholics would discriminate against Protestants.

● They believed that Belfast's industries would be ruined if Ireland won Home Rule.

The Labour movement

1. The Labour movement was led by **Big Jim Larkin** and **James Connolly**.
2. Larkin and Connolly founded the **Irish Labour Party** to represent workers in a new Home Rule parliament.
3. Larkin founded the **ITGWU** (Irish Transport and General Workers Union) to organise unskilled workers. This led to clashes with William Martin Murphy and the Employers Federation.
4. **Strike and Lockout**: Larkin planned a strike of tramway workers for Horse Show Week in Dublin in 1913. Murphy and the employers locked out the workers. The **Strike and Lockout** lasted for about five months and the workers went back to work without achieving their aims.
5. Connolly founded the **Irish Citizens Army** to protect workers during the Lockout.

The Home Rule Crisis, 1912–14

1. In Britain, the **Liberal Party** favoured Home Rule for Ireland, but the **Conservative Party** was opposed to it.
2. After elections in 1910, the Liberal Party was in government in Britain, but it needed the support of the Irish Home Rule Party. In return for that support, the Liberal Party brought in a Home Rule Bill for Ireland in 1912.
3. The House of Lords would only be able to delay the passing of the Bill for two years so that by 1914 Ireland would have a Home Rule parliament.

How did unionists organise opposition to Home Rule?

1. Carson and Craig held **demonstrations** against Home Rule.
2. Unionists signed the **Solemn League and Covenant**. They swore to defend the union with Britain by all means.
3. Unionists founded the **Ulster Volunteer Force** (UVF). They imported arms and ammunition from Germany through the port of **Larne**.
4. The Conservative Party supported the efforts of the unionists.
5. **Curragh Mutiny**: Officers of the British army in the Curragh said they would resign rather than enforce Home Rule in Ulster.
6. Nationalists organised the **Irish Volunteer Force**, led by Eoin McNeill. The Irish Volunteers brought in arms through **Howth**, Co Dublin.

War – the end of the Crisis

1. Attempts at getting a compromise between both sides failed, so it looked likely that Ireland was heading for civil war. Then the First World War broke out and both nationalists and unionists agreed to help the war effort.
2. The Home Rule Bill became law, but it was postponed until after the war was over.

Ireland in World War I

1. **Unionists** supported the war effort and joined the British army.
2. **Nationalists**: The Irish Volunteers split, most following Redmond, who wanted Irishmen to fight in the war.
3. A quarter of a million Irishmen joined the British army in World War I. They joined the Irish Guards, the Royal Munster Fusiliers and other regiments. They fought in the Western Front in France and in Gallipoli in Turkey.
4. The *Lusitania* was sunk by a German U-boat (submarine) off the Old Head of Kinsale in 1915.

The 1916 Rising

1. The **IRB** planned the 1916 Rising. They set up a **Military Council** to organise the rising. The Council included Patrick Pearse, Thomas Clarke and Séan McDermott.
   - They set Easter Sunday 1916 as the day for the rising.
   - They persuaded James Connolly and the Irish Citizens Army to join them.
2. **Roger Casement** was sent to Germany to get arms. They were loaded on board the *Aud* to be taken to Ireland, but the *Aud* was captured off the Kerry coast.
3. The Military Council gave a document to McNeill – called the **Castle Document** – which said that the British government was planning to arrest the leaders.
   - McNeill authorised manoeuvres for the Irish Volunteers, but he cancelled them when he found out the document was a forgery.
4. Pearse and the others decided to go ahead with a rising in Dublin on Easter Monday, 1916.
   - They took over key buildings such as the GPO. But they were easily defeated and they surrendered after a week.
   - The British government sent a gunboat up the Liffey which bombarded the GPO.

What were the results of the 1916 Rising?

1. Fifteen of the leaders were executed, including Pearse and Connolly.
2. Over 500 people were killed and 2,500 were injured; £3 million in damage was done to property.
3. The British imposed military (martial) law and interned (imprisoned without trial) 2,000 people.
4. Dubliners were angered by the destruction caused by the Rising and the resulting food shortages. But British actions – interning many and executing the leaders of the Rising – changed the minds of many. They began to support the actions and aims of the leaders of the 1916 Rising.
5. The British government called it the Sinn Féin Rising even though Sinn Féin had nothing to do with the Rising. Afterwards, Sinn Féin's popularity rose as younger members joined.

The rise of Sinn Féin

1. **Éamon de Valera** became president of Sinn Féin and president of the Irish Volunteers.
2. Sinn Féin's **popularity** grew because:
   - The British government tried to impose conscription in Ireland and Sinn Féin organised opposition to it.
   - The British government arrested Sinn Féin leaders in the so-called German Plot.
   - Sinn Féin won by-elections.

1918 general election

In this election Sinn Féin became the most popular party in Ireland.
- They now demanded a **republic** and they followed a policy of **abstentionism** (abstaining from parliament in London).

What were the 1918 general election results?

Sinn Féin	73
Home Rule Party	6
Unionists	23

The Independence Struggle or War of Independence, 1919–21

1. In 1919, Sinn Féin set up **Dáil Éireann** and an alternative government. De Valera was elected president of the Dáil, Griffith became Minister for Home Affairs and Michael Collins became Minister for Finance.
   - They declared a republic, they asked the Paris Peace Conference to recognise it and they set up Sinn Féin courts.

War

2. Local IRA (Irish Republican Army) units began a guerrilla campaign against British forces. In January 1919, the first attack was against an RIC (Royal Irish Constabulary) patrol in Soloheadbeg, Co Tipperary.
   - They attacked small RIC barracks in order to take its arms and ammunition.
3. Michael **Collins** was Director of Intelligence – he organised a spy network. He also organised the **Squad**, a group whose job was to kill spies and detectives.
4. The IRA organised **flying columns** – small groups of armed men who planned ambushes. In Cork, Tom Barry organised the Crossbarry and Kilmichael ambushes.

How did the British government respond?

1. **David Lloyd George**, the British prime minister, organised the **Black and Tans** (ex-soldiers) and the **Auxiliaries** (ex-officers) to fight the IRA.
   - They carried out reprisals against families and towns.

2. Lloyd George passed the **Government of Ireland Act, 1920**, which set up a parliament in Belfast and Dublin. But Sinn Féin rejected the Dublin parliament.

3. **Tomás Mac Curtain**, Lord Mayor of Cork, was shot in front of his family by the RIC.

4. **Terence MacSwiney**, Lord Mayor of Cork, died on hunger strike in Brixton prison in England.

5. **Bloody Sunday, 21 November 1920**: Collins's Squad killed a group of British agents sent to find him. Black and Tans shot into the crowd at a football match in Croke Park, killing 12 people.

6. Eighty IRA members were either captured or killed when the Dublin brigade attacked the Custom House in Dublin.

Peace

1. Both sides now wanted peace. The IRA was running out of arms and ammunition while the British government was criticised at home and abroad for the actions of the Black and Tans and the Auxiliaries.

2. De Valera came back from **America**, where he spent most of the War of Independence. He agreed a truce with Lloyd George, which came into effect in July 1921.

People in History

A named leader in the struggle for Irish independence, 1900–23: Michael Collins

You can use the information on Michael Collins to answer a *People in History* question on *A republican during the War of Independence in Ireland, 1919–21*.

Michael Collins was a leader in the struggle for Irish independence. He was born in Clonakilty in West Cork. He worked for a while in London, then came back to Ireland and fought in the **1916 Rising**. After the Rising, he was held in Frongoch Camp in Wales. Here he showed his abilities as a leader.

When he was released from jail, he built up the **IRB** (Irish Republican Brotherhood) and became its president. He was also involved with Sinn Féin and the Irish Volunteers. He warned **de Valera** and other Sinn Féin leaders about the British government's plans to arrest them in the so-called **German Plot** in 1918, but de Valera did not take Collins's advice and was arrested. Collins was made **Minister of Finance** in the Dáil government in 1919. He organised the **Dáil Loan**, which raised £350,000. He also organised the escape of de Valera from Lincoln jail.

During the War of Independence, Collins was **Director of Intelligence** for the IRA and that is how he organised a spy network. He was a wanted man by the British government, but they failed to capture him. His **Squad** – a team of trained killers – killed a group of

British spies on the morning of **Bloody Sunday**. This led to the Black and Tans attacking a football match in Croke Park, killing 12 people.

After the War of Independence, Collins was part of the Sinn Féin team which negotiated the **Anglo-Irish Treaty**. He knew the terms of the Treaty would not be acceptable to some republicans and that is why he said that he had signed his death warrant. In the Treaty debates, he argued that the Treaty was **a stepping stone** to independence. The Treaty was carried by 64 votes to 57.

After the Treaty vote, Collins was head of the **Provisional government** and the British handed over power to him. But relations between the Pro-Treaty and Anti-Treaty sides got worse. When the Anti-Treaty forces took over the **Four Courts** in the centre of Dublin and kidnapped a Free State general, Collins was forced to attack them. This was the beginning of the Civil War. While Collins was on a trip to West Cork, he was killed in an ambush in **Béal na mBláth** on his return. His death was a major blow as it deprived the country of an outstanding leader.

The Anglo-Irish Treaty, 1921

1. Sinn Féin sent a delegation led by Griffith and Collins to London to negotiate a treaty with the British government. De Valera refused to go.
2. The British delegation was more experienced; it was led by Lloyd George and Winston Churchill.
3. The terms of the **Anglo-Irish Treaty** on 6 December 1921 were:
   - Ireland was now known as the Irish Free State.
   - It was a member (dominion) of the British Commonwealth.
   - Members of parliament (TDs) in Dublin would have to take an Oath of Allegiance to the British king.
   - Three ports – the Treaty ports – at Cobh, Berehaven and Lough Swilly would be used by the British navy.
   - A Boundary Commission would be set up to decide the border between North and South.

Treaty Debates

1. The Dáil was divided over the terms of the Anglo-Irish Treaty.

Arguments For and Against the Treaty	
Pro-Treaty: Griffith and Collins	Anti-Treaty: de Valera, Cathal Brugha
• The IRA was too weak to continue fighting • The Treaty was a stepping stone to full independence	• The Treaty did not give Ireland a full republic • The Oath of Allegiance recognised the king

2. The Dáil voted in **favour** of the Treaty by 64 votes to 57.

The Civil War, 1922–23

1. The Pro-Treaty and Anti-Treaty sides grew further apart.

Two Sides of the Civil War	
Pro-Treaty	Anti-Treaty
Free State Army/government forces Regulars	Republicans Irregulars

2. The Anti-Treaty side took over the **Four Courts** in Dublin and captured a Free State general.
   - The Free State army, led by Collins, bombarded the Four Courts. The Free State army defeated the Irregulars in Dublin.
3. Then the Regulars attacked the Irregulars in the **Munster Republic**. They captured Cork.
   - **Griffith** died from a brain haemorrhage. **Collins** was killed in an ambush at Béal na mBláth, Co Cork.
4. Cosgrave and O'Higgins took over the Free State government. The Civil War got very bitter. It ended when de Valera got the IRA to call a ceasefire in May 1923.

The results of the Civil War

1. Over 900 people were killed. There was £30 million of damage done to property.
2. There was great bitterness between both Pro-Treaty and Anti-Treaty sides for many years after the Civil War.
3. The country lost able leaders, including Collins and Griffith.
4. The two main political parties owe their origins to the Pro- and Anti-Treaty sides in the Civil War.

Pro-Treaty	→	Cumann na nGaedheal	→	Fine Gael
Anti-Treaty	→	Sinn Féin	→	Fianna Fáil

The New State

Cumann na nGaedheal in power, 1922–32

Cumann na nGaedheal formed the government of the Irish Free State from 1922 to 1932. It was led by **W. T. Cosgrave**.

Law and order

1. The Constitution set up two houses of parliament; the Dáil and Seanad; the king's representative in Ireland was called the **Governor-General**.

2. The government set up the **Garda Síochána**, the court system was re-organised and a **Public Safety Act** gave the government wide powers of arrest.

3. The Free State government had to overcome the threat of the **Army Mutiny** in 1924. The victory of the government helped establish democracy in the country.

The economy

4. The Cumann na nGaedheal government improved agriculture by improving animal breeding methods, providing loans for farmers and keeping taxes low.

5. The government established the **Shannon Scheme** to build a hydroelectric station. The ESB was set up to build an electricity grid for Ireland.

What was the Shannon Scheme?

This was a hydroelectric plant built on the Shannon at Ardnacrusha to generate **electricity** for the country. It cost £5 million and it was one of the largest building projects in the state. The ESB was set up to construct a grid to take the electricity around the country.

Relations with Britain

6. **The Boundary Commission** was set up to decide the border between the North and the South. Nationalists hoped that the Commission would make the North of Ireland so small that it would be forced to join the South. Instead, the Commission only suggested small changes to the border so the Irish and British governments agreed not to make any changes.

7. **Ireland in the Commonwealth**: Cumann na nGaedheal worked to gain more independence for Ireland. The British government passed the **Statute of Westminster 1931**, which allowed Ireland to change any laws on Ireland passed by the British parliament.

Decline of Cumann na nGaedheal

8. De Valera founded **Fianna Fáil** when Sinn Féin would not agree to go into Dáil Éireann.

9. Why did Cumann na nGaedheal decline in popularity?
   - The Great Depression affected Ireland and unemployment increased.
   - The government cut the pay of teachers and gardaí.
   - De Valera and Fianna Fáil won the 1932 general election.

De Valera and Fianna Fáil in power, 1932–39

Dismantling the Treaty – relations with Britain

De Valera used the **Statute of Westminster** to give greater independence to Ireland. He did this by **dismantling** (taking apart) the Anglo-Irish Treaty.
   - He abolished the Oath of Allegiance and the office of governor-general.

- He removed the king as head of state.
- He wrote a new constitution, which gave greater power to the Irish people.

What did de Valera's constitution do?

It changed the name of the country from the Irish Free State to Ireland (or Éire). It made the president head of state. It claimed the right to rule over Northern Ireland. The head of government was now called *Taoiseach*.

The IRA and the Blueshirts

1. De Valera released IRA prisoners when he came to power. IRA members attacked meetings of Cumann na nGaedheal. These were protected by the **Army Comrades Association** (ACA).
   - The ACA were also known as the **Blueshirts**.
2. **Eoin O'Duffy**, former Garda Commissioner, became head of the Blueshirts. He favoured the ideas of Mussolini.
   - When he planned a march in Dublin to commemorate Griffith and Collins, it was banned by de Valera.
3. The Blueshirts joined with Cumann na nGaedheal to form a new political party, **Fine Gael**.
   - O'Duffy became its leader but was soon replaced by Cosgrave. Instead, he went off to Spain with 800 supporters to help Franco in the Spanish Civil War.
4. Relations between de Valera and the IRA worsened because of IRA murders and shootings. De Valera banned the IRA.

The Economic War – relations with Britain

1. De Valera refused to pay taxes due to **England** over land purchases.
   - Britain imposed taxes on Irish cattle imports and de Valera imposed taxes on English goods.
   - Eventually, both sides came to an agreement – the **Anglo-Irish Agreement**, 1938.
2. **Terms of the Anglo-Irish Agrement, 1938**:
   - De Valera agreed to pay a lump sum of £10 million for the payments due for land purchases.
   - The Irish government got back the three Treaty ports – Cobh, Berehaven and Lough Swilly.
3. **The Economy**
   - De Valera brought in a policy of **protectionism** (putting tariffs on imports to protect Irish industry).
   - The Irish Sugar Company and Aer Lingus were also set up.

The Emergency – Ireland in World War II

1. Ireland remained **neutral** in World War II because it wanted to stay independent and also because it was a small country.
2. De Valera passed the **Emergency Powers Act**, which gave it great power to control the country.
3. Irish neutrality was put in danger by the **IRA**, which tried to get help from Germany. But de Valera imprisoned the IRA leaders.
4. **Germany** planned Operation Green (the code name for the invasion of Ireland). But the distance to Ireland was too far. German bombers bombed the **North Strand** in Dublin, killing 34 people in 1941.
5. **Churchill**, prime minister of Britain, said Britain would end partition if Ireland joined the war. De Valera rejected Churchill's offer.
6. The **USA** was afraid that Ireland would be used as a base for German spies.

The economy – shortages and rationing

7. Séan **Lemass**, Minister of Supplies, got ships to bring supplies to Ireland. But there were severe shortages, so rationing of tea, sugar, clothes and footwear was introduced.
8. Electricity and gas were also rationed. This affected **factories**, so workers were laid off and unemployment increased.
9. Some went to England to get work in war industries or in the British army.

Northern Ireland in the war

In contrast to the South, Northern Ireland was involved directly in the war.

- Ships, planes, parachutes and shells were all produced for the war.
- Northern Ireland also contributed to **patrolling** the North Atlantic to protect shipping from U-boat attack.
- Later, the **USA** brought soldiers and sailors to Northern Ireland to prepare for D-Day.
- **Belfast** was bombed on a number of occasions in early 1941. Shipbuilding was disrupted, but the worst effects were the numbers of civilians who were killed.
- **Conscription** was not introduced to Northern Ireland but thousands still joined the British forces.

(See p. 135)

Ireland in the 1950s and 1960s

The First Inter-Party government

1. De Valera lost the 1948 general election. A new government, the First Inter-Party government, took over. It was led by **John A. Costello** (Fine Gael), and it was a coalition government composed of Fine Gael, the Labour Party, Clann na Poblachta and others.

2. The First Inter-Party government declared Ireland a **republic** and took Ireland out of the British Commonwealth.

3. The government began a scheme of **rural electrification** to bring electricity to homes and farms.

4. Dr **Noel Browne**, Minister for Health, introduced a scheme to bring **TB** (tuberculosis) under control. He also introduced the **Mother and Child Scheme**, which was a plan to provide free medical treatment to children under 16 and to mothers. But he failed to get this passed in the Dáil.

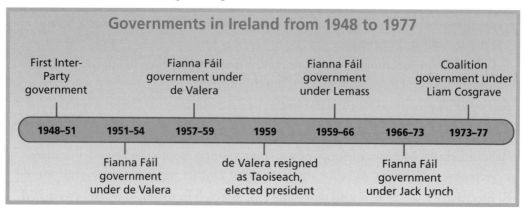

Ireland in the 1950s

5. Ireland experienced a great deal of unemployment and emigration in the 1950s.

6. The population declined.

Seán Lemass and the 1960s

7. De Valera resigned as Taoiseach and leader of Fianna Fáil in 1959. He was elected as **president** of Ireland and served for 14 years.
   - Seán **Lemass** took over as **Taoiseach**.

8. **The Economy**
   - Lemass introduced the **First Programme for Economic Expansion** to try to revive the Irish economy.
   - The programme encouraged exports and gave tax concessions to foreign companies to set up factories in Ireland.
   - More jobs were created and the population increased.

9. **Education**: Free secondary education was introduced by Minister for Education Donagh O'Malley. New schools were built and new courses were introduced.

10. **Northern Ireland**: Lemass went to Northern Ireland at the invitation of Terence O'Neill, the Northern prime minister. O'Neill returned the visit to Dublin. Relations between North and South improved.

11. **Social change in the 1960s**: People were better off.
    - The Catholic Church brought in many changes after the Second Vatican Council.
    - RTÉ was set up and television brought many new ideas into the country.
    - New towns and new shopping centres were built.

Ireland in the EEC

1. Ireland became a member of the **European Economic Community** (EEC) in 1973.
   - Irish farmers got guaranteed prices for their products and grants under the Common Agricultural Policy (CAP).
   - American companies were attracted to Ireland to set up factories here in order to gain access to the wider European market.
   - But some Irish factories closed due to foreign competition.
   - Ireland got grants for job training and road improvements.
2. Overall, Ireland **benefited** from membership of the European Economic Community.

Political leaders of modern Ireland

Seán Lemass was the Taoiseach who introduced a new economic policy to revive the Irish economy.

Éamon de Valera was Taoiseach for many years before becoming president in 1959.

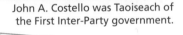

John A. Costello was Taoiseach of the First Inter-Party government.

Jack Lynch as Taoiseach was faced with the Arms Crisis. He also took Ireland into the European Economic Community.

Liam Cosgrave was Taoiseach of the Coalition government formed by Fine Gael and the Labour Party.

Charles Haughey was Taoiseach during the 1980s, when the country suffered economic difficulties.

Garret FitzGerald was Taoiseach during a period of economic difficulties in the 1980s. He also signed the Anglo-Irish Agreement (1985).

People in History

A named political leader in the Republic of Ireland: Seán Lemass

Fill in the blanks using the words in the list. (Words can be used more than once)

Seán Lemass was a political leader in Ireland after it got its independence from Britain. He helped de Valera found the _____ Party. He was **Minister of Industry and Commerce** in the de Valera government in the 1930s. He brought in a policy of _____ by putting _____ on imports to protect Irish industry. During the Emergency (Ireland in World War II), Lemass was **Minister for** _____. He set up Irish _____ to buy or charter ships to bring supplies to Ireland because of the _____. When de Valera resigned as _____ and leader of Fianna Fáil, Lemass succeeded him. Lemass brought in new, younger ministers such as Charles Haughey and Jack _____. He also brought in a **new economic policy** to solve the problems of _____ and emigration. Lemass's First Programme for _____ Expansion got rid of his old policy of protectionism. His new policy encouraged _____ and gave tax concessions and _____ to attract foreign industry. This policy worked as British and _____ companies set up factories here. There were more jobs, people's living standards improved and _____ stopped. Lemass also had a new policy for **Northern Ireland**. He believed that he would end _____ (the border between North and South) by making the South more prosperous. He went to Belfast to meet the prime minister of Northern Ireland, Terence _____, for the first time. _____ then met Lemass in Dublin. Lemass also encouraged his Minister for Education, Donogh _____, to bring in free secondary education. This led to a huge increase in numbers going to secondary school. When Lemass retired, he was succeeded as Taoiseach by Jack _____.

Use your textbook to check your answers when you are finished.

American	grants	protectionism	tariffs
Economic	Lynch	Shipping	unemployment
emigration	O'Malley	shortages	
exports	O'Neill	supplies	
Fianna Fáil	partition	Taoiseach	

Northern Ireland, 1920–85

Establishment of Northern Ireland

1. Northern Ireland was set up under the **Government of Ireland Act, 1920**.
2. The Unionist Party led by **James Craig** controlled power in Northern Ireland.
   - They regarded Catholics/nationalists with suspicion.
   - They discriminated against Catholics/nationalists through gerrymandering (rigging constituencies to ensure unionists were elected).
   - There were attacks against Catholics/nationalists in the early 1920s and the mid-1930s.

Northern Ireland during World War II

In contrast to the South, Northern Ireland was involved directly in the war.
   - Ships, planes, parachutes and shells were all produced for the war.
   - Northern Ireland also contributed to **patrolling** the North Atlantic to protect shipping from U-boat attack.
   - Later, the **USA** brought soldiers and sailors to Northern Ireland to prepare for D-Day.
   - **Belfast** was bombed on a number of occasions in early 1941. Shipbuilding was disrupted, but the worst effects were the numbers of civilians who were killed.
   - **Conscription** was not introduced to Northern Ireland, but thousands still joined the British forces.

(See pp. 130–31)

People in History

A person living in Northern Ireland during World War II, 1939–45

I lived in Belfast during World War II. I am a **unionist**, so I supported the war effort. I worked at **Harland and Wolff**, a great shipbuilding company. Thousands of new workers were taken on because the British government needed as many ships built as possible. These ships were needed to replace ships sunk at sea as they brought badly needed supplies to our country. Other industries in Belfast also thrived, such as the manufacture of **planes** and **parachutes**. Many people from Northern Ireland also joined the British forces and were active during **battles**, such as the Battle of Britain, the D-Day landings and the attack on Germany.

Northern Ireland also played a very important role in **patrolling** the North Atlantic as ships and planes based here went looking for German **U-boats**. Later on the Americans set up bases and stationed 120,000 soldiers and sailors here to protect the Atlantic trade and to get ready for the D-Day invasions.

Our government in Northern Ireland did not build up our **defences**, so Belfast was badly damaged when German bombers attacked in April and May 1941. We did not have enough anti-aircraft guns and balloons to protect the city. In all, 1,100 people were killed and thousands of houses were destroyed. Some people left the city to live in the countryside for a while. Harland and Wolff was put out of action for six months. We were thankful for the fire brigades which the Southern government sent to Belfast to stop the fires. But we were very angry with the offer **Churchill** made to de Valera of the Southern government. Churchill said he would end partition if the Southern government joined the war. De Valera rejected this offer.

Our leaders in government were too old; **Craig** was replaced as prime minister by **Andrews**, but Basil **Brooke**, who is younger, is doing a better job. We are hoping that after the war the conditions in Belfast will improve – there is a great deal of poverty in the back streets of the city. There is talk that Britain will bring in a 'welfare state', which will provide free education and health care. The people have worked hard during the war to produce for the war effort and to defend the country, so it is the least they deserve.

Northern Ireland after World War II

The **welfare state** was set up in Northern Ireland after World War II.

- There was free secondary education and free medical care for mothers and children.
- New houses were built.

Terence O'Neill as prime minister

Terence O'Neill succeeded Lord Brookeborough (Basil Brooke) as prime minister of Northern Ireland.

- O'Neill wanted to improve the **economy** of Northern Ireland by attracting new industries there.
- He tried to improve relations with **Catholics** by visiting Catholic schools.
- He improved relations with the **South of Ireland** by inviting Seán Lemass to Belfast, and by travelling down to Dublin later.
- He was criticised by Ian Paisley, leader of the Democratic Unionist Party.

The Civil Rights Movement

1. Tensions rose between Catholics and Protestants in Northern Ireland.
2. Catholics/nationalists felt that Protestants/unionists discriminated against them.
3. Nationalists now demanded their rights.
   - They wanted an end to gerrymandering.
   - They wanted one man, one vote in local elections.
   - The wanted a fair allocation of houses and jobs.
4. The **Civil Rights Association** was founded to achieve these aims. Its leaders included Gerry Fitt and John Hume.
   - The civil rights marches led to clashes with the RUC.
   - O'Neill was forced to resign after he brought in reforms for nationalists.

The Troubles

1. There were clashes between Catholics/nationalists and the RUC in Derry after an Apprentice Boys march in 1969.
   - This led to the **Battle of the Bogside**, when the RUC tried to get into a Catholic area.
   - There were also **riots** in Belfast, so the British army was brought in to stop the rioting.
2. The **Provisional IRA** ('Provos') attacked the British army and killed many people with bombs.
3. The Northern government led by Brian Faulkner brought in **internment** (imprisonment without trial). This led to increased bombings and shootings.
   - An anti-internment march in Derry was shot at by British troops, killing 13 people. This was called **Bloody Sunday**.
4. Soon after this the British government abolished the parliament in Stormont and ruled directly from Westminster.
   - They tried to bring peace to Northern Ireland with the **Sunningdale Agreement**, but this failed.
   - There was further trouble during the **Hunger Strikes**.
5. Eventually, the **Anglo-Irish Agreement** (1985) was signed and this gave a greater say to the South in the North of Ireland.
6. But it took many more years before the Troubles came to an end and peace was brought to Northern Ireland.

Past questions on *Political Developments in 20th-century Ireland*

Short-Answer Questions

1. Who was the founder of Sinn Féin in 1905?
2. What was the Solemn League and Covenant, 1912?
3. Mention **two** reasons why Sinn Féin won the 1918 general election.
4. Why were only 27 TDs present at the meeting of the First Dáil on 21 January 1919?
5. During the War of Independence, what were *Flying Columns?*
6. Give **two** reasons why there was a Civil War in Ireland during the years 1922–23.
7. During the Civil War, 1922–23, what was the *Munster Republic?*
8. What was the Shannon Scheme, 1927?
9. Give **two** reasons why there was an economic war between Britain and Ireland during the 1930s.

10. Give **two** terms of the Anglo-Irish Agreement, 1938.
11. Give **one** reason why Ireland was neutral during the Emergency, 1939–45.
12. Mention **one** way in which World War II had an impact on Irish life.
13. Name **two** political parties that were part of the First Inter-Party government, 1948–51.
14. Mention **two** achievements of the First Inter-Party government, 1948–51.
15. Mention **one** national project promoted by Dr Noel Browne as Minister for Health.
16. During the period 1959–66, mention **two** important decisions taken by the government of Seán Lemass.
17. Who was the founder of the Democratic Unionist Party?
18. Name **two** people who have been leaders of Fianna Fáil since the departure of Seán Lemass in 1966.
19. Name the **two** countries which joined the EEC with Ireland in 1973.
20. Give **one** reason why some unionists opposed the Sunningdale Agreement, 1973.
21. Name the Taoiseach **and** the British prime minster who signed the Anglo-Irish Agreement, 1985.

People in History

Ordinary level

1. A person involved in the struggle for Irish independence during the period 1916–23
   - *Hints*: Reasons for involvement; Important leaders; Tactics used and main events; Results of these events
2. A **named** leader of government in Ireland after 1945
   - *Hints*: Name of the leader; Problems faced by the leader; Achievements of leader; Any other relevant information

Higher level

1. A **named** leader involved in the struggle for Irish independence, 1916–23.
2. A person living in Northern Ireland during World War II, 1939–45.
3. A **named** political leader in the Republic of Ireland during the period 1960–85

Long-Answer Questions (Higher level)

1. (i) Mention **two** actions taken by unionists to prevent the introduction of Home Rule for Ireland during the period 1912–14.
   (ii) Match each of the following persons (1)–(6), with the corresponding event or organisation (a)–(f). (You do not need to write the full text in your answerbook, just the correct number and letter. Do not answer this question on your examination paper.)

Person	Event/organisation
1. Douglas Hyde	A. Clann na Poblachta
2. William T. Cosgrave	B. Founder of Sinn Féin
3. Séan MacBride	C. 1913 Strike and Lockout
4. Arthur Griffith	D. The Blueshirts
5. James Larkin	E. President of Ireland
6. Eoin O'Duffy	F. Cumann na nGaedheal

(iii) Write an account of **two** of the following:
    (a) The Easter Rising, 1916
    (b) The Anglo-Irish Treaty, 1921
    (c) The Economic War, 1932–38
    (d) The Civil Rights Movement in Northern Ireland.

2. (i) Give **two** reasons why the 1916 Rising was a failure.
  (ii) Mention **two** reasons why Sinn Féin won the 1918 election.
  (iii) Explain **three** of the following terms relating to the War of Independence, 1919–21: *The Squad; The Government of Ireland Act, 1920; The Auxiliaries; Flying Columns; The Anglo-Irish Treaty, 1921.*
  (iv) Write an account of **two** of the following:
    (a) The Civil War, 1922–23
    (b) Cumann na nGaedheal in government, 1923–32
    (c) Ireland during World War II
    (d) Northern Ireland, 1963–73

3. (i) Explain **three** of the following terms: *'The Squad'; Bloody Sunday (1920); The Irish Citizen Army; Gerrymandering; B- Specials*
  (ii) Write an account of **two** of the following:
    (a) The Home Rule Crisis, 1912–14
    (b) The Irish Free State, 1922–32
    (c) Ireland under de Valera, 1932–39
    (d) Seán Lemass as Taoiseach, 1959–66

12 Social Change in 20th-century Ireland

- To understand social change in 20th-century Ireland under each of the headings:
  - Rural and urban life and work
  - The status of women
  - Leisure and entertainment
  - Transport and communications

Social history and social change

1. **Social history** is concerned with the way people **live** – with their work, leisure, housing and transport.
2. **Social change** is concerned with how people's lives have **changed** and why the changes have occurred.

> From the **Chief Examiner's report** on '**social change**' (2008): 'In questions on social change, marks are only awarded for **clearly stated changes**. Candidates are expected to specify the changes that have occurred, showing '**the before and after**' of these changes and how the changes **affected people's lives**.'

Sources for social change

Explain how each of the following sources can help you in your study of social change in Ireland in the 20th century.

> Revise the definitions of *primary source, secondary source, bias* and *propaganda* in Chapter 1, pp. 14 –15.

Type of Source	Strength/Advantage	Weakness/Disadvantage
Census	Accurate information on population	Mistakes can be made
Diary	First-hand account Private views of writer	Could be biased
Newspaper	Daily record of events Eyewitness accounts	Could be biased Could be used for propaganda
Interview	First-hand account Could be eyewitness	Memory could be faulty Person could be biased
Autobiography	Eyewitness accounts of events	Could be biased Could exaggerate their own part
Photographs	Record of political, sporting and social history	Can be changed for propaganda purposes

Rural life and work

What is the meaning of 'rural'?

Rural = in the countryside

Changes in Rural Life in Ireland in the 20th Century		
	Before 1945/1950 (first half of the 20th century)	**After 1945/1950 (second half of the 20th century)**
Housing and living conditions	There was much **poverty**. Many people still lived in the countryside and there was little industry. Living conditions were difficult; houses were often damp and dark (for example, there was no electricity – oil lamps or candles provided light). A great deal of manual labour was required – washing clothes, cleaning the house, carrying water from a well or pump every day, hand milking of cows. **Landlords** were in decline as they sold their land to tenant farmers. They lived in the Big House. **Large farmers** were prosperous; they lived in two-storey slated houses with a parlour and three or four bedrooms; they had a garden. **Others** lived in single-storey thatched cottages with thick walls, two to five rooms, and outside toilets.	There were **improved** living conditions because the country became more **prosperous**. **Rural electrification** meant that power was available to run electric pumps for water; indoor plumbing meant that indoor toilets could be installed. The **economy** improved in the 1960s and in 1973 Ireland joined the **EEC**, so there was more money in the countryside. **New houses** were built – mostly bungalows with built-in furniture, central heating, televisions, living rooms separate from the kitchen; modern **kitchen appliances**, such as washing machines, cookers (gas or electric); **less manual work**; greater comfort for all with larger or smaller houses depending on the wealth of the farmers.
Social life	There were few pressures and a good social life depended on **gatherings** in neighbours' houses at night, conversation, stories, songs and dances; there were visits to the **pub**, **GAA** matches on a Sunday, market and fair days. But there was also emigration and rural depopulation as young people left.	Watching television replaced social gatherings in houses; the **car** gave greater mobility, so shopping was done in supermarkets in towns rather than the small local store; rural areas became less isolated. The **GAA** was still very important for matches and social gatherings. Market and fair days were gone – the **mart** replaced the fair day as a place to sell cattle. **Festivals** were organised in country towns during the summer.

Changes in rural work

Changes in Rural Work in Ireland in the 20th Century	
Before 1945/1950 (first half of the 20th century)	After 1945/1950 (second half of the 20th century)
More than **40 per cent of workers** worked on the land (but this was falling due to inheritance and emigration). Most farms were **small** – less than 50 acres (20 hectares), so it was difficult for farmers to make a living. Most farms depended on cattle rearing and dairying. There was very little machinery to lesson the **hard manual labour** required. Father and sons worked on the farm, but the farm was inherited by the eldest son only (the others **emigrated** – this caused rural depopulation); mother and daughters did the housework (cooking and cleaning) and fed hens and chickens. Farmers were **older** and tended to be **conservative** – they did not want to bring in changes. From the 1920s, **tractors** slowly replaced horses – there were 40,000 tractors by 1960; rural electrification in the 1950s helped to make work easier.	Improvements in farm work came with **rural electrification** in the 1950s – now milking machines could be used, and running water was supplied. Farmers benefited from Ireland's **membership of the EEC** in 1973 – they got better prices for their products and grants for farm improvement. Farms got **larger** with more **machinery** – milking parlours instead of milking machines, except in smaller farms in the West. There was a **decrease in manual labour** as tractors, combine harvesters and silage cutters became common. **Women** still did the housework, but some worked outside the home. Some farmers were **part-time** on the farm and held jobs in nearby towns. Fewer labourers were needed, so there was **migration** from the countryside to the cities or abroad – rural depopulation still continued.

Urban life and work

What is the meaning of 'urban'?

Urban = town/city

Changes in urban life

Changes in Urban Life in Ireland in the 20th Century	
Before 1945/1950 (first half of the 20th century)	After 1945/1950 (second half of the 20th century)
Housing: Only 30 per cent of people lived in large towns and cities. Living conditions depended on how well off people were. The influence of trains, trams, horses and carriages was changing the shape of cities such as Dublin; the city centre was used for business and for working-class tenements (blocks of flats) or terraced houses – the tenements had outdoor toilets and water from public pumps; often each room	**Housing**: Over 70 per cent of people lived in large towns or cities. There were improved living conditions for all except for the very poor due to the availability of electricity, growing prosperity and better building regulations. Cities such as Dublin developed the central business district (CBD); the main streets of the cities experienced inner-city decay and a rise in crime; later urban renewal schemes

Changes in Urban Life in Ireland in the 20th Century contd.	
Before 1945/1950 (first half of the 20th century) contd.	After 1945/1950 (second half of the 20th century) contd.
housed an entire family; damp living conditions led to TB and other sicknesses; there were terraced or semi-detached houses for skilled craftsmen and middle classes; some of these had electricity and piped gas; better-off middle-class and upper-class families moved to the suburbs into detached or semi-detached houses; they travelled to work in the city centre each day.	improved these streets; working-class families moved to new corporation houses or blocks of flats (for example, Crumlin or Ballymun in Dublin, Gurranabraher in Cork); middle-class and upper-middle-class families lived in semi-detached or detached houses in the suburbs; they worked in the CBD and shopped in new shopping centres in the suburbs. The general **standard of housing** improved – water supply, indoor toilets, central heating and new household appliances. But there were **more pressures** – travel to and from work, unemployment in the 1970s and 1980s, along with increased crime, drink and drugs.

Changes in urban work

Changes in Urban Work in Ireland in the 20th Century	
Before 1945/1950 (first half of the 20th century)	After 1945/1950 (second half of the 20th century)
Most of the work was done by men. There were many unskilled labourers – dockers, carters and general labourers in the cities. There was a surplus of labour, so wages were low – about £1 a week – and sometimes it was casual (daily) labour, so men were often unemployed. There were no unions for unskilled labourers until Big Jim Larkin founded the ITGWU (Irish Transport and General Workers Union); he fought for the rights of these workers and this led to the Dublin Strike and Lockout, 1913. Skilled craftsmen (tradesmen), such as carpenters and plumbers, were better paid; they served an apprenticeship and were unionised. Men also worked in clerical jobs – in the civil service, post office, banks and general offices; these were secure and respectable jobs. There were also businessmen and professionals, such as lawyers, doctors, and owners of large stores and factories.	Working patterns stayed much the same until about the 1960s; then the economy grew. There was a growth of manufacturing industry in industrial estates; later these declined as automation (machinery) was introduced; there was also a decline in crafts/skilled trades. There was a growth in service industries, such as transport, banks, law, insurance. More women were attracted to work outside the home. The small local shops declined as supermarkets and shopping centres grew. There was also a greater variety of employment (jobs) – there were new types of jobs in the chemical and electronic industries. There was no work for some as unemployment rose in the 1970s and 1980s; there were large pockets of unemployment – up to 80 per cent – in some working-class areas in Dublin and Cork.

The status of women

What does 'status of women' mean?

Status of women = role of women

People in History: An elderly woman describes changes in the role of women in Ireland between 1945 and 2000.

Changes in the status of women

Changes in the Status of Women in Ireland in the 20th Century	
Before 1945/1950 (first half of the 20th century)	**After 1945/1950 (second half of the 20th century)**
Women were regarded as second-class citizens in the early 20th century; they could not vote in general elections; they were expected to marry and have children; husbands were the breadwinners. Better-off married women supervised servants who did the housework and minded the children. Poorer married women worked as servants in houses of middle- and upper-class families, or as street traders in Dublin or Cork. In Belfast, women worked in the linen mills. In rural areas, women did the housework and kept poultry. Single women worked as domestic servants; some emigrated to the USA or Britain. Women were paid less than men. Married working-class women and single women worked in domestic service in the houses of middle- and upper-class families; they were paid 4 shillings a week, along with board and food. There was a campaign for votes for women – the suffrage movement led by Hanna Sheehy-Skeffington; women over age 30 got the vote in 1918 after World War I. Women were also involved in the independence movement in Ireland – the most famous was Countess Markievicz, who fought in the 1916 Rising and was the first woman elected to Westminster. (She did not take her seat because of Sinn Féin's policy of abstentionism.)	Women over 21 got the vote in 1922, but Ireland was a conservative society from the 1920s to 1960s; women's place was regarded as in the home and the 1937 Constitution recognised women's special role within the home. The marriage ban (or marriage bar) meant that women had to give up government jobs (e.g. teaching, civil service) when they married – the ban was not fully lifted until the 1970s. Changes in the status of women occurred because of increased availability of education, the fight for equality, changes in the law and new types of jobs. More women went to work outside the home; married women still worked after they married. Family size was limited. The women's movement campaigned for changes; they wanted equal pay and equal opportunities. More women became involved in politics and some became ministers (e.g. Gemma Hussey became Minister for Education and Mary Robinson became the first female president of Ireland). The Commission on the Status of Women recommended changes to the law (the Employment Equality Act, 1977, outlawed discrimination on the basis of sex or marital status). But problems still existed for women: women were still exploited in advertising; while more women became senior managers, they were still well outnumbered by men; some clubs and institutions still barred women as equal members.

Changes in leisure and entertainment

People in History: An old person describes changes in leisure and entertainment from the 1920s to the 1970s.

Changes in Leisure and Entertainment in Ireland in the 20th Century

Before 1945/1950 (first half of the 20th century)	After 1945/1950 (second half of the 20th century)
In the early 20th century people mostly provided their own entertainment, especially in the countryside; this was home-based with conversations, story-telling, music and card playing. In the cities, there was the beginning of mass entertainment; theatres such as the Gaiety and Abbey in Dublin or the Opera House in Cork produced plays, concerts and operas. There was also the beginning of cinema, which became more widespread in the 1920s and 1930s; radio began in the 1920s with 2RN which later became Radio Éireann; country people depended on battery-operated radios to hear news and GAA match reports on Sundays. Trains were used for leisure activities, such as day trips to the seaside (e.g. Tramore, Bray); the GAA was more popular in rural areas and the All-Ireland was a highlight; soccer was popular in working-class areas in Dublin and Cork.	Leisure and mass entertainment became big industries by the 1960s and 1970s. People had more time (shorter working week and longer holidays) and they were better off. Dance halls became common in the 1950s and 1960s; the popular music was rock and roll and country and western, which was played by big bands, such as the Royal Showband and the Dixies; the use of cars and organised bus trips led to the development of many dance halls in small towns; these went into decline with the arrival of the disco. RTÉ Television was set up in the early 1960s – the popularity of television gradually led to the decline of the cinema and larger cinemas closed down; there was a revival of cinema in the 1990s among the late teen and early 20s age groups; this was helped by the building of cineplexes, which increased the choice of movie. There was a greater variety of sports – the GAA was still popular, but it faced competition from soccer and rugby, which had international appeal. There was a rise in health consciousness with the use of sports complexes – health and fitness became more important due to the easy-going lifestyle of people. Amongst younger people, crazes developed, such as skateboarding, roller skating and roller blading. Teenagers became a big market for youth entertainment, with large pop-music concerts. Home entertainment also developed through the proliferation of videos, computer games and access to the internet.

Transport and communications

exam focus

From the **Chief Examiner's report** on the **differences between 'Transport'** and **'Communications'** (2001): 'In part (iii) a significant number wrote about 'transport' instead of 'communication'. This confusion has arisen previously, so it may be helpful to state plainly here that examiners interpret **'transport'** as being **the movement of people or goods**, while **'communication'** is taken to mean the **'transmission of messages, images and ideas'**.

Changes in transport

Changes in Transport in Ireland in the 20th Century	
Before 1945/1950 (first half of the 20th century)	**After 1945/1950 (second half of the 20th century)**
The horse and cart was used in the country and in the city for the transport of goods; horses and carriages were used by the better-off classes in the city and country for transport. The bicycle was developed with the pneumatic tyre, but many people went from place to place by walking. There were very few automobiles because of the cost of owning them. The train was important for longer journeys – it moved goods and passengers – and there were railway lines leading to many parts of the country. Horse and electric tramways were used in Dublin and Cork for passengers – they linked the city centre with the suburbs. Ships were used for overseas transport; ferries took passengers to England, transatlantic liners took emigrants from Cobh to the USA and merchant ships took goods to Britain. Transport developments influenced the location of workplaces and houses; the suburbs developed in Dublin and Cork and people commuted to work using suburban trains and tramways; trains also influenced day trips to the seaside (e.g. Tramore, Bray); more people could also travel to important inter-county GAA matches.	Trains and trams lost out to cars and lorries from the 1920s onwards; cars and lorries offered greater flexibility as people could use them to travel when and where they wished. The road system began to dominate the shape of cities as the suburbs spread out further; automobiles presented problems for the cities, which had narrow streets, resulting in pollution and traffic jams. Efforts were made to overcome these problems by building bypasses around towns and cities and also by encouraging people to use buses and (in Dublin) the DART. Aer Lingus was set up in 1936 when flying boats were used to make transatlantic flights; later, Shannon Airport was developed for US traffic; but air travel remained an expensive mode of travel until later in the century; Ryanair introduced low-cost flying, which made air travel more accessible; local and regional airports such as Cork or Farranfore, Co Kerry, were also developed, which made travel easier. Ferries were more popular than flying for families travelling on holidays; ferries sailed from Dun Laoghaire and Rosslare to Britain and France; the ferries became faster and more comfortable, but transatlantic liners lost out to air travel due to cost.

Changes in communications

Changes in Communications in Ireland in the 20th Century	
Before 1945/1950 (first half of the 20th century)	After 1945/1950 (second half of the 20th century)
All types of communications were slow or cumbersome early in the 20th century. Letters were used to send personal news to family and friends, while the telegraph was used to send urgent messages. Telegraph cables were laid between Britain, Ireland and the USA. The telephone was little used because few people had phones, due to their cost. Businesses used the telegraph and the telephone. Newspapers were the mass media which reached many people; there was a mix of serious and popular content (e.g. the *Freeman's Journal*, the *Irish Independent* and regional papers such as the *Cork Examiner*); some local newspapers were printed weekly; photographs were used. The *Irish Press* began in the 1930s as a paper supporting Fianna Fáil as other newspapers supported different political parties. Magazines also developed.	Post offices played an important part in communications; they sent letters, parcels and telegrams; later they were used as telephone exchanges. The telephone developed as one of the main types of personal communication – they were used by businesses as well; the fax and telex were used by businesses; later in the century the mobile phone and the internet were used, but mainly by businesses at first. Television, radio and newspapers were the mass media – newspapers competed with the others to provide the public with news. Radio developed from 2RN in 1926 and later became RTÉ 1, 2 FM; local channels also developed; radio was important for sport and news. RTÉ television began on New Year's Eve, 1961. The development of cable companies brought many satellite or cable channels into city houses. Television exposed Irish people to new ideas, which influenced and changed attitudes to women and religion; people became more aware of national and international news as Ireland became part of the global village. Newspapers remained largely as they were, featuring a mix of serious and popular content; tabloids from Britain provided competition later in the century; local papers also developed in towns and were made possible through advances in computer technology.

Past questions on *Social Change in 20th-century Ireland*

Short-Answer Questions

1. Mention **one** change in rural life since 1945.
2. Mention **one** change in the lives of women since 1945.
3. Mention **one** major change in farming in Ireland since 1945.
4. Mention **one** change in working life since 1945.
5. Mention **one** change in transport since 1945.

People in History

Ordinary level

1. An old person talking about changes in entertainment, housing, transport and communications that have taken place in Ireland since 1950
   - *Hints*: Changes in entertainment; Changes in transport; Changes in housing; Changes in communications
2. An old person talking about changes in life in the countryside or towns during the 20th century
   - *Hints*: Changes in housing; Changes in leisure and entertainment; Changes in transport and communications; Changes in the role of women
3. An old person talking about changes in leisure, sport and entertainment that have taken place during the 20th century
   - *Hints*: Leisure, sport and entertainment in the early 1900s; Changes in leisure activities; Developments in sport and entertainment; Effects of these changes

Higher level

1. An old person describing changes that have occurred in communications in Ireland since 1945
2. An old woman describing changes in the role of women in Ireland between 1945 and 2000
3. An old person describing social change in Ireland during the period 1930–60

Long-Answer Questions (Higher level)

1. (i) Identify **two** ways in which electricity changed life in Ireland.
   (ii) Mention **three** developments in air transport since the 1930s.
   (iii) Write about changes in **two** of the following areas since 1945:
      (a) Communications
      (b) Education
      (c) Housing
      (d) Religion

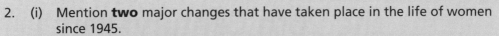

2. (i)   Mention **two** major changes that have taken place in the life of women since 1945.

    (ii) Mention **three** changes that have occurred in agriculture since 1945.

    (iii) Write an account of the changes that have taken place in **two** of the following since 1945:

        (a) Housing

        (b) Transport

        (c) Work

        (d) Leisure Activities

3. (i)   Explain how **three** of the following sources would be useful in studying social change in Ireland: *Church records; School roll books; Census reports; Diaries.*

    (ii)   Identify **three** changes in urban housing in Ireland since the 1920s.

    (iii) Identify **three** changes in education since 1960.

    (iv) Write about the impact on Irish life of the changes in communications since 1960.

4. (i)   Identify **three** types of primary source that a historian could use to find out about social change in Ireland.

    (ii) Mention **three** major changes that have occurred in the role of women since 1960.

    (iii) Give **three** major changes that have occurred in rural life since 1973.

    (iv) Describe the main changes that have occurred in communications since 1960.

International Relations in the 20th Century: Part 1

aims
- To understand the impact of the Treaty of Versailles
- To assess the rise to power of Mussolini and Hitler and their impact
- To consider the origins of World War II
- To understand the progress of World War II and the role of key battles

Peace and war in Europe, 1920–45

The Paris Peace Conference

The conference was held after Britain, France and the USA defeated Germany and Austria-Hungary in World War I.

- **President Wilson** of the USA wanted Germany to be treated fairly; he also suggested a League of Nations to keep peace after the war.
- **David Lloyd George**, prime minister of Britain, wanted to impose harsh terms on Germany.
- **President Clemenceau** of France (the 'Tiger') wanted revenge for France; he wanted to keep Germany weak.

Treaty of Versailles

1. The Treaty of Versailles was made with **Germany**.
   - The Rhineland was demilitarised (no German soldiers could be there).
   - Germany lost the Polish Corridor to Poland.
   - Union with Austria (Anschluss) was forbidden.
   - The German army was reduced to 100,000 soldiers.
   - Germany had to accept the War Guilt Clause (that is, admit that it caused the war).
   - Germany had to pay reparations (compensation) of £6.6 billion to the victorious Allies.
2. Germany had to sign the Treaty, but Germans were very angry with the terms.

The League of Nations

1. The League of Nations was set up to maintain **peace** between countries.
2. The League had a headquarters in **Geneva**; it had an **Assembly** where decisions had to be unanimous and a **Council** where decisions also had to be unanimous.
3. The League sorted some small disputes between countries, but it could not stop bigger countries doing what they wanted to do.
   - Japan invaded Manchuria (China).

- Italy invaded Abyssinia (Ethiopia).
- Hitler and Germany often broke the terms of the Treaty of Versailles.

Reasons for failure:

4. The League had no army; it only used sanctions or boycotts to force countries to follow its decisions.
5. The Council and Assembly had to be **unanimous**.
6. The most powerful countries (such as the USA) were not members.

Democracy and dictatorship: The rise of fascism, 1920–33

Mussolini and Fascist Italy

How did Mussolini rise to power in Italy?

1. Mussolini founded the **Fascist Party**, also known as the **Blackshirts**, after World War I. He rose to power in Italy because:
   - Italy suffered during World War I and Italians were unhappy that they did not get land they were promised.
   - The Italian **economy** also suffered so that unemployment and inflation were high after the war.
   - Businesses and industrialists feared the **spread of communism** in Italy; they wanted a strong leader to stop communists.

What was communism in Russia?

The Communist Party led by Lenin and later Stalin took over power in Russia in 1917. They set up a dictatorship and took over land and industry. Many people outside of Russia feared that communists would do the same in other European countries.

   - The **Fascist Party** (Blackshirts) grew stronger as they used violence against socialists.
   - The **March on Rome**: the Fascists planned a March on Rome to demand a place in government; the king, Victor Emmanuel, was tired of all the changes in government so he asked Mussolini to become prime minister of Italy.

What was fascism?

Fascists believed in dictatorship, control of the press and radio. They were anti-communist and favoured extreme nationalism.

The fasces – symbol of Mussolini's Fascist Party

Mussolini's dictatorship

2. Mussolini established a **dictatorship**:

People in History: A member of Mussolini's Fascist Party describes what life was like in Italy under Mussolini.

- He passed a law which said the party which got the majority of the votes in the next election would get two-thirds of the seats in parliament; the Fascists became the largest party.
- After the murder of a socialist leader, **Matteotti**, by the Fascists, the Socialist Party withdrew from parliament. This made Mussolini stronger.
- He banned other political parties, except the Fascist Party.
- He set up the secret police, the OVRA.
- He controlled press and radio.

3. **Propaganda** was important to Mussolini:

- He called himself *Il Duce* (the Leader) and organised a cult of personality around himself.
- He got the press, radio and cinema to glorify Fascist successes.
- In schools, students were taught to praise Mussolini; boys and girls joined Fascist youth organisations.

4. **Fascist changes and achievements**:

- Mussolini improved the **road** system by building *autostrada* (motorways).
- He drained the **Pontine Marches** near Rome.
- He promoted the **Battle for Grain** and the **Battle for Births**.
- He signed the **Lateran Treaty** with the Catholic Church, which made peace with the Church after 50 years of disagreement.

Mussolini's foreign policy

5. Mussolini wanted to expand the power of Italy around the Mediterranean Sea.

- In 1935, Italy invaded **Abyssinia** and easily defeated its native tribes.
- He was opposed by the League of Nations, but he was supported by Hitler.

6. Mussolini and Hitler improved their relations.

- They signed the **Rome–Berlin Axis**, which was a treaty of friendship; also, Mussolini agreed to Hitler's takeover of Austria.
- Then they signed the **Pact of Steel** under which they pledged to help each other in war.

7. But Italy was very weak in **World War II**; Hitler had to send Rommel to North Africa to help the Italian army there.

8. When the Allies invaded Italy, Mussolini was captured and killed by Italians who were opposed to him.

Hitler and Nazi Germany

How did Hitler rise to power in Germany?

The swastika, symbol of the Nazi Party

1. **The Weakness of the Weimar Republic**: The Weimar Republic, a parliamentary government, was in place in Germany after World War I. It was blamed for defeat in World War I and for accepting the harsh terms of the Treaty of Versailles.

2. **The Great Depression**: After the Wall Street Crash of 1929, the Great Depression spread to Germany. German unemployment rose to 6 million by 1932. The Weimar Government could not solve the economic problems.

3. **Hitler's Nazi Party**: Hitler intended to get power by democratic means and after that to establish a dictatorship, as Mussolini had done in Italy. The Nazi Party won many seats in the elections and it became the largest party in the Reichstag (German parliament).

4. **Hitler's policies**: Hitler made sure his policies appealed to as many people as possible; his opposition to the Treaty of Versailles appealed to everybody; his anti-communism appealed to businessmen and industrialists; he also promised to revive the economy and end unemployment.

5. **Propaganda**: Hitler and the Nazis used clever propaganda techniques to get their message across to people; he blamed Germany's troubles on the Treaty of Versailles, the Jews and the communists; he was an outstanding speaker.

6. **The SA and the SS**: The SA (Brownshirts) and SS (Blackshirts) used violence to attack opposition parties.

7. President Hindenburg appointed Hitler **Chancellor of Germany** on 30 January 1933.

How did Hitler establish dictatorship?

8. Hitler called an **election** and the SA and SS attacked opposition parties. Hitler increased the number of seats in parliament.

9. When a Dutch communist burnt down the **Reichstag** building, Hitler banned the Communist Party.

10. Hitler passed the **Enabling Law**, which allowed him to rule by decree.

11. Hitler banned trade unions, and he used the secret police, the **Gestapo**, to put down the opposition.

12. Hitler used the SS to kill the leader of the SA, Röhm, and others who threatened his power in the **Night of the Long Knives**.

13. When President Hindenburg died, Hitler made himself president as well as chancellor of Germany. He became *der Führer* (the Leader).

Nazi propaganda

14. **Goebbels** became the Minister for Propaganda. He controlled the press, radio newspapers and cinema. He controlled the news they sent out.

- Hitler was glorified in a cult of personality.
- The Nuremberg Rallies and torchlight parades were held.
- In schools, students were told to glorify Hitler; boys and girls had to join the **Hitler Youth** and the **League of German Maidens**.

The Nazi economy

15. Hitler improved the German economy:

- He reduced unemployment from 6 million to no unemployment by 1939.
- He built *autobahns* (motorways).
- He began rearmament with more ships, submarines and planes. He began conscription to increase the size of the German army.

The Nazis and the Jews

16. Hitler hated the Jews (anti-Semitism).

- He passed the **Nuremberg Laws** to deprive Jews of German citizenship, banned them from marrying non-Jews and forced them to wear the **Star of David**.
- In the **Night of the Broken Glass** (*Kristallnacht*), Jewish shops and synagogues were attacked and 90 Jews were killed.
- Many of Germany's Jews emigrated after this, including the great scientist Albert Einstein.

17. During **World War II**, Hitler undertook the mass murder of Jews. This was called the **Final Solution** by the Nazis; it is now called the **Holocaust**.

- Jews were rounded up in **ghettoes** and **concentration camps**, such as **Auschwitz**.
- Himmler's SS organised their mass execution, beginning with the gassing of women, children and older men.
- Others were used as slave labour until they died.
- Some were buried in mass graves and others were burnt in ovens.
- About 6 million Jews were killed.

People in History

A member of the Nazi Party describes what life was like in Germany under Hitler

I am a member of the Nazi Party and now our leader, Adolf Hitler, is in power as **chancellor** of Germany. It is now time for us to establish a **dictatorship** for the good of Germany. Hitler called elections and our SS and SA attacked the socialists and communists. Hitler then passed the **Enabling Act**, which gave him power to rule by decree and put an end to democracy. This is very good for life in Germany.

Our Minister of Propaganda, **Goebbels**, controls newspapers, radio and cinema so that the people know what to think. This is necessary because everybody must support Nazi ideas. Our Nuremberg Rallies and torchlight parades are great spectacular events and they show all Germans how powerful we are. We did a great job organising the Olympic Games in Berlin. Hitler is now *der Führer* because Hindenburg died and Hitler took the title of president as well. We have to control education so that the boys and girls are brought up adoring Hitler and being good Nazis. We also want them to join the Hitler Youth and the League of German Maidens.

We don't like the Jews (anti-Semitism) because they are an inferior race. The **Nuremberg Laws** have been imposed on them – they are no longer German citizens, they can't marry non-Jews and they must wear the Star of David. After a Polish Jew killed a German diplomat in Paris, I helped on the **Night of the Broken Glass** to attack Jewish shops and synagogues. About 90 Jews were killed that night and others were put into concentration camps.

Hitler has built up Germany so much that our economy is booming and unemployment, which was 6 million, is falling fast. Rearmament – the manufacture of ships, submarines and planes – and building motorways (*autobahns*) have provided more jobs.

Hitler has had great success with his **foreign policy**. We are now masters of central Europe as he has remilitarised the Rhineland, taken over Austria (*Anschluss*) and the Sudetenland, the rest of Czechoslovakia and now the Polish Corridor. I support Hitler's war on Poland. I know we will be successful with our blitzkrieg tactics.

The drift to war in Europe, 1933–39

18. Hitler's **aims** in foreign policy were:
- To create a greater Germany of all German-speaking people
- To acquire *Lebensraum* (living space) in Eastern Europe for raw materials and food
- To destroy the Treaty of Versailles

19. Hitler's foreign policy in action:
- The Saar, a coal-producing area given to France after World War I, voted to return to Germany.
- Hitler began **rearmament** with conscription and building submarines, warships and planes.
- Hitler **remilitarised** the Rhineland by sending in German troops.
- Hitler's relations with **Mussolini** improved because of the Italian invasion of Abyssinia (Ethiopia) and the Spanish Civil War.

Hitler and Mussolini

1. Hitler and Mussolini agreed the **Rome–Berlin Axis**; this allowed Hitler to annex (takeover) Austria in the *Anschluss*.

- Later they agreed the **Pact of Steel**, where they committed to help each other in war.

2. **Policy of Appeasement**: Britain and France did not take action when Hitler broke the Treaty of Versailles on a number of occasions; they followed a policy of appeasement in which they believed that if they gave in to Hitler's demands they would prevent a war.

> ### Why did Britain and France follow a policy of appeasement?
>
> They thought Germany had been harshly treated in the Treaty of Versailles and they did not want a repetition of the horrors of World War I.

- Hitler demanded the **Sudetenland** – a German-speaking area – from Czechoslovakia. Czechoslovakia refused.
- The **Munich Conference** was held with Mussolini, Hitler, Daladier (France) and Chamberlain (Britain); they agreed to force Czechoslovakia to hand over the Sudetenland to prevent war.
- Hitler came to a surprise agreement with **Stalin**, the leader of communist Russia; they signed the **Nazi–Soviet Pact**, which included a 10-year non-aggression pact; they also agreed to divide Poland between them.
- Hitler demanded the **Polish Corridor**, a strip of Polish territory which separated most of Germany from an eastern province, East Prussia. Poland refused.
- Despite their support of Poland, Hitler thought Britain and France would not do anything if he acted, so he ordered the **invasion of Poland** on 1 September 1939.

3. Two days later, Britain and France declared war on Germany. World War II had begun.

Political leaders in the modern world

Mussolini, leader of Fascist Italy

Hitler, leader of the Nazi Party and of Germany

Goebbels, propaganda minister in Nazi Germany

Himmler, leader of the SS in Nazi Germany

Chamberlain, prime minister of Britain who favoured the policy of appeasement before World War II

Churchill, prime minister of Britain from 1940 onwards who led Britain to victory over Germany

Stalin, leader of communist Soviet Russia

Roosevelt, president of the United States of America during World War II

World War II in Europe, 1939–45
German victories, 1939–42

1. Hitler defeated **Poland** in five weeks using blitzkrieg tactics. Germany and the Soviet Union divided Poland between them.
   - After this attack, there was no fighting during the winter of 1939–40 in what people called the **Phoney War**; both sides built up their weapons.
2. Next Hitler conquered **Denmark and Norway**.
   - He wanted Norway to protect the supply route of **iron ore**, which came from Sweden during the winter; this was vital for his war industries.

Hitler's conquests

- Land under direct German control
- 'Puppet' governments
- Land occupied by USSR
- German invasions
- Mussolini advances

What was *Blitzkrieg* (or 'lightning war')?

It was a German war tactic that combined the use of tanks, infantry, artillery and air power. In Poland, the German air force (Luftwaffe) destroyed the Polish air force on the ground, the German Panzer tank units cut off the Polish army, and the German infantry defeated the Polish army. Germany also used this tactic in France and Soviet Russia.

3. Then Hitler attacked **Belgium, Holland and France**. Hitler used blitzkrieg tactics and cut off the British and French armies at Dunkirk, in France.

   - In **Operation Dynamo**, the British sent over hundreds of boats to rescue thousands of soldiers from the beaches of Dunkirk.
   - Hitler easily captured the **Maginot Line** (a French defensive line); then he divided France, ruling part of it directly, the other part was ruled as **Vichy France** under German control.

4. **Churchill**, prime minister of Britain, organised British resistance to Hitler in the **Battle of Britain**.

   - Hitler's plan to invade Britain was called **Operation Sea Lion**. But first he had to gain control of the air over the English Channel. The Royal Air Force (RAF) and the Luftwaffe fought for control of the air in the Battle of Britain.
   - Britain defeated the Germans with the help of **radar**, which told them where the Germans were going to attack.

5. The Battle of Britain was followed by the **Blitz** – the Luftwaffe attack on British cities over the winter of 1940/41.

   - Cities such as London and Coventry were attacked; some people evacuated to the countryside, but many stayed in the cities.
   - In London people slept in the Underground.
   - The Blitz ended when Hitler ordered the attack on Soviet Russia.

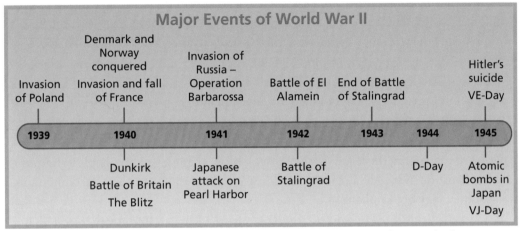

Major Events of World War II

1939	1940	1941	1942	1943	1944	1945
Invasion of Poland	Denmark and Norway conquered / Invasion and fall of France	Invasion of Russia – Operation Barbarossa	Battle of El Alamein	End of Battle of Stalingrad		Hitler's suicide / VE-Day
	Dunkirk / Battle of Britain / The Blitz	Japanese attack on Pearl Harbor	Battle of Stalingrad		D-Day	Atomic bombs in Japan / VJ-Day

6. **Operation Barbarossa** – the invasion of the Soviet Union: Hitler attacked Russia because he hated communists and he wanted *Lebensraum*.

   - He attacked towards Leningrad, Moscow and Kiev with **blitzkrieg** tactics.
   - **Stalin**, leader of Russia, encouraged the people to fight in what the Russians called the **Great Patriotic War**. He ordered that industries be moved behind the Ural Mountains, away from German attack. He ordered a **scorched-earth policy** of destroying all crops so that the Germans could not use them as they advanced.
   - The Germans' advance was halted by the **winter snow**.
   - **Battle of Stalingrad**: In the following year, Hitler ordered an attack on Stalingrad; there was vicious street fighting and the German army was trapped in Stalingrad; 200,000 German soldiers had to surrender; this was a major turning point in the war.

7. **America** joined the war when Japan attacked Pearl Harbor in December 1941; America became the **arsenal of democracy**, supplying Britain with food and weapons.

8. **The War at Sea**: Britain and America won the war at sea (also known as the **Battle of the Atlantic**), a battle against German U-boats as they attacked convoys bringing supplies to Britain; the Allies won because of increased shipbuilding and the use of Ultra, which cracked the German codes sending messages to their submarines.

9. **The War in the Air**: Britain and America bombed Germany by day and by night; they bombed major German cities such as **Hamburg**; 30,000 people were killed on a raid on **Dresden**.

   - The Germans counter-attacked by using **V1 flying bombs** and **V2 rockets** against Britain.

HL

People in History

A German soldier who took part in Operation Barbarossa (the invasion of Russia, 1941)

I am a German soldier who took part in Operation Barbarossa, which was the German invasion plan for the Soviet Union in 1941. Hitler wanted to invade the Soviet Union because he hated **communists** and he wanted to gain *Lebensraum* (living space) so that we could get raw materials and food. He had agreed the **Nazi–Soviet Pact** with the Soviet Union before the war, but we knew that this was only to allow us to conquer Poland.

Our attack on Russia began in June 1941 and I was in a **tank** as part of the attack on Moscow; there were other attacks towards Leningrad and Kiev. We used **blitzkrieg tactics** – our Luftwaffe planes bombed the Soviet planes to give us control of the air; our Panzer tanks moved rapidly over the wide Russian plains and our infantry mopped up any Russian soldiers.

We heard that **Stalin**, the leader of the Soviet Union, encouraged his people to fight the 'Great Patriotic War'. He already moved heavy industry beyond the Ural Mountains, out of the range of our planes.

We moved quickly into the Soviet Union because the Russian **Red Army** retreated. But they used a **scorched-earth policy** so they burnt all the crops, knocked down bridges and blew up railway lines so that we could not use them. SS troops followed us and they rounded up Jews who were killed or sent to concentration camps. Some of our troops found evidence of the massacre of Polish army officers by the Russians in the **Katyn Forest**, which the Soviet Union denied that they did.

Our troops had no trouble taking Kiev, but we were slowed down as we advanced towards Moscow and Leningrad. The heavy autumn rains muddied the land and after that the snow and ice froze our lorries, tanks and planes. We were not ready for this severe winter. Neither were the infantry soldiers because their clothes were not warm enough and some of them froze to death on duty.

We were halted outside Moscow and Leningrad for the winter. There is talk that Hitler plans to attack Stalingrad and the oil fields of the Caucasus next year.

The Allies advance, 1942–45

10. The Allies advanced from the south through Italy; **Mussolini** was deposed by the Italians and he was captured and shot; his body was hung publicly in Milan.

11. The Soviet Union advanced from the east.

12. **D-Day, Operation Overlord:** the Allies planned a landing on the coast of Normandy in France. They used the coastline's shallow water, sandy beaches and proximity to England to surprise the Germans.
    - General Eisenhower commanded the Allied forces; Allied planes bombed the German defences of the Atlantic Wall; paratroopers dropped behind enemy lines; warships and landing craft landed American, British and Canadian troops on five beaches (called Omaha, Utah, Gold, Juno and Sword).

- The Allies built PLUTO (Pipeline under the Ocean) to supply oil and Mulberry Harbours (floating artificial piers) in order to land trucks and tanks.
- They advanced on Paris.

13. **Hitler's Suicide**: Hitler committed suicide in his bunker in Berlin as the Allied armies closed in on Berlin. Germany surrendered.

People in History
A soldier in the D-Day landings
Fill in the blanks using the words in the list. (Words can be used more than once)

I was an American soldier in D-Day. This was the day American, British and Canadian armies invaded France in **Operation** _____ to open a second front against Hitler. This was organised by **General** _____, our commander-in-chief. At this time, most of the fighting in Europe was being done by the Russians so _____, the leader of the Soviet Union, demanded that we should open up a _____ front in the west. Our commanders selected the _____ coast in France because it had large beaches with _____ water and also it was close to Britain. But they had to fool the Germans into thinking that we were attacking around _____ because that was nearer to England.

On the morning of D-Day, our planes bombed the German defences and dropped _____ behind enemy lines. Our planes gave us _____ of the air so that German _____ planes could not attack us. The warships shelled the _____ coast while I went in a _____ **craft**. This was a flat-bottomed boat which could sail in shallow water and the front flap would open out to let out the soldiers. Our invasion force of 130,000 soldiers attacked _____ **beaches**, which were code named _____, Utah, Gold, Juno and Sword. My landing craft sailed into _____ where many American soldiers landed. We eventually captured the strong German defences. This was part of Hitler's _____ **Wall**, which he had built to defend the coast with _____ bunkers. To ensure we got supplies of tanks and trucks, the army and navy set up _____ **Harbours** (floating artificial piers). They also built _____ (Pipeline under the Ocean) in order to supply the tanks and trucks with oil.

After D-Day, we advanced onto _____ and northern France, heading for Berlin. Hitler was being attacked from all sides now.

Use your textbook to check your answers when you are finished.

Atlantic	five	Omaha	second
Calais	landing	Overlord	shallow
concrete	Luftwaffe	paratroopers	Stalin
control	Mulberry	Paris	
Eisenhower	Normandy	PLUTO	

Why did the Allies win the war?

1. The Allies had a larger population and larger armies than Germany, Italy and others.
2. America produced huge numbers of tanks, planes and weapons to keep the Allies going during the war.
3. The Allies produced more oil than the Germans.
4. The Allies won the major battles of the war – Battle of Britain, Stalingrad, D-Day.

What were the results of World War II?

1. 55 million people, civilians and soldiers, died.
2. Cities, industries, roads and railways were destroyed.
3. Nazi war criminals such as Goering were tried in the **Nuremberg Trials**.
4. As agreed at the Yalta Conference between Roosevelt, Churchill and Stalin, Germany was **divided** in two between the Soviet-controlled East Germany and Allied-controlled West Germany. The two were re-united when communism collapsed in 1990.
5. Relations between America and the Soviet Union worsened and turned into the **Cold War** after World War II was over; the Soviet Union installed communist governments in Eastern European states.
6. The USA and the Soviet Union became the **superpowers** and Europe was weakened.
7. European leaders began a drive to **European unity** after the war.

Past questions on *International Relations in the 20th Century: Part 1*

Short-Answer Questions

1. Give **two** reasons why Germans were unhappy with the Treaty of Versailles.
2. Which European leader was known as *'Il Duce'*?
3. Mention **two** actions taken by Hitler to become dictator of Nazi Germany.
4. What was the *Night of the Long Knives*, 1934?
5. What was the *Maginot Line*?
6. What was *appeasement*?
7. What did Hitler and Stalin agree in the Nazi–Soviet Pact, 1939?
8. From your study of *International Relations in the Twentieth Century*, give **one** reason why World War II broke out in 1939.
9. Name **two** countries invaded by Hitler in April 1940.
10. During World War II, explain why the Battle of Stalingrad was so important.
11. During World War II, what was *Operation Overlord*?

12. Name the leader of the USSR **and** a leader of the United States during World War II.

13. Mention **one** decision made by the Allied leaders at the Yalta Conference, 1945.

14. From your study of *International Relations in the Twentieth Century*, mention **one** historic event which followed from World War II.

15. Name the British prime minister who attended the Munich Conference, September 1938.

16. Give **one** reason why there was division in Europe at the end of World War II.

17. Tick **one** of the following terms and explain your chosen term: *Dictator; Superpower; Common Market; Empire.*

People in History

Ordinary level

1. A leader involved in the twentieth-century international event below: War in Europe, 1939–45
   - *Hints*: Name of the leader; Problems faced by the leader; Achievements of the leader; Any other relevant information

Higher level

1. A member of the Nazi Party describes how Hitler came to power in Germany

2. A pilot in the Royal Air Force or the German Luftwaffe during the Battle of Britain, 1940

3. A Russian soldier on the Eastern Front, 1941–45

4. A British or American soldier who took part in D-Day (Allied landings in France, June 1944)

Long-Answer Questions (Higher level)

1. (i) In your answer-book, supply the missing words in the following sentences (1)–(6). You should number the words correctly, but you need not rewrite the sentences.

   (1) Mussolini's followers were known as the ___.

   (2) After World War I, many Italians were unhappy with the Treaty of ___.

   (3) Many businessmen feared the spread of ___ and therefore supported fascism.

   (4) After the March on ___, Mussolini was appointed prime minister of Italy.

   (5) The ___ Treaty, signed with the Pope in 1929, recognised the Vatican City as an independent state.

   (6) In 1935, the Italians invaded ___.

   (ii) Give **two** reasons why Hitler came to power in Germany in January 1933.

   (iii) Explain **three** of the following terms relating to Germany under Nazi control, 1933–39: *The Enabling Act; The Night of the Long Knives; The Nuremberg Laws; Kristallnacht; The Gestapo.*

(iv) Write an account of the events, from 1933 until 1939, which led to the outbreak of World War II.

2. (i) Give **two** reasons why fascism became popular in Europe in the 1920s and 1930s.

(ii) Give **two** reasons why Germans were dissatisfied with the Versailles settlement.

(iii) Name **two** European countries created after World War I.

(iv) Write an account of **one** of the following:
(a) The Blitz, 1940
(b) Operation Barbarossa
(c) The Holocaust

3. (i) Give **two** reasons why Fascist leaders gained support in Europe in the 1920s and the 1930s.

(ii) Write an account of **one** of the following:
(a) Mussolini's political achievements, 1922–39
(b) Education and youth control in Nazi Germany
(c) Hitler's treatment of the Jews, 1933–39

(iii) Give **two** reasons why the League of Nations failed to keep the peace in Europe during the 1930s.

4. (i) Explain **two** of the following terms relating to Italy under Mussolini, 1922–39: *March on Rome; Lateran Treaty; OVRA; Battle for Grain; Pact of Steel.*

(ii) Mention **two** reasons why major European countries were willing to appease Hitler during the 1930s.

(iii) **World War II.**

Match each item in column **A**, (1)–(6) with its corresponding item in column **B**, (a)–(f).

You do not need to write the full text in your answerbook, just the correct number and letter.

Column A	Column B
1. Blitzkrieg	(a) German invasion of the USSR
2. Phoney War	(b) Nazi plan to invade Britain
3. Dunkirk	(c) USA provides Britain with military materials
4. Operation Sea Lion	(d) Swift mechanised, military attack
5. Lend-Lease	(e) British and French troops evacuated to England
6. Operation Barbarossa	(f) The winter of 1939–40

(iv) Give **two** reasons why Germany was defeated in World War II.

International Relations in the 20th Century: Part 2 (The Options)

 aims

- To understand the causes of the Cold War
- To assess the causes, progress and consequences of three crises in the Cold War
- To understand the main trends in the development of European unity
- To understand the main trends after 1945 which led to Indian independence

The rise of the Superpowers, 1945–91

 exam focus

Who were the Superpowers?

The superpowers were the USA and the USSR (Soviet Union) because they were so much more powerful than Britain, France and other countries.

Higher level: You have a choice of doing **one** of the following: (1) The Rise of the Superpowers, (2) Moves towards European Unity, or (3) Asian nationalism after 1945 – Gandhi and Indian independence. Your teacher will already have selected the topic you are doing.

HL

What was the Cold War?

The Cold War was a period of hostility between the USA and the USSR which began after World War II.

What caused the Cold War?

1. **Political differences**: The USA believed in democracy and private industry (capitalism) while the Soviet Union believed in dictatorship and government ownership of business and industry (communism).
2. **Disagreements during World War II**: America had the secrets of the atomic bomb and would not share them with the Soviet Union.
3. **Post-war disagreements**: Stalin said he installed communist governments in Eastern European countries to protect the Soviet Union; America said that was Soviet expansionism.
   - Winston Churchill said an '**iron curtain**' was dividing Europe.
4. **The Truman Doctrine**: President Truman of the USA said he would help countries resisting the spread of communism; this became the basis for the US policy of containment to stop the spread of communism.

5. **The Marshall Plan**: America offered to help Europe's economy recover after the war; Stalin prevented Eastern European countries from getting help from the Marshall Plan or European Recovery Program.

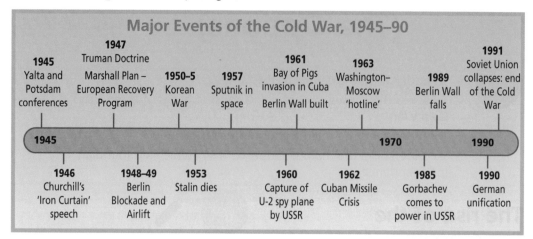

Major Events of the Cold War, 1945–90

1945 Yalta and Potsdam conferences

1947 Truman Doctrine Marshall Plan – European Recovery Program

1950–5 Korean War

1957 Sputnik in space

1961 Bay of Pigs invasion in Cuba Berlin Wall built

1963 Washington–Moscow 'hotline'

1989 Berlin Wall falls

1991 Soviet Union collapses: end of the Cold War

1945 ———————————————————————— 1970 ———————— 1990

1946 Churchill's 'Iron Curtain' speech

1948–49 Berlin Blockade and Airlift

1953 Stalin dies

1960 Capture of U-2 spy plane by USSR

1962 Cuban Missile Crisis

1985 Gorbachev comes to power in USSR

1990 German unification

Political leaders in the era of the superpowers

Truman, president of the USA during the Berlin Blockade and the Korean War

Stalin, leader of the Soviet Union during the Berlin Blockade and the Korean War

Mao-Tse Tung (Mao Zedong), leader of communist China during the Korean War

Kennedy, president of the USA during the Cuban Missile Crisis

Khrushchev, leader of the Soviet Union during the Cuban Missile Crisis

Castro, leader of Cuba during the Cuban Missile Crisis

Case study 1: The Berlin blockade, 1948–49

1. After World War II, Germany was divided into four zones and Berlin was divided into four sectors.
   - These were controlled by the USA, Britain and France on one side, and the Soviet Union on the other.
2. The USA wanted to revive the German economy. They wanted a strong democratic government.
3. The Soviet Union disagreed and took reparations from their part of Germany.
4. **President Truman** of the USA wanted to use Marshall Aid funds to revive the German economy. The USA and their Allies launched a new currency – the Deutschmark.
5. **Stalin**, leader of communist Russia, cut off all road, rail and canal links to West Berlin.
6. **The Berlin Airlift**: The USA and its Allies organised **Operation Vittles** to fly supplies into Berlin.
   - Large cargo planes used three air corridors to fly into three airports in West Berlin.
   - At the peak, they were flying in every 90 seconds with 8,000 tons of goods a day.
   - The goods included food, medical supplies, petrol and coal.
7. Berlin suffered because there were shortages so rationing was used.
   - Stalin also cut electricity into West Berlin.
   - Industry suffered and 120,000 lost their jobs.
8. The spirit of the people was kept up by huge public meetings.
9. Stalin realised that he was not going to win – he wanted Truman to drop the currency or leave Berlin.
   - Stalin lifted the Blockade.

Results:

10. The USA won the first victory in the Cold War battle with the Soviet Union.
11. After the Blockade was lifted, **NATO** (North Atlantic Treaty Organisation) was formed to defend its members against potential Soviet attacks. It included the USA, Canada and ten Western European countries.
12. Germany remained **divided** until the Cold War ended in 1990.
13. Berlin remained a **source of tension** during the Cold War, especially as East Germans left their side to get work in the more prosperous West. Eventually the Soviet and East German government built the Berlin Wall.

People in History

A named leader involved in one of the crises during the rise of the superpowers (Berlin Blockade, Korean War, Cuban Missile Crisis): Truman

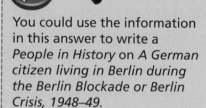

You could use the information in this answer to write a *People in History* on *A German citizen living in Berlin during the Berlin Blockade or Berlin Crisis, 1948–49.*

President Truman was a leader involved in the **Berlin Blockade**. Truman was president of the USA and he supported the **Truman Doctrine** and the **Marshall Plan** to stop the spread of communism in Europe. The Berlin Blockade was the first major test of the **Cold War**, a period of tension and hostility between the USA and the Soviet Union which lasted for 45 years.

Truman agreed to the division of Germany after World War II into four occupied zones and Berlin into four sectors controlled by the USA, Soviet Union, Britain and France. Truman used the Marshall Plan to revive the German economy. He was opposed to the Soviet Union, which wanted reparations (compensation) and took machinery from their zone. He launched a **new currency**, the Deutschmark, and this led to Stalin and the Soviet Union cutting off all road, rail and canal links from West Germany to Berlin.

Truman said he was not going to leave Berlin. Instead he decided he would supply West Berlin along three 20-mile-wide air corridors. He organised **Operation Vittles** to use large cargo planes to fly into three airports in West Berlin. They flew in food, medical supplies and drums of petrol. Planes landed every 90 seconds, bring in 8,000 tons of cargo a day at their busiest times. Truman insisted that the planes continue over the winter in spite of bad weather and harassment by Soviet planes.

Truman realised things were **very difficult** in Berlin. He knew that food was rationed, but he supported the will of the West Berliners not to give in. He knew they lived on dehydrated potatoes, and powdered milk and eggs brought in by the planes.

Stalin believed it would be impossible for Truman to keep Berlin supplied. He wanted Truman to leave Berlin or to drop his currency plans. But Truman refused to give in. Stalin saw that he could not win so in May 1949 he lifted the blockade. Truman had won the first victory of the Cold War.

As a result of the tension of the Berlin Blockade, Truman set up **NATO** (North Atlantic Treaty Organisation) with 11 other countries to defend Western Europe from attack by the Soviet Union. He and his allies set up the Federal Republic of Germany, while the Soviet Union set up the German Democratic Republic. The division of Germany lasted until the end of the Cold War.

Case study 2: The Korean War, 1950–53

1. After World War II, Korea was divided along the 38th parallel.
   - North Korea was supported by the Soviet Union.
   - South Korea was supported by the USA.
2. In 1950, North Korea invaded the South.
   - They took most of the country.
3. President Truman of the USA moved to help South Korea. He believed in a policy of containment to stop the spread of communism.
4. The United Nations organised armies from the USA and 15 other countries to help the South Koreans.
   - The UN forces led by Douglas MacArthur pushed the North Koreans back.
5. Then the communist government in China, led by **Mao Tse-Tung**, joined the war, backing North Korea.
   - They drove the UN forces down south.
6. Truman fired MacArthur because MacArthur wanted to attack China; he also proposed using the atomic bomb.
7. The war dragged on until 1953. By this time Truman had been replaced by Eisenhower as president, and Stalin had been replaced by Khrushchev.
   - Peace was agreed and both sides held onto the same border on the 38th parallel.

   Results:
8. There were 54,000 Americans soldiers killed, 400,000 South Koreans, about half a million North Koreans and between 200,000 and 500,000 Chinese.
9. America got a new ally in Japan, which helped out by supplying materials for the war.
10. The USA made alliances with other countries in order to contain communism in China.

Case study 3: The Cuban Missile Crisis, 1962

1. Fidel **Castro**, a communist leader, overthrew Batista, dictator of Cuba.
   - Castro **nationalised** American businesses and the US refused to buy sugar from Cuba.
   - Cuba got help from the Soviet Union led by **Khrushchev**.
2. President Kennedy of the USA gave the go-ahead for the **Bay of Pigs** invasion, which failed to overthrow Castro.
3. Then a **U2 spy plane** photographed Soviet missile bases being built in Cuba.
   - These bases would bring major US cities such as Washington, D.C. and New York City within the range of Soviet nuclear missiles.

4. Kennedy decided to **blockade** Cuba until the missiles were removed.
- The world was on the brink of **nuclear war**.

5. Then the USA and the Soviet Union came to an agreement.
- Khrushchev said he would dismantle the missiles in Cuba if the USA promised not to invade the island.
- Kennedy accepted this.

Results:

6. Both sides agreed that they would never risk a nuclear war again.

7. A telephone hotline was set up between Washington and Moscow so that both leaders would be in direct communication.

8. The USA and the Soviet Union agreed to sign a Nuclear Test Ban Treaty.

9. The USA dismantled missiles which it had in Turkey.

Moves towards European unity

People in History

A named leader in the movement for European unity between 1945 and 1992: Robert Schuman

Fill in the blanks using the words in the list. (Words can be used more than once)

Robert Schuman

Robert Schuman was a leader of European unity after 1945. He was born in Luxembourg but lived in _____. when he was a boy. He grew up with a strong pride in _____.

After World War II, he was prime minister of France on two occasions before he became _____ Minister.

He was afraid of a _____ Germany. He knew France had been invaded _____ times by Germany. He thought that the only way to make peace between the two countries was to unite their _____. Then France and Germany would work for a peaceful Europe.

Schuman attended the _____ Congress along with many of Europe's leading politicians, such as _____, Churchill and De Gasperi. This Congress led to the **Council of** _____. He believed Europe should be based on human _____ and fundamental freedoms. He was also involved as Foreign Minister in forming _____ (the North Atlantic Treaty Organisation) for the defence of Europe, against the threat of _____.

He was persuaded by **Jean** _____ to propose the _____ **Plan**. This plan was based on the idea that if the French and German _____ and steel industries were dependent on each other, this would lessen the chances of war between them. Schuman persuaded Adenauer, chancellor of West Germany, to support the plan. Schuman's plan led to the formation of the **European Coal and Steel Community** (_____). Six countries – France, Germany, the Netherlands, Belgium, Luxembourg and _____ – signed the Treaty of _____ in 1951. The six agreed to put all coal and steel production under a joint authority that included representatives from all six countries. For the first time in European history, these countries handed over some of their power to an outside body.

Schuman became _____ of the European Movement in 1955 to continue to promote the idea of European unity. In 1957, he supported the foundation of the European Economic Community (_____) and became president of the European Parliament. He died in 1963. He was honoured as one of the Founding _____ of European unity.

Use your textbook to check your answers when you are finished.

Adenauer	EEC	Italy	Schuman
Alsace-Lorraine	Europe	Monnet	strong
coal	Fathers	NATO	three
communism	Foreign	Paris	
economies	France	president	
ECSC	Hague	rights	

Asian nationalism after 1945 – Gandhi and Indian independence

People in History

A named leader in the struggle for African or Asian independence after 1945 – Gandhi

Fill in the blanks using the words in the list. (Words can be used more than once)

Mahatma Gandhi was a leader of Indian independence. Gandhi and the **Indian** _____ **Party** wanted independence (_____) for India from Britain. Gandhi believed in _____ **and non-cooperation** to achieve his aims. He said that Indians should make life

Mahatma Gandhi

difficult for the British by _____ British goods, schools and courts. After World War II ended in 1945, Gandhi saw that Britain was **weaker** because of the war, and that Indians were now **more**

exam focus

You are only allowed **2 marks for background information**, so when answering this question on **'after 1945'**, make sure most of your information comes from after 1945.

involved in running their own civil service and the army. By then, Gandhi was _____ old so his role in the Indian independence movement was much less important than before 1945. Gandhi was **not involved** in the main negotiations between the _____ Party, the _____ League and the British government. But _____, the leader of the party and one of the main negotiators, **consulted Gandhi** on key issues. The British government sent Lord _____ as Viceroy to India to organise Indian independence. Gandhi was **opposed** to _____ plan to end British rule. _____ believed the only way for Britain to withdraw from India was to divide the country into **two states** – one for the _____, and one for the _____ (the **partition plan**). But Gandhi wanted to maintain the unity of India and to keep _____ and _____ together. He even proposed a plan to put Muslims in charge. Nehru and the other leaders of the Congress Party realised that the only way to prevent a **Hindu–Muslim** _____ **war** was to agree to the partition plan. They persuaded Gandhi to accept the plan because they knew he had widespread support around the country. After independence, there was serious conflict between Hindus and Muslims. Gandhi went on a _____ **strike** (fast-unto-death) to try to stop the violence. He broke his fast when leaders said they would give up the violence. But a Hindu fanatic, **Nathurum** _____, shot Gandhi on 20 January 1948 because he felt that Gandhi had betrayed Hindus by agreeing to the _____ of India and Pakistan. Before this, Gandhi had refused police protection saying, 'God is my protector.' Gandhi's **methods** of non-violence had set the Indian Congress Party on the road to independence. After his death, others, such as **Martin Luther** _____, followed his methods to fight for civil rights for _____ Americans.

Use your textbook to check your answers when you are finished.

76 years	division	Mountbatten	non-violence
black	Godse	Mountbatten's	self-government
boycotting	Hindus	Muslim	
civil	hunger	Muslims	
Congress	King	Nehru	

Past questions on *International Relations in the 20th Century: Part 2 (The Options)*

Short-Answer Questions

1. Explain **one** of the following terms from *International Relations in the Twentieth Century: Peaceful co-existence; Decolonisation; Common market.*

People in History

Ordinary level

1. A **named** leader involved in **one** of the twentieth-century international events below:
   - The rise of the superpowers (The Cold War), 1945–92
   - Moves towards European unity, 1945–92
   - African or Asian nationalism, 1945–92
   - *Hints*: Name of the leader and country; Difficulties; Achievements; Influence

Higher level

1. A news reporter describing a major event during the Cold War, 1945–63

   or

   A historian describing the main events in the movement towards European Unity, 1945–92

   or

   A supporter of an independence movement in a **named** African or Asian country after 1945

2. A **named** leader involved in **one** of the crises during the rise of the superpowers (Berlin Blockade; Korean War; Cuban Missile Crisis)

   or

   A **named** leader in the struggle for African or Asian Independence after 1945

   or

   A **named** leader in the movement for European Unity between 1945 and 1992

Long-Answer Questions

1. Write an account of **one** of the following:
   (a) A **named** crisis during the Cold War, 1945–63
   (b) Events leading to European unity, 1945–73
   (c) The struggle for independence of a named African or Asian country after 1945

2. Choose topic 1 **or** 2 **or** 3 below:

Topic 1 Rise of the Superpowers

Write an account of **one** of the following crises and how it affected relations between USA and USSR:

(a) Korean War, 1950–53

(b) The Cuban Missile Crisis

Topic 2 Moves towards European Unity

Write an account of the growth of the European Union between 1973 and 1992.

Topic 3 African and Asian nationalism

In the case of a **named** African or Asian country, write an account of the challenges it faced after achieving independence in the period after 1945.

3. **Choose Topic 1 or 2 or 3 below:**

Topic 1 – Rise of the Superpowers.

(a)   (b)   (c)

Name **one** of the leaders shown above (a), (b) or (c) **and** write an account of a major crisis in the Cold War, 1945–63, in which that leader was involved.

Topic 2 – Moves towards European Unity

Name **one** important personality in the movement for greater European Unity, 1947–72, **and** write an account of that person's role in the movement.

Topic 3 – African and Asian Nationalism

Name **one** leader involved in the movement for independence in a **named** African **or** Asian country since 1945 and write an account of that leader's role in the movement.

Glossary

Abbot head of a monastery

A.D. Anno Domini; after the birth of Christ

Amphitheatre a round arena such as the Colosseum used for gladiator contests in ancient Rome

Aos Dána people with special skills in Celtic times, e.g. druids

Appeasement policy of British government in 1930s which held that if governments gave in to Hitler's small demands then a world war could be prevented

Aqueduct bridge for carrying water in ancient Rome

Archaeology the study of the past through material remains

Artefact object made by people, e.g. sword, axe

Astrolabe navigation instrument used in the Age of Exploration to find latitude

Atrium central courtyard in a Roman house

Autobiography story of a person's life written by that person

Auxiliaries ex-British army officers who were enlisted in the Royal Irish Constabulary during the War of Independence

Bailey courtyard or open space in a motte and bailey or medieval stone castle

Battle of Britain air battle between the Royal Air Force and the German Luftwaffe during World War II

Bawn walled enclosure built for defence in the Plantation of Ulster

B.C. before the birth of Christ

Biography the story of a person's life written by somebody else

Black and Tans ex-British army soldiers who were enlisted in the Royal Irish Constabulary during the War of Independence

Black Death plague caused by fleas on rats which spread in the Middle Ages

Blackshirts name given to Mussolini's Fascist followers or to Hitler's SS

Blitzkrieg lightning war tactics used by Germany in World War II, using planes, tanks and infantry

Blitz German bombing of British cities after the Battle of Britain during World War II

Bloody Sunday, 1920 a day during the War of Independence in which Michael Collins's Squad killed British spies and, in revenge, the Auxiliaries killed 12 people in Croke Park

Blueshirts originally called the Army Comrades Association, which protected Cumann na nGaedheal meetings from attack by IRA members in the 1930s

Book of Kells a manuscript copy of the Four Gospels created in early Christian Ireland

Brehon a judge in Celtic Ireland

Bronze metal made from a mixture of tin and copper

Brownshirts name given to Hitler's Stormtroopers or SA

B-Specials part-time police in Northern Ireland

Carbon dating technique used to date ancient objects by measuring the amount of carbon-14 in them

Caravel ship used by Portuguese and Spanish sailors to explore the coasts of Africa and the Americas

Catacombs underground tombs used by Christians in ancient Rome for burials and to hold masses

Cathach example of a manuscript in early Christian Ireland

Charter permission granted by kings or lords to towns to trade

Chronology the study of time and dates; putting events in order of time

Church abuses practices such as nepotism, simony, pluralism and absenteeism which were common in the Catholic Church before the Reformation

Cist burial/grave burial in a small rectangular grave

Circus Maximus arena in ancient Rome for chariot racing

Clinker-built overlapping planks of wood used in building caravels in the Age of Exploration

Cloister covered walking area in a medieval monastery for monks praying

Coffin ships name given to badly maintained ships used to transport emigrants to America during the Great Famine

Coalition government government formed by a number of political parties, usually applied to Fine Gael–Labour Party government of the 1970s

Cold War period of hostility between the USA and its allies and the Soviet Union and its allies which lasted from after World War II to the collapse of communism in the early 1990s

Collective security policy of the League of Nations that each member state was responsible for the security and safety of all other members

Colosseum arena in ancient Rome used for gladiator fighting

Communism political belief associated with Soviet Russia and holding that the state (or government) should control industry and agriculture

Conacre land rented out in Ireland for 11 months for growing potatoes or corn

Conquistadores Spanish conquerors who defeated native empires in Central and South America

Corbelling a method of building a roof where flat stones were put on top of one another

Council of Trent meeting of cardinals, bishops and the Pope held in northern Italy aimed at reforming the Catholic Church after the Reformation

Counter-Reformation efforts by the Catholic Church to reform itself and stop the spread of Protestantism

Court cairn tombs in the Neolithic period with an open entrance, an inner burial chamber and covered by a mound of stones

Craftsman skilled person trained as an apprentice during the Middle Ages, e.g. a carpenter

Crannóg artificial island dwelling used during the Iron Age

Democracy political system which holds that political power comes from the people who vote for leaders in a general election

Derbhfine royal family in Celtic society

Dig (excavation) digging up the earth in order to look for historical objects (artefacts)

Domestic system the making of goods (such as thread and cloth) in people's houses before the Industrial Revolution

Dominion status membership of the British Commonwealth agreed by Ireland in the Anglo-Irish Treaty, similar to Canada and Australia

Drawbridge bridge over a moat in a medieval castle

Druid priest in Celtic society

Dendrochronology (tree-ring dating) finding out the age of timber by studying the pattern of rings

Economic War conflict in 1930s between Ireland and Britain over land annuities where Britain imposed taxes on Irish imports and Ireland responded with taxes on British imports

Emergency name given to the period in Ireland during World War II

Enabling Act law passed by Hitler which gave him power to rule by decree

Enclosure the division of the three open fields and the common into individual farms during the Agricultural Revolution in England

Eviction when tenant farmers were thrown off the land in 19th century Ireland for failure to pay rent

Excavation (dig) digging up the earth to look for historical objects (artefacts)

Fasces symbol of axe and rods of Mussolini's Fascist Party

Fascism political belief of Mussolini in Italy and Hitler in Germany which was anti-democratic and anti-communist

Feudalism system of land ownership and government during the Middle Ages

Final Solution policy of Hitler and the Nazis of killing all Jews during World War II

File poet in Celtic society

Flying columns small units of the IRA which ambushed British forces during the War of Independence

Forum the marketplace in the city centre in ancient Rome

Fresco painting style in ancient Rome and in the Renaissance where painting is done on damp plaster

Führer (Leader) title of Hitler after he combined the office of president and chancellor

Fulacht Fiadh method of cooking in the Bronze Age using a hole filled with water and lined with flat stones

Gerrymander system of rigging the boundaries of constituencies in Northern Ireland to ensure unionist control

Gladiator a slave who a specially trained fighter in ancient Rome

Gothic style of architecture in the Middle Ages which featured pointed arches and windows

Guild a trade association in the Middle Ages for craftsmen and merchants

Hawking hunting with hawks in the Middle Ages

High Cross tall stone cross in monasteries in early Christian Ireland

Hill fort large circular forts on high ground with ditches all around ,e.g. Hill of Tara in Co Meath

History the story of the past, using evidence

Home Rule Irish nationalist policy which wanted self-government in Ireland with a parliament in Dublin dealing with internal Irish affairs

Humanism the study of the writings of ancient Greece and Rome

Il Duce (Leader) title used by Mussolini

Inquisition Catholic Church court in Italy and Spain used to try Protestants and Jews

Insula apartment block in ancient Rome

Internment the arrest and imprisonment without trial of people suspected of being involved in violence in Northern Ireland during the Troubles

Jesuits religious order founded by Ignatius Loyola to spread the teachings of the Catholic Church

Jousting fighting between knights in the Middle Ages

Justification by faith Luther's belief that only faith in God would allow a person to go to heaven

Keep tower in a medieval castle where the lord or king lived

Knight specially trained warrior in the Middle Ages

Lazybeds long ridges of land ready for growing potatoes

Lebensraum (living space) Nazi policy to use Eastern Europe and Russia to provide raw materials and workers for the Nazis

Legion a division of the army in ancient Rome, usually 5,000 soldiers

Legionary a soldier in a legion in ancient Rome

Log and line used in ships of the Age of Exploration to work out the speed of the ship

Logbook used in ships of the Age of Exploration to record events during the voyage

Luftwaffe German air force during World War II

Lunula neck ornament of the Bronze Age

Manor a village and the land around it in the Middle Ages

Manuscript a hand-written book

March on Rome Mussolini's plan to march Fascist groups on Rome to demand members in government, led to him becoming prime minister

Medieval society life and how it was lived in the Middle Ages

Megalith large stone

Mesolithic the Middle Stone Age

Middlemen a person in 19th century Ireland who rented land from a landlord and then rented out that land to farmers

Mother and Child Scheme public health scheme of First Inter-Party government which planned to give free medical aid to mothers and to children under age 16

Motte and bailey castle built of timber in the Middle Ages, with a mound and a courtyard

Moat trench filled with water around a medieval castle

Neolithic New Stone Age

Neutrality policy of Irish government during World War II not to take part in the war

Night of the Broken Glass (*Kristallnacht*) night when Hitler's SA attacked Jews, their shops and synagogues after a Polish Jew killed a German diplomat in Paris

Night of the Long Knives night when Hitler used the SS to arrest and kill leaders of the SA, including Röhm, because they threatened his leadership

Nuremberg Laws Nazi laws against the Jews, which deprived them of German citizenship, banned marriages with non-Jews and forced them to wear the Star of David

Ogham standing stone with ogham script on it

Operation Barbarossa German battle plan for the invasion of Soviet Russia during World War II

Operation Overlord code name for Allied plan to invade France during World War II

Oral sources interviews or tape recordings of people's memories of events

Oratory a church

Panzer German tank during World War II

Passage tomb/grave a tomb with a passage that leads to one or more burial chambers, covered by a mound of stones or earth (e.g. Newgrange)

Patron supporter of the artists during the Renaissance

Penal laws laws passed in 17th- and 18th-century Ireland to control and discriminate against Catholics and Presbyterians

Perspective technique used by artists in the Renaissance to create the illusion of depth (3D effect)

Pillory a timber frame where people punished in the Middle Ages had to place their hands and head

Plantation policy of the English government to bring in English and Scottish planters to Ireland

Portolan charts earliest maps used during the Age of Exploration which showed places along the coast joined by straight lines

Portcullis iron-and-timber grill at the entrance to a castle, for defence

Portal tomb/dolmen tombs made of huge upright stones with a giant capstone on top

Page first stage in the training of a knight in the Middle Ages

Pollen produced by plants; analysis of pollen found in ancient sites helps archaeologists to find out what plants were growing at the time, when forests were cleared and when farming spread

Primary sources sources which come directly from the time that is being studied (e.g. weapons, tools, paintings, letters)

Promontory fort fort built on a headland

Propaganda use of information to influence opinions of people to ensure power

Quadrant navigation instrument used in the Age of Exploration to find latitude

Reformation a movement that protested against abuses in the Catholic Church and led to the establishment of the Protestant churches.

RAF Royal Air Force (British Air Force)

Rationing use of coupons and ration books to control the amount of food, clothes, footwear and petrol given to each person during the Emergency (World War II) in Ireland (also in Britain and Germany)

Refectory dining room in a monastery in early Christian Ireland or in a medieval monastery

Renaissance time of revival of interest in learning of ancient Greece and Rome, begun in Italy

Republicanism political belief in Ireland which wanted complete independence from Britain and to establish a republic (a government without a monarch), by physical force (rebellion)

Rí king in Celtic society

Ring fort A farmstead surrounded by one or more banks of earth and ditches

Romanesque type of architecture in the Middle Ages which followed the style of ancient Rome

Round tower tall tower built in monasteries in early Christian Ireland for safety

Rule by decree situation in which rulers such as Mussolini and Hitler make laws without the need to ask for them in parliament

Sanctuary protection given by monasteries to people who were threatened with arrest or violence

Scorched-earth policy war tactic used by the Soviet soldiers during World War II of burning crops and destroying bridges and towns as they retreated before the Germans

Scriptorium the manuscript room in a monastery in early Christian Ireland or in a medieval monastery

Secondary sources sources which come from after the time which is being studied (e.g. a history book)

Serf A peasant who worked the land for a lord in the Middle Ages

Servitors English soldiers and officials who were granted land in the Plantation of Ulster

Sfumato painting technique associated with Leonardo da Vinci which used blended colours

Shannon Scheme Cumann na nGaedheal government plan in the 1920s to build hydroelectric scheme on the Shannon

Socialism political belief which favours state (government) control of industry and agriculture

Souterrain underground passage or storage area in a ring fort

Spices used to give flavour to food, brought from the Spice Islands

Squad group of IRA volunteers formed by Michael Collins to kill British spies and others during the War of Independence

Statute of Westminster law passed by British government which gave power to Commonwealth countries, including Ireland, to change any laws passed by the British government for that country

Stola long dress worn by women in ancient Rome

Stone circle standing stones arranged in a circle

Stratigraphy a method of dating objects where the oldest layers are at the bottom and the youngest layers are at the top

Swastika Nazi symbol taking the form of a crooked cross

Tánaiste next in line to be Taoiseach in a Gaelic clan

Taoiseach another name for a king or rí in ancient Ireland

Toga a long robe for men in ancient Rome

Torc a circular neck ring used by the Celts

Tuath kingdom in Celtic society

Tunic short garment worn by men and women in ancient Rome

U-boat German submarine

Undertakers English planters who received land during the Plantation of Munster, or English and Scottish planters who received land during the Plantation of Ulster

Ulster Solemn League and Covenant declaration of Ulster unionists to resist Home Rule by all means, signed by over 200,000 people

Unionism political belief which held that Ireland's union with Britain must be retained and that Parliament in Westminster should continue to make laws for Ireland

Vassal person who has been granted land by a lord in the Middle Ages

Vernacular the language of the people

Villa a country house or estate in ancient Rome

Visual sources photographs, paintings

Wattle and daub interwoven sticks covered by mud and used to make walls

Wedge tomb tomb with large flat stones, some at the side acting as walls, and large capstones on top; wedge-shaped in design

Workhouse a place where poor people can live if they have no recourses; used in 19th-century Ireland (and England)

SATs Skills

Reading Comprehension Workbook

9–10 years

OXFORD

UNIVERSITY PRESS

Different types of question

You will find several different types of questions in this book:

- short answers which need one word or a few words
- several line answers which need one or two sentences
- longer answers where you need to explain in more detail, give several points and use evidence from the text.

Some questions have multiple choice answers which may need ticking or circling. For some questions you may need to draw lines or complete a table.

Tips: Always look at the number of marks available and the amount of space provided for your answer. Use this as a guide to know how much to write.

If the question asks for evidence, make sure you include some short, relevant quotations from the text which help support your point.

Always use the text for evidence; do not rely on the pictures.

OXFORD
UNIVERSITY PRESS

Great Clarendon Street, Oxford, OX2 6DP, United Kingdom

Oxford University Press is a department of the University of Oxford. It furthers the University's objective of excellence in research, scholarship, and education by publishing worldwide. Oxford is a registered trade mark of Oxford University Press in the UK and in certain other countries

Text © Oxford University Press 2017

Author: Michellejoy Hughes
The moral rights of the author have been asserted

First published in 2017

British Library Cataloguing in Publication Data
Data available

978-0-19-274959-8

10 9 8 7 6 5 4 3 2

Paper used in the production of this book is a natural, recyclable product made from wood grown in sustainable forests. The manufacturing process conforms to the environmental regulations of the country of origin.

Printed in China

Acknowledgements

Cover illustration: Lo Cole
Page make-up and illustrations by Aptara

Although we have made every effort to trace and contact all copyright holders before publication this has not been possible in all cases. If notified, the publisher will rectify any errors or omissions at the earliest opportunity.

Links to third party websites are provided by Oxford in good faith and for information only. Oxford disclaims any responsibility for the materials contained in any third party website referenced in this work.

Cactus Garden

Read the text below and answer the questions that follow.

Estanislao Gonzáles Ferrer was a plant expert, called a botanist, who collected lots of cactus plants from different parts of the world. He gave his collection to the famous artist, architect and environmentalist César Manrique (born in 1919) who created the cactus park in Lanzarote. The park is set inside an old, circular quarry, which is a deep pit like a mine where rock, stone or other material has been taken 5 from. The park has an upper and lower layer around the perimeter to show the plants at their best. There are over 10 000 plants on show with over 1000 different species covering a huge variety of colour, size, shape and country of origin. As Lanzarote is a volcanic island belonging to Spain with no rivers, streams or lakes, the cactus plants are ideal as they require so little water and they can store the 10 water they do need in their fleshy, thick body or leaves. This means that cacti (the word for more than one cactus) can survive in very dry places.

The cactus park is a miniature world of peace and calm where little lizards run freely and the only noise is from the gentle chatter of visitors as they sit under the shade in the small café. The cactus garden took 20 years to perfect and was completed in 15 1990. Manrique himself died just two years after completing the park.

For a wonderful experience, the Jardín de Cactus is somewhere that everyone should visit at least once in their life. You would be amazed at how beautiful a cactus garden can be. Until then, there are some fantastic photographs of the park online. 20

Did you know...?

Cactus plants have spines that do a range of important jobs:

1 They provide protection to stop the plant being eaten by animals.

2 They help the cactus to remain camouflaged.

3 They help to create water by trapping air around the surface of the cactus.

4 They can reduce the loss of water by providing shade for the cactus which 25 lowers the temperature of the plant.

Ⓐ How did Ferrer help César Manrique? [1]

_____

_____

_____

_____

Ⓑ What shape is the cactus park? [1]

_____

Ⓒ *The park has an upper and lower layer around the **perimeter** to show the plants at their best.*

Tick the word below which is closest in meaning to the word *perimeter* in this sentence.
Tick **one**. [1]

centre ☐

area ☐

edge ☐

top ☐

Ⓓ *He **gave** his collection to the famous artist, architect and environmentalist César Manrique*

Which word below could be used to replace the word *gave* in this sentence?
Tick **one**. [1]

stole ☐

donated ☐

sold ☐

bought ☐

(E) Use a line to join the dates to the events. [1]

César Manrique dies	1919
The Jardín de Cactus is completed	1970
César Manrique is born	1990
The creation of the Jardín de Cactus is begun	1992

(F) Why are cactus plants well-suited to Lanzarote? [2]

_____

_____

_____

(G) Find and copy a group of **nine** words that shows how someone can see the cactus park without having to visit Lanzarote. [1]

_____

(H) Tick the following statements to show whether they are **true** or **false**. [1]

	True	False
César Manrique cared about the environment.		
Lanzarote belongs to Canada.		
There are beautiful lakes on Lanzarote.		
The spines on cactus plants help the plant's survival.		

5

ⓘ Look again at the 'Did you know…?' text and find the sentence: *They help the cactus to remain* **camouflaged**

Tick the word below which is closest in meaning to the word *camouflaged* in this sentence. Tick **one**. [1]

safe ☐

vulnerable ☐

protected ☐

disguised ☐

Ⓙ How is the cactus park described as a quiet place?

Find and copy **three** words or short phrases. [1]

_____

_____

_____

Ⓚ Give **two** reasons why the author thinks that everyone should visit the cactus park. [2]

_____

_____

_____

_____

Ⓛ *There are over 10 000 plants on show with over 1000 different* **species** *covering a huge variety of colour, size, shape and country of origin.*

Tick the word below which is closest in meaning to the word *species* in this sentence. Tick **one**. [1]

types ☐

animals ☐

trees ☐

special ☐

5

Secret Signs

Read the text below and answer the questions that follow.

Jess walked along the path through the woods searching for clues. She had first seen the three sticks lying neatly next to each other with the middle stick pointing towards a path and this had been followed with another three sticks pointing to this path. Parts of the woods were light and bright where missing trees gave the sunshine chance to penetrate, but this section of the woods was 5 densely planted and in full leaf. There was still enough light to see around her, but Jess could no longer see too far ahead. She didn't know how far this path would take her but at that moment, she spotted a pair of crossed sticks. Her heart raced a little as she stood still but turned her head slowly around until she saw a mark in the ground. A circle, two lines crossed inside it and three squares 10 to the right hand side of it. Jess knew exactly what this meant. She left the path and counted three trees to the right of her and then two trees behind this tree. At the base of this final tree she crouched down and found a piece of paper folded into a tiny square and wrapped in a see-through sandwich bag and stuck with sticky-tape to the tree... 15

Four children huddled around the bench at the bottom of Grace's garden.

"What about Jess?" asked James. He had been the first to return with his piece of paper, but they had now all been back for ages.

"It's been three hours now," said Grace checking her watch and glancing up the garden path, but Jess was not there. 20

"I don't like this at all," said Tom who was nervously nibbling the skin around his bitten fingernails. "I think we should tell her dad."

The four children looked at each other and slowly nodded in agreement.

"OK, come on then," said Megan. "But..." she began until a noise stopped her. The children all turned their heads towards the house and breathed in relief as Jess 25 jogged up the garden path and flopped on the ground beside them. Jess had a red face and her fringe stuck to her forehead. She looked so tired and was struggling to bring her breathing down to normal. After a few minutes, she was able to speak.

"I have the paper, but it was so far to go and it took ages to find it. I just hope it makes sense." 30

She fished the paper from her jacket pocket and smoothed it out as the other children put their pieces of paper on the ground. They all stared at the pieces until they could put them in order, like a jigsaw that didn't make sense until all of the paper pieces were put into the right place. 35

"Oh wow!" began Tom. "This is a map of the old allotment plots on Hollybank Lane. Look, there is the bus stop and that is the entrance next to the church."

Grace said, "Yeah, I think you're right Tom, but the allotment gates are massive and always locked. How can we get in?"

"Ah!" said James. "Mimi has a key as she has the plot that Grandpa used to have. I could ask when she is next there and she could let us in." 40

The children all nodded enthusiastically.

"Do we know how to solve these strange clues?" asked Megan.

"Well..." said Jess, "they look like the symbols that we found in the first letter. Who has the first letter?" 45

"I do," replied James. "I'll bring it with me next time." He looked at his watch. "I have to go – Mum will be worried. Are we meeting here tomorrow morning?"

They all nodded. Today had been a difficult and tiring day, but they were now one huge step closer to solving the mystery...

Ⓐ Why is Jess in the woods?

Give **two** reasons. [2]

_____

_____

_____

_____

2

(B) *this section of the woods was **densely** planted*

Tick the word below which is closest in meaning to the word *densely* in this sentence. Tick **one**. [1]

daintily ☐

thickly ☐

stupidly ☐

surprisingly ☐

(c) What are the names of the five children in the story? [1]

_____

_____

(D) According to the text, how does Tom feel and how do you know? [2]

_____

_____

_____

_____

(E) Find and copy a group of **three** words that shows what all of the children do when they first see Jess. [1]

_____

(F) When Jess appears in the garden, how does she look and why might she look like this? [2]

_____

_____

_____

_____

7

(G) *She **fished** the paper from her jacket pocket*

Tick the word below which is closest in meaning to the word *fished* in this sentence. Tick **one**. [1]

returned ☐   replied ☐

retrieved ☐   refused ☐

(H) Tick the following statements to show whether they are **true** or **false**. [1]

	True	False
The allotment is locked.		
Jess has a jigsaw puzzle in her jacket pocket.		
The story is set in the winter.		
There is a church near to the allotment plots.		

(I) *Jess jogged up the garden path and **flopped** on the ground beside them.*

Which word below could be used to replace the word *flopped* in this sentence?
Tick **one**. [1]

jumped ☐   back-flipped ☐

perched ☐   collapsed ☐

(J) Find **two** examples in the text that explain why the title is 'Secret Signs'. [2]

_____

_____

_____

_____

(K) Look at the last sentence. Why has the author not ended the sentence with one full stop? [2]

_____

_____

_____

7

PLUTO

Read the text below and answer the questions that follow.

Dear Sir,

I am writing in reference to codename PLUTO. As requested, here are the details of the operation to date. As confidentiality is of the utmost importance, I trust that this letter will be destroyed once the information has been understood. We have a coded message in our files and no other information has been kept. Naturally, staff are informed strictly on a 'need to know' basis.

5

Operation Overlord is due to take place with the Allied invasion of Normandy. Arthur Hartley, our chief engineer, has recognised the immense amount of fuel that we will need for the invasion. Oil tankers in the English Channel are never going to be able to supply enough fuel, especially with enemy action taking place. Hartley needs to create a safe pipeline for the fuel and he has suggested that we lay 1609 kilometres of pipework, which we can lay at night, to transport fuel from the ports of Liverpool and Bristol under the ocean, which can reach as far as the Rhine allowing the Allied troops to push forward as far as necessary.

10

We have considered that, at first, we might not be able to transport as much fuel as we should like until we can iron out any potential problems. Once we have done this, we are reasonably optimistic that we could pump as much as 4000 tons of fuel every day to where it is most needed. The prototype pipeline would be around 7 cm in diameter and made of flexible steel. Engineers who have developed the design have looked at how cotton thread is wrapped around a cotton reel and think that piping could be wrapped around a large drum then unwrapped as far as it is needed. In June we will be laying lengths of cable in the River Clyde and then some pipe will be loaded on board HMS Holdfast – a ship that will perform a rehearsal of Operation PLUTO. We hope to lay pipes across the Bristol Channel to connect Ilfracombe and Swansea. We will then be able to roll out the operation in full.

15

20

25

It is anticipated that we will have pipes from the Isle of Wight to Cherbourg and from Dungeness to Pas-de-Calais. We will store the pumps in buildings that will be disguised as either houses, garages or shops. Pipes will then run under the River Mersey, underground until they reach the Isle of Wight and beyond. The people of England and Wales will have no idea that beneath them will lie a long snake of pipes carrying the fuel and as long as the pipes are laid deep enough, they should be less at risk from enemy attack.

30

We believe that we can successfully run the D-Day Landings with this plan and although this is an ambitious scheme, we are confident that it can be done. The sooner we can end this appalling war, the better — and tanks, planes and all machinery need fuel. This part of the war effort should provide a quick and successful outcome.

35

(A) What do you think Operation PLUTO stands for? [1]
Tick **one**.

Place Lines Until The Operation ☐

Pipeline Under The Ocean ☐

Push Lead Up The Opposition ☐

Petrol Links UK To Overseas ☐

(B) *until we can iron out any **potential** problems*

Tick the word below which is closest in meaning to the word *potential* in this sentence.
Tick **one**. [1]

possible ☐

important ☐

insignificant ☐

dramatic ☐

(C) Find **three** examples in the text that tell you this letter was secret. [3]

_____

_____

_____

(D) Who was the chief engineer on the operation? [1]

_____

6

Ⓔ According to the text, why might it not be possible to pipe as much fuel in the early days? Tick **one**. [1]

A larger size pipe might need to be manufactured. ☐

The flexible steel might break. ☐

There might be issues that need to be solved first. ☐

The cost of the operation might be too expensive. ☐

Ⓕ Which of these drawings best represents the piping?
Tick **one**. [1]

☐

☐

☐

☐

Ⓖ Tick the following statements to show whether they are **true** or **false**. [1]

	True	False
HMS Holdfast is a ship.		
Pipes will connect Cherbourg to Dungeness.		
The prototype pipeline will be around 7 mm in diameter.		
Operation Overlord is connected to the Allied invasion of Normandy.		

Ⓗ *The sooner we can end this **appalling** war the better*

Tick the word below which is closest in meaning to the word *appalling* in this sentence.
Tick **one**. [1]

expensive ☐ poor ☐

appealing ☐ dreadful ☐

4

(I) Why will the pipes be less at risk from enemy attack? [1]

_____

_____ 5

(J) Why is fuel needed for Operation Overlord? [1]

_____

_____

(K) Do you think the pumps will be attacked by the enemy?
Circle **one**. [2]

Yes   No   Maybe

Give **two** reasons from the text which support your answer.

_____

_____

_____

(L) Below are some summaries of different paragraphs from the text.

Number them from 1 to 5 to show the order in which they appear in the text. [1]

The end of the war is in sight.   _____

A rehearsal is suggested.   _____

England and Wales will have pipes underground.   _____

Secrecy is everything.   _____

A solution is recognised.   _____

Cookies

Read the text below and answer the questions that follow.

Cookies and biscuits make a delicious treat, but buying them from a shop means that they might be full of additives, contain too much sugar, salt or fat and it is easy to eat too many of them. There is nothing nicer than baking your own batch of cookies and being able to make them exactly to your own taste. In fact, why not make your own recipe book with notes to help you remember what recipes work well and which additional ingredients you have tried using?

These cookies are perhaps more like a cross between a cake and a cookie. They are softly baked and are ideal for people who are gluten-intolerant as they have no flour in them. Porridge oats are an excellent source of fibre and help reduce cholesterol. Coconut provides lots of nutrients and fibre to keep our bodies healthy and it provides a natural sweetness, but as it is high in saturated fat, there isn't too much in this recipe. The recipe can be easily varied – there are some ideas at the end. Even better, you can place one or two cookies in a sandwich bag or freezer tub to freeze once they have been baked and cooled. They will defrost in a couple of hours so you can eat just as many as you want. Otherwise, a batch will store in a biscuit tin or container for a week, if they last long enough!

Coconut Oat Cookies

Ingredients:

50 g butter or coconut oil
40 g sugar
1 egg lightly whisked
200 g porridge oats
150 g desiccated coconut

Method:

1. Ask an adult to help you preheat the oven to 160° / Gas Mark 3.

2. Put all of the ingredients in a bowl together and stir well.

3. Place a heaped teaspoonful on to a non-stick baking sheet or well-greased baking tray.

4. Bake them for 10 minutes before checking them every 5 minutes until they are golden. Always get an adult to help you take trays in and out of the oven.

Variations:

- If you use finely ground oats, or even oat flour, the cookies will be smoother; using chunky or jumbo porridge oats will make them crumblier.

- You can flatten the cookies or leave them lumpier for a more rugged look.

- You can vary the flavour of these cookies by adding $\frac{1}{2}$ teaspoon of cinnamon, ginger or mixed spice at stage 2.

- You could add finely chopped cherries, dates, or some sultanas, currants or chopped nuts at stage 2. Some chopped or flaked almonds or unsalted peanuts are especially tasty.

- You could add some chocolate chunks at stage 2 or place a chocolate button on the top of each cookie at the end of stage 3.

Ⓐ What does the text suggest are the problems with buying cookies from a shop? Tick **two**. [2]

They are more expensive than baking your own. ☐

They might be full of additives. ☐

There is an excess of packaging to have to throw away. ☐

They might contain too much sugar, salt or fat. ☐

They are never as tasty as home-baked cookies. ☐

Ⓑ Explain why having your own recipe book is useful.

Find **two** reasons. [2]

_____

_____

_____

_____

C Tick the following statements to show whether they are **true** or **false**. [1]

	True	False
Flour can contain gluten.		
Porridge oats are high in fibre.		
Coconut is low in saturated fat.		
You could use less sugar if you use coconut in a recipe.		

D Find and copy **one** word used in the text to mean 'beaten'. [1]

_____

E Using the information in the text, circle the correct option to complete each sentence below. [4]

To make a crumblier cookie, you need to use oats that are...

smaller   larger   wetter   drier

The cookies will need to cook for...

at least 10 minutes   up to 10 minutes

under 10 minutes   exactly 10 minutes

Any nuts can be used for variety such as....

whole almonds and salted peanuts   flaked almonds and whole peanuts

chopped almonds and flaked peanuts   flaked almonds and unsalted peanuts

The cookies could be baked on...

a lightly oiled baking tray   a heavily greased pudding bowl

a non-stick baking sheet   an extra-large baking tray

6

(F) *or leave them lumpier for a more* **rugged** *look*

Tick the word below which is closest in meaning to the word *rugged* in this sentence.
Tick **one**. [1]

craggy ☐

silky ☐

square ☐

dense ☐

(G) Explain why an adult is needed to help to make the cookies. [1]

_____

_____

(H) Freezing the cookies allows you to eat as many as you want at a time. What other benefit of freezing the cookies can you think of? [1]

_____

_____

(I) Find and copy a **seven**-word phrase that shows that cookies should not be eaten every day. [1]

_____

_____

(J) What is meant by the phrase *if they last long enough*?
Tick **one**. [1]

The recipe doesn't make many cookies. ☐

They are delicious and will be eaten quickly. ☐

They begin to go stale or mouldy. ☐

They begin to break into crumbs. ☐

5

Hopituh Shi-nu-mu

Read the text below and answer the questions that follow.

It is another beautiful day. Sitting here it is easy to praise Masau-u, the
ancient Creator who has power over seeds and crops. It is also sad that
our old ways are being replaced with new ways, like the tiny plant that
we grow: it swells, provides us with the corn, then the old plant withers
and dies. My parents and grandparents sat here looking out at the huge   5
expanse of land, but I must take you back to the beginning...

My name is Kay and I am from the village of Moencopi, but myself, my
parents and many generations before were all born in Oraibi. These are
villages in northeast Arizona, America. There are twelve villages in the
Hopi area, but the old Oraibi was split and my people moved to Hotevilla   10
and then to Moencopi. My people settled in Moencopi, which means
'Place of the Stream that is Flowing', in 1906, but of course I was only
two years old then. Our village is divided into two communities and I live
in the lower village. My parents and grandparents are no longer living
and I am now old myself. My family talked of old Oraibi and what a   15
wonderful place it was. We had lots of chiefs who had responsible tasks
to do. We had a crier chief, a war chief, a village chief, a sun chief – so
many people to keep our village running smoothly.

We are all Hopi people – it is short for Hopituh Shi-nu-mu which means
'The Peaceful People' as that is how we were. We were happy to be   20
peaceful with our neighbours and to be left to follow our own culture,
our religion, our language and our ways of life. In our society we
believed that everyone and everything that has life is related. We show
gratefulness to the sun for warmth, for the clouds that bring rain, to the
corn that feeds us. We greet every stranger as a brother or sister and we   25
respect all. We keep our minds and souls free of evil thoughts and deeds.

Our clans are headed by women and when a baby is born, all of the
women in the family name the new baby and then our parents choose
their favourite. My parents tended the land like most of our friends
and family. Agriculture is so important to us. We grow squash, melons,   30
beans and, of course, corn. We are known for our basket-making, weaving,

> pottery making, carving and silver jewellery work. We are artistic in our heart and soul. In addition to making our art, we keep all of the old rituals. We have the Snake and Antelope priests who perform our Kachina rites and they anchor our traditional ways.
>
> 35

(A) What is *Masau-u*? [1]

_____

(B) Find and copy a **two**-word phrase that shows the land is vast. [1]

_____

(C) In what year was Kay born? [1]

_____

(D) What does the name Moencopi mean? [1]

_____

(E) *so many people to keep our village running* **smoothly**

Tick the word below which is closest in meaning to the word *smoothly* in this sentence. Tick **one**. [1]

slippery ☐

greasily ☐

awkwardly ☐

effortlessly ☐

5

(F) Complete the sentences below. [4]

The types of food the Hopi people grow are:

_____

The villages Kay's people lived at are:

_____

The types of chiefs from Oraibi were:

_____

The types of artwork Hopi people make are:

_____

(G) Find and copy **one** sentence that shows how Hopi babies are named. [1]

_____

_____

_____

(H) Look again at the last paragraph.

Which **one** word is used to mean 'farming'? [1]

_____

(I) Why is Kay sad? [1]

_____

(J) Find and copy **one** sentence that shows how the Hopi people were naturally creative. [1]

_____

_____

8

Unit 5

(K) *We keep our minds and souls free of evil thoughts and* **deeds**

Tick the word below which is closest in meaning to the word *deeds* in this sentence.
Tick **one**. [1]

promises ☐

omens ☐

actions ☐

deaths ☐

(L) Place the following words into the correct space: [1]

clouds   culture   related   respect   warmth

The Hopi people wanted to be left so that they could follow their own _____.

They greeted strangers with _____ and believed that all living things

were _____ to each other. They were grateful for the sun

that brought them _____ and the _____ that brought them rain.

(M) *My parents* **tended** *the land like most of our friends and family.*

Tick the word below which is closest in meaning to the word *tended* in this sentence.
Tick **one**. [1]

neglected ☐

managed ☐

softened ☐

built on ☐

3

Answers

Unit 1

(A) Ferrer gave his cactus collection to César Manrique. [1]

(B) Circular / round [1]

(C) edge [1]

(D) donated [1]

(E) All correctly matched for 1 mark: César Manrique dies = 1992 / The Jardín de Cactus is completed = 1990 / César Manrique is born = 1919 / The creation of the Jardín de Cactus is begun = 1970. [1]

(F) 1 mark each for any two: Cactus plants do not need much water / They can store water in their thick, fleshy stems / Lanzarote has no water other than the sea. [2]

(G) *There are some fantastic photographs of the park online* [1]

(H) All correct for 1 mark: True, False, False, True [1]

(I) disguised [1]

(J) All correct for 1 mark (in any order): *peace / calm / gentle chatter* [1]

(K) 1 mark for each: The cactus park is a *wonderful experience* / It is a *beautiful* place. [2]

(L) type [1]

Unit 2

(A) 1 mark each for any two: Jess is searching for clues / Jess is following secret signs / Jess is looking for a piece of paper. [2]

(B) thickly [1]

(C) All correct for 1 mark (in any order): Jess, Grace, James, Tom, Megan. [1]

(D) 1 mark for each: Tom is nervous / He is *nervously nibbling the skin around his bitten fingernails*. [2]

(E) *breathed in relief* [1]

(F) 1 mark for any one: *Jess had a red face* / Her fringe was *stuck to her forehead* / She looked *tired* / She was struggling to breathe normally. 1 mark for any one: Jess had been rushing around / Jess had been hurrying / Jess had been running. [2]

(G) retrieved [1]

(H) All correct for 1 mark: True, False, False, True [1]

(I) collapsed [1]

(J) 1 mark each for any two: Jess was *searching for clues* / She had found a series of sticks / She saw a *mark in the ground* / The children each had a part of a secret map / Megan referred to solving *strange clues* / The story ends with the words *solving the mystery*. [2]

(K) 1 mark each: The three dots (ellipsis) are used to show the reader that this isn't the end of the story / It suggests suspense. [2]

Unit 3

(A) Pipeline Under The Ocean [1]

(B) possible [1]

(C) 1 mark each for any three: The operation is using a codename / *As confidentiality is of the utmost importance* / *I trust that this letter can be destroyed* / *We have a coded message in our files* / *no other information has been kept* / *staff are informed strictly on a 'need to know' basis*. [3]

(D) Arthur Hartley [1]

(E) There might be issues that need to be solved first *(until we can iron out any potential problems)*. [1]

(F) The drawing looking like a large cotton reel is correct, showing that *piping could be wrapped around a large drum then unwrapped as far as it is needed*. [1]

(G) All correct for 1 mark: True, False, False, True [1]

(H) dreadful [1]

(I) The pipes will be laid deep enough under the ocean and underneath England so as not to be accessible. [1]

(J) Tanks, planes and all machinery need fuel. [1]

(K) 1 mark each for any two to support whichever answer is chosen:

Yes: Because there is enemy fire / Because there is a wartime situation / Because the operation is risky.

No: Because the pump houses would be disguised as other buildings / Because the pumps would not be noticeable.

Maybe: Because there is enemy fire / Because there is a wartime situation / Because the operation is risky / Because the pump houses would be disguised as other buildings / Because the pumps would not be noticeable. [2]

(L) All in the correct order for 1 mark: 1: Secrecy is everything / 2: A solution is recognised / 3: A rehearsal is suggested / 4: England and Wales will have pipes underneath them / 5: The end of the war is in sight. [1]

Unit 4

(A) 1 mark for each: They might be full of additives / They might contain too much sugar, salt or fat. [2]

(B) 1 mark each for any two: You can make notes / You can remind yourself which recipes worked well / You can write which additional ingredients you have tried / You can use it to make the same recipe in the future / You can use it to help make the recipe more to your own taste. [2]

(C) All correct for 1 mark: True, True, False, True [1]

(D) whisked [1]

(E) 1 mark for each: larger / at least 10 minutes / flaked almonds and unsalted peanuts / a non-stick baking sheet. [4]

(F) craggy [1]

(G) Answer should include a reference to ovens being hot. [1]

(H) 1 mark for any suitable answer such as: There are always cookies ready to eat / They don't take long to defrost / You can make batches of different flavours / You can bake in advance for special occasions / You could buy the ingredients when they are reduced in price and bake cookies for future occasions / There is no need to buy packs of biscuits. [1]

(I) *Cookies and biscuits make a delicious treat.* [1]

(J) They are delicious and will be eaten quickly. [1]

Unit 5

(A) *The ancient Creator* [1]

(B) *huge expanse* [1]

(C) Kay was born in 1904 (in 1906 she was 2 years old). [1]

(D) *Place of the Stream that is Flowing* [1]

(E) effortlessly [1]

(F) 1 mark for each: squash, melons, beans, corn / Oraibi, Hotevilla, Moencopi / crier, war, village, sun / basket-making, weaving, pottery, carving, silver jewellery. [4]

(G) *Our clans are headed by women and when a baby is born, all of the women in the family name the new baby and then our parents choose their favourite.* [1]

(H) *Agriculture* [1]

(I) Kay is sad because the old ways are being replaced with the new ways. [1]

(J) 1 mark for any one: *We are known for our basket-making, weaving, pottery making, carving and silver jewellery work / We are artistic in our heart and soul*. [1]

(K) actions [1]

(L) All correct for 1 mark: The Hopi people wanted to be left so that they could follow their own <u>culture</u>. They greeted strangers with <u>respect</u> and believed that all living things were <u>related</u> to each other. They were grateful for the sun that brought them <u>warmth</u> and the <u>clouds</u> that brought them rain. [1]

(M) managed [1]

Unit 6

(A) 1 mark for any one: *The beaches are clean and truly beautiful and the huge range of lagoons, caves and gentle bays make it ideal for families / It is a mountainous country with huge snow-tipped mountain ranges, but the lakes, natural springs and beaches will have something for every holidaymaker.* [1]

(B) The woods in the Llogara National Park. [1]

(C) There is a tremendous amount of birds, fish and mammals with over 90 endangered species. [1]

(D) The Rozafa Castle in Shkodra. [1]

(E) All correct for 1 mark: False, True, True, False [1]

(F) tasty [1]

(G) All correctly matched for 1 mark: Apollonia = interesting place to discover a Greek built city / Llogara = ideal for walkers / Tirana = great for historic artefacts / Shkodra = perfect for exploring the castle / Butrint = good for wandering around an ancient ruined city. [1]

(H) 1 mark for each: byrek / dollma / cannoli. [3]

(I) All correct for 1 mark: Fact, Fact, Opinion, Opinion [1]

(J) amazing [1]

(K) *archaeological artefacts* [1]

(L) 1 mark each for any two: To see the best time for visiting Albania / To see the difference between the minimum and maximum temperature / To see how the weather changes over the year. [2]

Unit 7

(A) All correct for 1 mark: *sauntering* / *slinks* / *darts* [1]

(B) neighbourhood [1]

(C) 1 mark for any one: *Not every night, but quite often* / *But tonight is different.* [1]

(D) 1 mark for any suitable answer such as: The fox is happy / The fox is alert / The fox looks healthy / The fox is sniffing for food / The fox is comfortable in his surroundings. [1]

(E) 1 mark each for any three: There is a *hawthorn tree* in the garden / There is *shrubbery that skirts around the house* / *To the right of [the] tree is the path to the woods* / Part of the garden is not lit up by the streetlight / Part of the garden is private / The garden can be seen by the poet. [3]

(F) All correct for 1 mark: True, False, False, True [1]

(G) The poet expects the worst – that the fox has been killed/hit by the car. [1]

(H) 1 mark each for any two: It is dark so she cannot see well / She is elderly and may not have perfect eyesight / She sees the colour ginger and assumes it is a cat / She has heard a sound in the shrubbery and assumes it is a cat / The fox is so near the house that the lady assumes it is a pet cat. [2]

(I) All correct for 1 mark: The fox scratches like *a thoughtful old man* / The fox stretches like *an athlete warming up* / The fox is seen as *a bold explorer*. [1]

(J) 1 mark each for any two: The car has had a near accident which has shaken or upset the driver / The driver doesn't want to hit the fox if he darts out into the road / The driver is looking out for the fox. [2]

(K) The fox lived (he is called a *survivor* and we know that he was hiding under a car). [1]

Unit 8

(A) 1 mark each for any two: They *design a building that looks better than others* / They design *in an amazing new way* / They *use materials in a revolutionary way*. [2]

(B) A building that is *important and specially protected*. [1]

(C) All correct for 1 mark: Carl Bernard Bartels and James Doulton [1]

(D) All correctly matched for 1 mark: W. Aubrey Thomas dies = 1934 / The Tower Building is completed = 1908 / The Royal Liver Building is completed = 1911 / W. Aubrey Thomas is born = 1859 [1]

(E) All correct for 1 mark: True, False, False, True [1]

(F) *hard and durable* [1]

(G) The Royal Liver Friendly Society [1]

(H) *legend* [1]

(I) 1 mark for each: copper / glazed terracotta / reinforced concrete / granite [4]

(J) maritime [1]

(K) He included turrets on the building. [1]

Unit 9

(A) On the Lido deck. [1]

(B) All correct for 1 mark: life jacket / warm clothing / a hat / shoes. [1]

(C) He heard someone crying. [1]

(D) *This was not an exciting adventure*. [1]

(E) 1 mark each for any three, with an example to support it: Ben doesn't speak in proper sentences, e.g. "*Gonna go lifeboats*?" / Ben confuses his words, e.g. "*Mustard Station*" / Ben needs help tying his laces, e.g. *as she knotted Ben's laces* / Ben needs to hold hands, e.g. *Beth held Ben's hand*. [3]

(F) A place to meet. [1]

(G) To distract Ben to stop him from being upset. [1]

(H) 1 mark each for any three: There are *three pirate boats* / The pirates are *nearby* / They are in small boats / Pirate attacks on cruise ships are rare. [3]

(I) A ship that is zigzagging makes it a moving target and means it is harder to catch, board or attack. [1]

(J) accompanied [1]

(K) Beth begins the story excited and happy. At the end she is nervous and needs reassurance. [1]

Unit 10

(A) To teach using examples. [1]

(B) All correct for 1 mark: True, False, False, False [1]

(C) remembering [1]

(D) All correct for 1 mark: Tables and Grids / Mnemonics / Mind Maps / Music. [1]

(E) 1 mark for each: linking / word / replace. [3]

(F) 1 mark for one of the following: You can learn lots of information easily / It allows you to remember a long string of facts / You can remember information quickly / You can use your brain and memory to do amazing things. [1]

(G) everyday [1]

(H) Answer should refer to it being a map of somewhere familiar with places linked to information. As you mentally picture the map, you also picture the information linked to each landmark. [1]

Albania

Read the text below and answer the questions that follow.

Natural beauty – a playground for families

Albania is a small country with a long coastline. It is full of natural beauty
with such a stunning natural landscape and wonderfully warm Mediterranean
weather. It is a mountainous country with huge snow-tipped mountain ranges,
but the lakes, natural springs and beaches will have something for every
holidaymaker. The beaches are clean and truly beautiful and the huge range of   5
lagoons, caves and gentle bays make it ideal for families. Should the weather
become too hot, the cooling woods in the Llogara National Park make a welcome
change and are perfect for hikers and ramblers. Albania is recognised for
having an amazing depth of plant diversity. Nearly a third of all plant species
throughout Europe can be found in Albania. Unsurprisingly, the number of birds,   10
fish and mammals is also tremendous. There are over 90 endangered species in
Albania, so it really is a bird and animal watchers' paradise.

Awe-inspiring ancient history

If you are interested in history, Albania has an ancient history and culture that
dates back for many thousands of years. The National History Museum – in the
capital, Tirana – has many amazing archaeological artefacts while the ruins of   15
the UNESCO heritage site of the city of Butrint show a glimpse of life in the past.
There is a wonderful view from the Rozafa Castle in Shkodra or perhaps take a
trip to Apollonia for an amazing exploration of the ancient Greek city.

Climate

Albania has a typical Mediterranean climate, so the winters are mild and the summers are hot and sunny. This is the minimum and maximum temperature in degrees Celsius for the capital, Tirana. The weather in the mountains will be significantly colder.

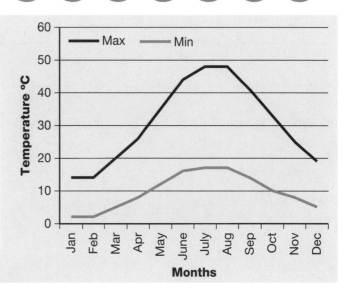

Tasty treats to try...

Albanian food has been influenced by its neighbours Greece, Italy and the other Balkan states. The extremely fertile land produces fresh salads and vegetables which are the basis of most meals, but here are some other delicious specialities that you must try:

Buke misri: tasty bread made with corn   5
Byrek: a nourishing pastry pie often stuffed with spinach and cheese
Cannoli: a sweet wafer roll filled with flavoured ricotta cheese
Dollma: delicious stuffed vegetables
Sardele me limon: a mouth-watering dish of sardines with lemon
Tarator: a cold, refreshing cucumber and yoghurt soup or drink   10

(A) Find and copy **one** sentence that shows Albania is suitable for children to visit. [1]

_____

_____

_____

(B) Where can people go to look for shade? [1]

_____

(C) Why is Albania *a bird and animal watchers' paradise*? [1]

_____

_____

(D) Which historical place can be visited for scenic views? [1]

_____

4

(E) Tick the following statements to show whether they are **true** or **false**. [1]

	True	False
The weather is the same across the whole of Albania.		
It is easy to grow crops in Albania.		
Albania is a great holiday destination for nature lovers.		
Albania is a land-locked country.		

(F) *here are some other **delicious** specialities that you must try*

Tick the word below which is closest in meaning to the word *delicious* in this sentence.
Tick **one**. [1]

delicate ☐   charming ☐

tasty ☐   handsome ☐

(G) Draw lines to match the places below to the activity. [1]

Apollonia		good for wandering around an ancient ruined city
Llogara		great for historic artefacts
Tirana		perfect for exploring the castle
Shkodra		ideal for walkers
Butrint		interesting place to discover a Greek-built city

(H) Add the correct word so that these statements are correct. [3]

I would eat _____ if I wanted a spinach and cheese pie.

I would eat _____ if I wanted some stuffed vegetables.

I would eat _____ if I wanted a ricotta cheese-filled roll.

6

Unit 6

ⓘ Tick the following statements to show whether they are **fact** or **opinion**. [1]

	Fact	Opinion
There is snow on the mountain tops.		
The temperature can be over 40°C in the summer.		
Buke misri is a tasty corn bread.		
There is a wonderful view from the Rozafa Castle.		

Ⓙ *the number of birds, fish and mammals is also* **tremendous**

Tick the word below which is closest in meaning to the word *tremendous* in this sentence. Tick **one**. [1]

amazing ☐

average ☐

awful ☐

assorted ☐

Ⓚ Find and copy a **two**-word phrase that is used mean 'old items'. [1]

_____

Ⓛ The text is taken from a page in a travel brochure.

Give **two** reasons why you think a weather chart might be included in a travel brochure. [2]

_____

_____

_____

5

Lone Fox

Read the poem below and answer the questions that follow.

He sits under the hawthorn tree in our front garden at night.
Not every night, but quite often.
He comes from the woods at the back
Sauntering across the road to our tree.
To the right of our tree is the path to the woods.   5
To the left of it is the dense shrubbery that skirts around the house.
He is hidden from the street light.
He is hidden from spectators.

It takes him a couple of minutes to look around, to take in the night air.
Then he begins the ritual of cleaning himself.   10
He sticks his front leg up in the air, it is not elegant.
He scratches underneath his chin, like a thoughtful old man.
He stretches his back legs, like an athlete warming up.
Now he yawns – he is probably waking up for a night on the prowl.
There is food in the vicinity and he knows it.   15
His nose twitches, his eyes glow and he almost seems to be smiling.

He sometimes sits and waits – I wonder what he is thinking.
Then when he is ready – leisurely, and in his own time,
He slinks off, making his way along the street
To see if any bins might provide a feast.   20
There are butchers' and greengrocers' back yards to explore,
There is a chip shop and the supermarket car park –
Not too far for a bold explorer,
And each with the potential for rich pickings.

But tonight is different.   25

Our fox sits, cleans himself and sniffs the night air.
When a group of people suddenly appear from the house over the road.
Visitors who now cross the usually silent road to their parked car.
The fox reacts quickly, but sees that he is trapped.
The car blocks his exit, the people block his other escape route. 30
He squeezes himself into the shrubbery, but he has been spotted.
"Hello puss-cat!" says an elderly lady peering into the garden.
It is dark and she can no longer see 'the cat'.
"Aww," she says, "there is a big ginger cat living at that house."
She opens the car door as soon as it is unlocked. 35
The engine starts and the car reverses backing off the pavement.
The fox spies his escape and darts from under the shrubbery,
But the car has now moved forward into the path of the fox.
The car slams on the breaks with a squeal.
Then silence. 40

I hold my breath and expect the worst.
My stomach feels sick and I feel faint.
The car drives off slowly,
But fortunately, our fox is nowhere to be seen.
I begin to breathe but my knees feel shaky. 45
And then I catch sight of him,
A little foxy face cowering underneath a parked car.
He remains there for a little time, before regaining his confidence.
He may be a little shaken, but he is used to living on the edge.
He is a survivor. 50

A Find **three** words that tell us how the fox walks. [1]

_____

_____

_____

1

(B) *There is food in the **vicinity** and he knows it*

Tick the word below which is closest in meaning to the word *vicinity* in this sentence.
Tick **one**. [1]

garden ☐   neighbourhood ☐

fridge ☐   viciousness ☐

(C) Find and copy **one** line from the poem that tells us this is not the first time the fox has visited the garden. [1]

_____

_____

(D) *His nose twitches, his eyes glow and he almost seems to be smiling*

What impression does this gives you about the fox? [1]

_____

_____

(E) Write down **three** things that you are told about the poet's garden. [3]

_____

_____

_____

_____

(F) Tick the following statements to show whether they are **true** or **false**. [1]

	True	False
The road outside the house is usually quiet.		
There are woods to the left of the hawthorn tree.		
There are no street lights near the house.		
There are some shops within the neighbourhood.		

7

(G) Why does the poet feel sick and faint? [1]

_____

_____

(H) Why do you think that the lady believes she has seen a cat? Give **two** reasons. [2]

_____

_____

_____

_____

(I) Circle the **three** people that the fox is likened to. [1]

an old man   the poet   an explorer

an athlete   a lady   a butcher

(J) Give **two** reasons why you think the car _drives off slowly_. [2]

_____

_____

_____

_____

(K) What was revealed at the end of the poem?

Tick **one**. [1]

The fox died.   ☐

The fox was badly injured.   ☐

The fox lived.   ☐

Nobody knows what happened to the fox.   ☐

7

Walter Aubrey Thomas

Read the text below and answer the questions that follow.

An architect is someone who designs buildings and makes sure that they are built to the design. Every building has an architect, from homes and schools to offices and shops. Some architects are well-known because they design a building that looks better than others, or because the architect designs in an amazing new way or uses materials in a revolutionary way. **5**

Walter Aubrey Thomas (W. Aubrey Thomas) was born on the Wirral in 1859. He was an architect and many of his buildings are listed, which means they are important and specially protected. Some of the buildings are not only known in this country, but are recognised all around the world.

One of the most famous buildings that W. Aubrey Thomas designed is the **10** Royal Liver Building on Liverpool waterfront, with the liver birds on top of the two clock towers. The building is one of the 'Three Graces of Liverpool' next to the Cunard Building and the Port of Liverpool Building and was built for the Royal Liver Friendly Society. The building work began in May 1908 and was completed in July 1911. **15**

The building was built as a steel frame with reinforced concrete and then covered in granite – a stone which is hard and durable. The two clock faces were designed to be large enough for any passing ship or boat to be able to see. The two liver birds were designed by Carl Bernard Bartels and are made of copper, which is why they are green. They both carry a **20** sprig of seaweed in their beaks as Liverpool was made through seafaring trade. The **legend** is that one bird looks over the city of Liverpool to keep everyone safe. The other bird looks over the port of Liverpool to keep the waterfront safe.

Opposite the Royal Liver Building is another building designed by **25** W. Aubrey Thomas: the Tower Building. The Tower Building was built on the site of the old Tower of Liverpool, which housed the jail for holding prisoners. W. Aubrey Thomas included turrets on the building to remind people of the Tower of Liverpool's history. It was designed out of a steel

frame that is then covered in granite like the Liver Building, but then   30
faced with white glazed terracotta, which was made by the pottery maker,
James Doulton. W. Aubrey Thomas thought that the white tiles would help
stop smoke pollution from turning the buildings black. The building was
completed in 1908.

W. Aubrey Thomas died in 1934 and left behind children and   35
grandchildren, but to the rest of the world, he left behind some of the most
recognisable and well-loved buildings.

(A) Give **two** reasons why an architect might be well known. [2]

_____

_____

_____

_____

(B) What is a listed building? [1]

_____

_____

_____

_____

(C) Find **two** other people who helped W. Aubrey Thomas complete his buildings. [1]

_____

_____

4

(D) Draw lines to match the dates below to the events. [1]

W. Aubrey Thomas dies	1911
The Tower Building is completed	1934
The Royal Liver Building is completed	1859
W. Aubrey Thomas is born	1908

(E) Tick the following statements to show whether they are **true** or **false**. [1]

	True	False
The Royal Liver Building took 3 years and 2 months to build.		
The liver birds carry a tree branch in their beaks.		
The Tower Building is one of the 'Three Graces of Liverpool'.		
W. Aubrey Thomas was a father.		

(F) Find and copy a **three**-word phrase that describes why granite was used to face the Royal Liver Building. [1]

_____

(G) For whom was the Royal Liver Building designed?
Tick **one**. [1]

The Cunard Building ☐   The Royal Liver Friendly Society ☐

The Port of Liverpool ☐   The Three Graces of Liverpool ☐

(H) Look at the fourth paragraph beginning *The building was built as a steel frame…*

What word is used in the paragraph to mean 'story'? [1]

_____

5

(I) Circle the correct option to complete each sentence below. [4]

The liver birds were made from...

granite   reinforced concrete   copper   glazed terracotta

The Tower Building was faced with...

granite   reinforced concrete   copper   glazed terracotta

The Royal Liver Building frame was built as a metal frame with...

granite   reinforced concrete   copper   glazed terracotta

The outside of the Tower Building had a steel frame covered in...

granite   reinforced concrete   copper   glazed terracotta

(J) *as Liverpool was made through **seafaring** trade*

Tick the word below which is closest in meaning to the word *seafaring* in this sentence.
Tick **one**. [1]

fishing   ☐   seaside   ☐
maritime   ☐   fairy   ☐

(K) What did W. Aubrey Thomas do to remind people that the Tower Building was on the site of the Tower of Liverpool? [1]

_____

_____

6

Pirate Attack

Read the text below and answer the questions that follow.

"This is Carole giving a huge shout out to the Octopus Club. The 'Inflatable Challenge' will start in ten minutes on the Lido Deck."

"Nan, come and watch us!" Beth shouted with excitement.

Rose smiled and grabbed her mobile so she could take photographs of Beth and Ben. This holiday was a once-in-a-lifetime adventure and she wanted them to remember every second of it, but suddenly the tannoy changed.   5

"This is your Captain speaking, please return to your cabins immediately to collect your life jacket, warm clothing, a hat and shoes. Then go to your Muster Station. Do not run. Do not panic. Follow the emergency procedures."

Beth blinked and looked around. Did she really just hear the Captain? The   10 emergency alarm sounded. Holidaymakers began moving off the sun-loungers and gazing around at each other as they moved towards their cabins. Rose held the hands of Beth and Ben and pulled them carefully towards the stairs while her mind raced.

Rose walked purposefully down the corridor and into their cabin. Without   15 speaking, the children pulled on their socks and shoes and put on their hooded coats before grabbing their life jackets. Rose tried to stop her hands from shaking as she knotted Ben's laces and pulled her own hooded fleece and rain-mac over her head. They could hear the sound of someone crying in a cabin above them and this made Ben panic.   20

Rose tried to smile brightly as she ushered them out of their cabin. "I'm sure the Inflatable Challenge will be on later so don't worry, but first we have another challenge and this is a really fun adventure."

Beth held Ben's hand and joined in with the 'challenge' story.

"Do you remember the emergency drill we did on the first day? We all put on our   25 life jackets and gathered at our Muster Station," Beth said to her brother.

"What's Mustard Station?" asked Ben.

"Not mustard, it's muster!" Beth said.

"It's where we gather ready to join the lifeboats," Rose added.

Ben's eyes grew huge and scared, "Gonna go lifeboats?" 30

"I don't know," Rose said swallowing hard. "We're about to find out."

As they reached their Muster Station, instead of being taken to the lifeboats, the passengers were directed through the staff doorways and down white, metal stairs to the staff decks. Some passengers were crying and they all looked worried. This was not an exciting adventure. 35

"Please sit on the floor next to the wall here," said the staff member who looked calm, but serious. He called out passengers' names and crossed off cabin numbers, radioing confirmation to the Captain's bridge.

"What's happening?" Beth asked, her lower lip trembling.

"We have three small pirate boats nearby. It is very rare for pirates to attack 40 cruise ships, but ships like ours have a silent alarm to connect us to the closest ship that can help us and until then, the safety of the ship, the passengers and the staff is the Captain's sole concern."

Beth looked around at the other passengers, unable to take it in.

Everyone looked at each other in stunned silence. Without warning, the ship 45 turned sharply in one direction as everyone leant to the right and then it swung to the opposite direction throwing everyone back to their initial position. Sitting on the shiny floor with nothing to hold on to made balance impossible. This zigzagging lasted for some time and Beth understood the sensation of seasickness. Then loud shouts from the ship's crew could be heard on the radio. 50

Ben clung to Rose and she tried to calm him. There were enough passengers on this corridor who were crying and several children and babies were clearly terrified. One mother attempted a group sing-along of 'Ten Green Bottles', but most passengers did not want to be distracted. They wanted to know how this was going to end. The staff were constantly on their walkie-talkies and still the 55 shouting could be heard and the ship continued to zigzag until, at last, there was news.

"The Captain has made contact with the navy and they are coming to our rescue. We are being escorted to safety right now. Please remain where you are until the Captain gives further announcements." 60

"Nan," began Beth nervously, "are we okay?"

Rose couldn't stop her hand from shaking; an involuntary reaction to the shock. "Yes darling, we're okay."

Ⓐ Where was the Inflatable Challenge taking place?

Tick **one**. [1]

At the Octopus Club ☐

At Carole's ☐

On the Lido deck ☐

Along the corridor ☐

Ⓑ What are the **four** items that passengers had to take to the Muster Station? [1]

_____   _____

_____   _____

Ⓒ What made Ben panic when he was in the cabin?

Tick **one**. [1]

He wanted to do the Inflatable Challenge. ☐   He heard someone crying. ☐

He had to put his warm clothes on. ☐   He was scared of the lifeboats. ☐

Ⓓ Find and copy **one** sentence that shows the holiday was no longer enjoyable. [1]

_____

_____

Ⓔ Ben is three years old. Find **three** examples in the text to support this. [3]

_____

_____

_____

_____

Ⓕ What is the main purpose of a Muster Station?

Tick **one**. [1]

A place to read information ☐

A place to find the Captain ☐

A place to store life jackets ☐

A place to meet ☐

8

Unit 9

(G) Why does Rose tell Ben a *'challenge'* story?
Tick **one**. [1]

To make Ben walk faster towards the
Muster Station ☐

To distract Ben to stop him from
being upset ☐

To give Ben something to look forward
to later on ☐

To give Rose something to focus on ☐

(H) Write down **three** things that you are told about the pirates. [3]

_____

_____

_____

(I) Why does the ship zigzag? [1]

_____

_____

_____

(J) *We are being* **escorted** *to safety right now.*

Tick the word below which is closest in meaning to the word *escorted* in this sentence.
Tick **one**. [1]

accompanied ☐

isolated ☐

ignored ☐

sailed ☐

(K) How does Beth change from the beginning of the story to the end? [1]

_____

_____

_____

7

Kings and Queens

Read the text below and answer the questions that follow.

Today we are going to show you a magic trick that will impress your family and friends. In just a few minutes, you will be able to use your mind to learn every king and queen of Great Britain, from 1707 to our present queen, in order of their reign. The magic trick will include these kings and queens, so let's look at the information and the first way of recalling the **facts**. 5

Here is a quick way of remembering the order of these kings and queens:

Reign:	Name:
1707–1714	Queen **A**nne
1714–1727	King **G**eorge I
1727–1760	King **G**eorge II
1760–1820	King **G**eorge III
1820–1830	King **G**eorge IV
1830–1837	King **W**illiam IV
1837–1901	Queen **V**ictoria
1901–1910	King **E**dward VII
1910–1936	King **G**eorge V
1936–1936	King **E**dward VIII
1936–1952	King **G**eorge VI
1952–current	Queen **E**lizabeth II

Always
Give
Gorillas
Green
Grapes,
While
Vanilla
Eclairs
Get
Elephants
Greatly
Excited

Tables and Grids:

If we look at the table, we can see that only the main **facts** and figures are given. Whenever we look at information in a table, grid or box, it is easier to remember than reading it in a paragraph. If you want to learn information, 10 try putting it into a table or grid.

Mnemonics:

A **mnemonic** is a way of helping us remember information. The example here forms a funny sentence that takes the first letter of each king or queen in the order that they reigned, and creates another word that helps our memory. You could take any information to create your own **mnemonic**. 15 It doesn't matter how silly the rhyme might be to help you recall **facts**!

Now let's look at another two memory aids that can help you remember information:

Mind Maps:

Using a map and linking information to places on the map can be successful. In the map, each king or queen is linked to one of 12 places, but it works best with a map that you already know. Think about 12 places you might see on **20** a regular journey you have: your house, a post box and so on. Add each king or queen so that when you want to remember the order, think about that journey and the kings and queens that you have added to each place.

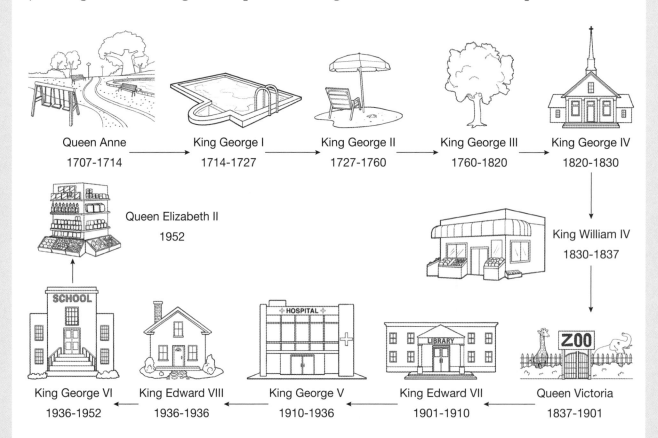

Music:

Have you always wondered why you cannot remember what you have to do for homework, but you remember all of the words of an annoying song **25** when you've only heard it a couple of times? Find a tune you know or even better, a song that you can replace the words to. You can try this now by singing 'The Twelve Days of Christmas,' replacing the gifts with each king or queen and keeping the partridge in a pear tree: "On the first day of Christmas my true love sent to me one Queen Anne and a partridge in **30** a pear tree..."

Hopefully you now have some techniques to remember the names and dates of all of the kings and queens from 1707 to our present queen. Keep testing yourself each couple of days until you can easily recall them all.

(A) What is the main aim of the text?
Tick **one**. [1]

| To teach using examples | ☐ | To threaten using warnings | ☐ |
| To thrill using fear | ☐ | To entertain using stories | ☐ |

(B) Tick the following statements to show whether they are **true** or **false**. [1]

	True	False
Four kings and queens reigned in the 1700s.		
Five kings and queens reigned in the 1900s.		
There were seven King Georges.		
Two kings reigned in 1936.		

(C) *and the first way of **recalling** the **facts***

Tick the word below which is closest in meaning to the word *recalling* in this sentence.
Tick **one**. [1]

| remembering | ☐ | using | ☐ |
| forgetting | ☐ | proving | ☐ |

(D) Write down the **four** methods that can be used to help our memory. [1]

_____

_____

_____

_____

_____

4

Unit 10

(E) Circle the correct option to complete each sentence below. [3]

Using a mind map works by _____ places to information.

singing   writing   linking   drawing

A *mnemonic* can take the first letter to make another _____ .

letter   word   memory   link

We can also use a song to _____ words that will fit with a tune that we already know.

sing   add   subtract   replace

(F) Why do you think this is referred to as a *magic trick*? [1]

_____

_____

_____

_____

(G) *places you might see on a **regular** journey*

Tick the word below which is closest in meaning to the word *regular* in this sentence. Tick **one**. [1]

popular ☐   everyday ☐
unknown ☐   spectacular ☐

(H) Explain how a mind map works. [1]

_____

_____

_____

_____

6

Key Words

fact:
information that is true and can be proven; not someone's point of view

legend:
a traditional tale sometimes thought to be true, but not proven

mnemonic:
a system, such as a pattern of letters, as a way of remembering something

opinion:
information that is someone's point of view and can't be proven

Progress chart

How did you do? Fill in your score below and shade in the corresponding boxes to compare your progress across the different tests and units.

50% 100%

Unit 1, p4 Score __ / 4

Unit 1, p5 Score __ / 5

Unit 1, p6 Score __ / 5

Unit 2, p8 Score __ / 2

Unit 2, p9 Score __ / 7

Unit 2, p10 Score __ / 7

Unit 3, p12 Score __ / 6

Unit 3, p13 Score __ / 4

Unit 3, p14 Score __ / 5

Unit 4, p16 Score __ / 4

Unit 4, p17 Score __ / 6

Unit 4, p18 Score __ / 5

Unit 5, p20 Score __ / 5

Unit 5, p21 Score __ / 8

50% 100%

Unit 5, p22 Score __ / 3

Unit 6, p28 Score __ / 4

Unit 6, p29 Score __ / 6

Unit 6, p30 Score __ √ 5

Unit 7, p32 Score __ / 1

Unit 7, p33 Score __ / 7

Unit 7, p34 Score __ / 7

Unit 8, p36 Score __ / 4

Unit 8, p37 Score __ / 5

Unit 8, p38 Score __ / 6

Unit 9, p41 Score __ / 8

Unit 9, p42, Score __ / 7

Unit 10, p45 Score __ / 4

Unit 10, p46, Score __ / 6